D0424007

Style: Language Variation and Identity

Style refers to ways of speaking – how speakers use the resource of language variation to make meaning in social encounters. This book develops a coherent theoretical approach to style in sociolinguistics, illustrated with copious examples. It explains how speakers project different social identities and create different social relationships through their style choices, and how speech-style and social context inter-relate. Style therefore refers to the wide range of strategic actions and performances that speakers engage in, to construct themselves and their social lives. Coupland draws on and integrates a wide variety of contemporary sociolinguistic research as well as his own extensive research in this field. The emphasis is on how social meanings are made locally, in specific relationships, genres, groups and cultures, and on studying language variation as part of the analysis of spoken discourse.

NIKOLAS COUPLAND is Professor and Research Director of the Cardiff University Centre for Language and Communication Research. He is a founding co-editor of the *Journal of Sociolinguistics*.

KEY TOPICS IN SOCIOLINGUISTICS

Series editor:
Rajend Mesthrie

This new series focuses on the main topics of study in sociolinguistics today. It consists of accessible yet challenging accounts of the most important issues to consider when examining the relationship between language and society. Some topics have been the subject of sociolinguistic study for many years, and are here re-examined in the light of new developments in the field; other are issues of growing importance that have not so far been given a sustained treatment. Written by leading experts, the books in the series are designed to be used on courses and in seminars, and include suggestions for further reading and a helpful glossary.

Already published in the series:
Politeness by Richard J. Watts
Language Policy by Bernard Spolsky
Discourse by Jan Blommaert
Analyzing Sociolinguistic Variation by Sali A. Tagliamonte
Language and Ethnicity by Carmen Fought

Forthcoming titles:
World Englishes by Rakesh Bhatt and Rajend Mesthrie
Bilingual Talk by Peter Auer

Style
Language Variation and Identity

NIKOLAS COUPLAND

CAMBRIDGE UNIVERSITY PRESS

CAMBRIDGE UNIVERSITY PRESS
Cambridge, New York, Melbourne, Madrid, Cape Town,
Singapore, São Paulo, Delhi, Tokyo, Mexico City

Cambridge University Press
The Edinburgh Building, Cambridge CB2 8RU, UK

Published in the United States of America by Cambridge University Press, New York

www.cambridge.org
Information on this title: www.cambridge.org/9780521618144

© Nikolas Coupland 2007

This publication is in copyright. Subject to statutory exception
and to the provisions of relevant collective licensing agreements,
no reproduction of any part may take place without the written
permission of Cambridge University Press.

First published 2007
Reprinted 2009

A catalogue record for this publication is available from the British Library

Library of Congress Cataloguing in Publication Data

Coupland, Nikolas, 1950 – Language variation and identity / Nikolas Coupland.
p.   cm. – (Key topics in sociolinguistics)
Includes bibliographical references and index.
ISBN-13: 978-0-521-85303-3 (hardback)
ISBN-13: 978-0-521-61814-4 (paperback)
1. Language and languages – Variation.   2. Language and languages – Style.
3. Sociolinguistics.   4. Identity (Psychology)   I. Title.   II. Series.
P120.V37C68   2007
417′.7 – dc22   2006039240

ISBN 978-0-521-85303-3 Hardback
ISBN 978-0-521-61814-4 Paperback

Cambridge University Press has no responsibility for the persistence or
accuracy of URLs for external or third-party internet websites referred to in
this publication, and does not guarantee that any content on such websites is,
or will remain, accurate or appropriate. Information regarding prices, travel
timetables, and other factual information given in this work is correct at
the time of first printing but Cambridge University Press does not guarantee
the accuracy of such information thereafter.

Contents

Figures and tables

Figures:

The International Phonetic Alphabet

Tables:

Preface and acknowledgements

In the new world of sociolinguistics, the simple concept of 'style' has a lot of work to do. The idea of 'stylistic variation' emerged from William Labov's seminal research on urban speech variation and language change, and it existed there in order to make a few key points only. As Labov showed, when we survey how speech varies, we find variation 'within the individual speaker' across contexts of talk, as well as between individuals and groups. Also, when individual people shift their ways of speaking, survey designs suggested that they do it, on the whole, in predictable ways that are amenable to social explanation.

From this initially narrow perspective, crucial as it was in establishing a basic agenda, a sociolinguistics of style has steadily come to prominence as a wide field of research, whether or not researchers use the term 'style' to describe their enterprise. Style used to be a marginal concern in variationist sociolinguistics. Nowadays it points to many of the most challenging aspects of linguistic variation, in questions like these: How does sociolinguistic variation interface with other dimensions of meaning-making in discourse? What stylistic work does variation do for social actors, and how does it blend into wider discursive and socio-cultural processes? Are there new values for variation and for style in the late-modern world?

When we work through issues like these, some important boundaries shift. For one thing, the study of sociolinguistic variation becomes very much wider. The canonical study of language variation and change will always remain a pillar of sociolinguistics, but it need not be an autonomous paradigm. One of my ambitions for the book is to show what variation study is like when it 'goes non-autonomous'. The boundary between 'dialect variation' and the social construction of meaning in discourse starts to collapse. Theories and sensitivities from different parts of sociolinguistics start to coalesce – interactional sociolinguistics, pragmatics, anthropological linguistics and even conversation analysis do not need to stand outside of variationism, nor it outside them.

My own thinking on sociolinguistic style has spanned two-and-a-half decades, although it remains to be seen whether this particular quantitative index (like some other quantitative measures that come up for review in the book) makes a meaningful difference. I was enthused to write this book mainly because of the acceleration of sociolinguistic interest in things 'stylistic' and 'contextual' and 'socially meaningful' in the last decade, prompted by some remarkable new waves of research. I won't attempt to list the relevant names and paradigms here – they fill out the pages of the book. But I would like to make a few biographical notes, by way of personal acknowledgement.

I had begun writing about style in the late 1970s, when the theme emerged from my doctoral research on sociolinguistic variation in Cardiff, the capital city of Wales. I was fortunate to start long-running dialogues, soon after that, with Allan Bell and Howard Giles. In their own research they developed new relational perspectives on spoken language variation that opened up an entirely new theoretical chapter for sociolinguistics. I continued to collaborate with Howard Giles over many years on various themes that lay at the interface between sociolinguistics and social psychology. I have been fortunate to be able to develop some of that work, more recently, in collaboration with Peter Garrett and Angie Williams in Cardiff, and more recently still with Hywel Bishop.

After some scratchy ink and pen exchanges about his evolving theory of audience design in the very early 1980s, Allan Bell and I maintained close links, latterly in co-editing the *Journal of Sociolinguistics*. That particular collaboration ensured we would have no time to write collaboratively about style, although we had firmly intended to do this. I have no doubt that this book would have been much the better if Allan and I had achieved our aim of writing a similar book together.

As the Centre for Language and Communication Research at Cardiff University grew and diversified through the 1980s and 1990s, several of my colleagues there were involved in developing new sociolinguistic fields, particularly critical and interactional approaches to language and society. The study of style needed the sorts of insight that they were developing in their own and in our joint research. In particular there has been the formative effect of my many collaborations with Adam Jaworski, for example on metalanguage, sociolinguistic theory and discourse analysis. My other Cardiff colleagues, including Theo van Leeuwen and Joanna Thornborrow, have again been important sources of inspiration. My research collaborations with Justine

Coupland, for example on the theme of discourse and ideology, social identities in later life and on relational talk, have been where I developed most of the ideas behind the present book, although her contributions to this book are far too pervasive to summarise.

Apart from those already mentioned, a long list of people have made very valuable input into my thinking and writing about 'style', whether they recall it or not. No doubt with unintended omissions, let me thank Peter Auer, Mary Bucholtz, Janet Cotterill, Penelelope Eckert, Anthea Fraser Gupta, Janet Holmes, Tore Kristiansen, Ben Rampton and John Rickford. Thanks also to Rachel Muntz and Faith Mowbray for their help in connection with the BBC *Voices* research that has a walk-on part in Chapter 4. Reading groups convened by Julia Snell, Emma Moore and Sally Johnson fed back some valuable criticisms on parts of the text. Ayo Banji made extremely helpful input into compiling the Index. Allan Bell, Adam Jaworski and Natalie Schilling-Estes, as well as Rajend Mesthrie, read and commented on the whole manuscript in draft form, for which I am extremely grateful.

I have summarised and rewritten parts of my previously published writing in this book. The main sources in this connection, listed in the References section, are Coupland 1980, 1984, 1985, 1988, 2000b, 2001b, 2001c, 2003, in pressa, in pressb, Coupland and Bishop 2007, Coupland, Garrett and Williams 2005, Coupland and Jaworski 2004. I am particularly grateful to my co-authors for letting me rework some parts of this material here. Figures 2.1 and 2.2 are adapted from Figures 7.23 and 7.11 in Labov (2006).

The disciplinary boundary-shifting that I referred to above has presented me with the problem of knowing where to draw the line around style in this book. I have given most space to those studies of how classical forms of sociolinguistic variation – what most people call accent and dialect features – are worked into discursive social action and where they make meaning at the level of relationships and personal or social identities. As I say later, this is a rather artificial boundary to try to police, because my motivating concerns for the book are social meaning and social identity, much more than sociolinguistic variation itself. For example, I would have liked to include some detail on the discursive management of age-identities in later life (an area of my own my research with Justine Coupland). But this would have taken the book away from indexical meanings linked to the domains of social class, gender and racial/ethnic identities, which is where style research has been most active to date.

This book can be read as a critique of variationist sociolinguistics. Meaning-making through talk has not been what variationists have generally tried to explain, although it has seemed to me a strange omission. It is all the more strange when we think of William Labov's commitment to the politics of language variation, his interest from the outset in the social evaluation of varieties, and his ground-breaking work in narrative analysis and interactional ritual. His followers in the field of variationist sociolinguistics have not often been able to maintain that breadth. In order to bridge back into questions of social meaning, I have found it important to challenge some of the assumptions of variationist research. These are mainly its dogged reliance on static social categories, its imputation of identity-values to numerical patterns (quantitative representations of linguistic variation), and its thin account of social contextualisation.

I fully recognise that, and celebrate the fact that, variationist sociolinguistics has taken great strides through keeping within these constraints, when research questions have been formulated at the level of linguistic systems and how they change. But I think we need a sociolinguistics of variation *for people* and *for society*, as well as (not instead of) a sociolinguistics of variation *for language*. 'Sociolinguistic style' has been the rubric under which quite a lot of that extension of the programme has already been achieved, and where further progress is clearly in prospect. 'Stylistics', as a label for a sub-discipline of linguistics, has a dated feel to it, and so does 'style'. But in the context of sociolinguistics, style nevertheless points us to a range of highly contemporary phenomena. We seem to find meaning in our lives nowadays less through the social structures into which we have been socialised, and more through how we deploy and make meaning out of those inherited resources. How social reality is creatively styled is a key sociolinguistic question, and the main question in what follows.

NC
July 2006

Transcription conventions

Where necessary, International Phonetic Alphabet (IPA) symbols are used to identify consonant and vowel qualities, as in the following charts (as shown over).

THE INTERNATIONAL PHONETIC ALPHABET

EXTRACTS OF TRANSCRIBED CONVERSATION

These are numbered consecutively within each chapter. Where possible, I have re-transcribed data extracts from the original sources in the interests of simplicity and consistency. Wherever possible, these transcriptions use orthographic conventions, but with the following additions and deviations:

(.)	a short untimed pause of less than one second
(2.0)	a timed pause, timed in seconds
[quietly]	stage directions and comments on context or spoken delivery
[ ]	between lines of transcript, denotes overlapping speech, showing beginning and end points of overlap
:	lengthened sound
::	more lengthened sound
<u>you</u>	(underlined) said with heavy stress
?	marks question intonation not interrogative syntax
(( ))	inaudible speech sequence or unreliable transcription
italics	sequences of particular analytic interest, explained in the text

Any other conventions used in particular extracts are explained in the text.

CONSONANTS (PULMONIC)

	Bilabial	Labiodental	Dental	Alveolar	Post alveolar	Retroflex	Palatal	Velar	Uvular	Pharyngeal	Glottal
Plosive	p b			t d		ʈ ɖ	c ɟ	k g	q ɢ		ʔ
Nasal	m	ɱ		n		ɳ	ɲ	ŋ	ɴ		
Trill	ʙ			r					ʀ		
Tap or Flap				ɾ		ɽ					
Fricative	ɸ β	f v	θ ð	s z	ʃ ʒ	ʂ ʐ	ç ʝ	x ɣ	χ ʁ	ħ ʕ	h ɦ
Lateral fricative				ɬ ɮ							
Approximant		ʋ		ɹ		ɻ	j	ɰ			
Lateral approximant				l		ɭ	ʎ	ʟ			

Where symbols appear in pairs, the one to the right represents a voiced consonant. Shaded areas denote articulations judged impossible.

VOWELS

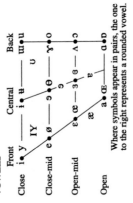

Where symbols appear in pairs, the one to the right represents a rounded vowel.

The International Phonetic Alphabet (revised to 1993, updated 1996)

1 Introduction

1.1 LOCATING 'STYLE'

'Style' refers to a way of doing something. Think of architectural styles and the striking rustic style of house-building in rural Sweden. That particular style – what allows us to call it a style – is an assemblage of design choices. It involves the use of timber frames, a distinctively tiered roofline, a red cedar wood stain and so on. We can place this style. It belongs somewhere, even if the style is lifted out of its home territory and used somewhere else. It has a social meaning. The same is true for styles in all other life-domains. Cultural resonances of time, place and people attach to styles of dress and personal appearance in general, to styles in the making of material goods, to styles of social and institutional practice, perhaps even to styles of thinking. We could use David Machin and Theo van Leeuwen's (2005) idea of 'social style' to cover all these. The world is full of social styles.

Part of our social competence is being able to understand these indexical links – how a style marks out or indexes a social difference – and to read their meanings. The irony is that, if we ourselves are closely embedded in a particular social style, we may not recognise that style's distinctiveness. Reading the meaning of a style is inherently a contrastive exercise. You have to find those red cedar buildings 'different' in order to see them as having some stylistic significance. This is the old principle of meaning depending on some sort of choice being available. But style isn't difference alone. When we use the term 'style' we are usually attending to some aesthetic dimension of difference. Styles involve a degree of crafting, and this is why the word 'style' leaks into expressions like 'having style', 'being in style' or 'being stylish'. The aesthetic qualities of styles relate, as in the case of the Swedish red cedar buildings, to a process of design, however naturalised that process and its results might have become in our experience. We talk about 'style' rather than 'difference' when we

1

are aware of some holistic properties of a practice or its product. A style will 'hang together' in some coherent manner. Engagement with style and styles, both in production and reception, will usually imply a certain interpretive depth and complexity. Although we are considering 'style' as a noun at this point, when we refer to 'a style' and to 'styles' (plural), and giving styles a quality of 'thing-ness', the idea of style demands more of a process perspective. I think we are mainly interested in styles (noun) for how they have come to be and for how people 'style' (verb) meaning into the social world. 'Styling' – the activation of stylistic meaning – therefore becomes an important concept in this book.

This general account of style can of course be applied to *linguistic* forms and processes too. We are all familiar with the idea of linguistic style, and most people will think first of language in literary style. Literary style relates to the crafting of linguistic text in literary genres and to an aesthetic interpretation of text. This book is about *style in speech* and about *ways of speaking*, not about literary style, although it would be wrong to force these areas of study too far apart. The book is about style in the specific research context of sociolinguistics, where concepts very similar to 'social style' have been established for several decades. The general sociolinguistic term used to refer to ways of speaking that are indexically linked to social groups, times and places is *dialects*. Dialects are social styles. Some dialects are in fact rather like red cedar timber buildings, redolent with meaningful associations of rurality and linked to particular geographical places. They have strong cultural associations, especially when we look at them contrastively. Dialectologists have traditionally looked for boundaries between dialect regions, and traced the evolution of dialects over time and the consequences of dialects coming into contact with each other (Chambers and Trudgill 1999).

We are likely to think of dialects in this sense as being the social styles of yesteryear, largely out of step with the social circumstances of contemporary life. But dialect differences are of course a characteristic of modern life too. Dialects are evolving social styles and they can be read for their contemporary as well as their historical associations – associations with particular places (geographical dialects) and with particular social groups (social dialects). Dramas associated with dialect are played out as much in cities as in rural enclaves, and sociolinguistics for several decades has enthusiastically teased out the complexities of language variation in urban settings. The human and linguistic density of cities invites an analysis in terms of 'structured difference'. Cities challenge the view that one discrete social style (e.g. a dialect) is associated with one place, which was the basic assumption in the analysis of rural dialects. It has become the norm to consider cities as sociolinguistic systems that organise linguistic variation in complex ways. But understanding the social structuring of styles, even in the sophisticated manner of urban sociolinguistics, is not enough in itself. We need to understand how people *use* or *enact* or *perform* social styles for a range of symbolic purposes. Social styles (including dialect styles) are a resource for people to make many different sorts of personal and interpersonal meaning. As I suggested might be generally true for intellectual interest in style, what matters for linguistic style is more to do with process than with product, more to do with use than with structure. Stylistic analysis is the analysis of how style resources are put to work creatively. Analysing linguistic style again needs to include an aesthetic dimension. It is to do with designs in talk and the fashioning and understanding of social meanings.

So this is not a book about dialectology either. My starting point is certainly the sociolinguistics of dialect, as it has been carried forward by variationist sociolinguistics in the tradition of William Labov's research. This is where the term 'style' was first used in sociolinguistics, and one of my aims for the book is to map out the main steps that sociolinguists have taken using the concept of style. This will initially be a critical review, focusing on the limited horizons of style research in variationist sociolinguistics. The positive case to be made, however, is that, under the general rubric of style, sociolinguistics can and should move on from the documenting of social styles or dialects themselves. It should incorporate the priorities I have just sketched – analysing the creative, design-oriented processes through which social styles are activated in talk and, in that process, remade or reshaped. This means focusing on particular moments and contexts of speaking where people use social styles as resources for meaning-making. It means adding a more active and verbal dimension ('styling social meaning') to sociolinguistic accounts of dialect ('describing social styles').

To set the scene for later arguments and debates, several core concepts need to be explored in this introductory chapter. First we need to consider variationist sociolinguistics and its general approach to style. Then we will look back at the early history of stylistics (the general field of research on style in linguistics), to appreciate the climate in which sociolinguistics first came to the idea of style. The idea of social meaning then comes up for initial scrutiny. Looking ahead to the more contemporary research that this book mainly deals with, we will then consider research methods and the sorts of sociolinguistic data that we can deal with under the heading of style research. The wider relevance of style to contemporary social life, which can be characterised by the term 'late-modernity', is then reviewed. Finally in this chapter, I give a short preview of the structure of the rest of the book.

1.2 VARIATIONISM IN SOCIOLINGUISTICS

Sociolinguistics is, as they say, a broad church. The blander definitions of sociolinguistics refer to studying language 'in society' or language 'in its social context'. Other definitions focus on studying linguistic diversity or language variation. What these simple definitions have in common is that they give priority to language, then add some summary idea of what aspect of language is to be given priority (its variability) or what sort of data is to be given priority (social manifestations of language). Definitions like these have to be understood historically. It was once important to stress 'social contexts' in defining sociolinguistic priorities in order to challenge types of linguistics where actual occurrences of spoken language were not given priority. Even though most people would agree that using language is an inherently social process, sociolinguists needed to make a case for observing language as it is used in everyday life and for not relying on intuited or fabricated instances of language. Stressing variability has been important in order to resist the ideological assumption that what matters in language is linguistic uniformity and 'standardness'. William Labov used the notion of *secular linguistics* to describe his approach to language variation and change. The idea was that studying variable language forms, 'non-standard' as well as 'standard' forms, challenges what we might think of as the high priesthood of theoretical linguistics and its reliance on idealised linguistic data. It also challenges the belief that 'standard' language is more orderly and more worthwhile than 'non-standard' language.

But the study of language variation and change has been in the mainstream of sociolinguistics for four decades. *Variationist* sociolinguistics, as the approach developed by Labov is generally called, has developed its own powerful principles of theory and method (Chambers 1995/2003; Labov 1966, 1972a, 1972b, 1994, 2001a; Chambers, Trudgill and Schilling-Estes 2004). In this book I intend to take the considerable achievements of variationist sociolinguistics for granted, and to ask what it has *not* achieved, particularly in relation to the notion of style and the active dimension of styling. So, as I have mentioned, my orientation is a critical one, although I intend it to be constructively so. The negative part of my argument is that variationist sociolinguistics has worked with a limited idea of social context – and styling is precisely the *contextualisation* of social styles. The survey designs of variationist research, which have been remarkably successful in revealing broad patterns of linguistic diversity and change, have not encouraged us to understand what people meaningfully achieve through linguistic variation. Variationist sociolinguistics has produced impressive descriptions of social styles, but without affording much priority to contextual styling.

What then are the general features of the variationist approach? Sociolinguistic surveys of language variation give us detailed descriptions of how linguistic details of regional and social accents and dialects are distributed. ('Dialect' is a general term for socially and geographically linked speech variation, and 'accent' refers to pronunciation aspects of dialect.) Speakers are not fully consistent in how they use accent or dialect features. Their speech will often, for example, show a mixture of 'standard' and 'non-standard' forms of the same speech feature. Nor are individuals within any particular social category identical in their speech. So the sort of truth generated in variationist research is necessarily one based in generalisations and statistical tendencies. These are 'probabilistic' truths, expressing degrees of relative similarity and dissimilarity within and across groups of speakers and social situations. The convention is to produce averaged statistical values (e.g. percentages of people's use of a particular linguistic feature in a particular social situation, or factor loadings in statistical tests) to represent patterns of linguistic variation. So, accent variation between two different groups of speakers is usually represented as the difference between one statistical value (perhaps a percentage) and another.

Variationist research has very expertly shown that 'speaking differently' has to be defined in several stages. Stage one is typically to identify a group of people who share a geographical characteristic, such as living in the Midlands city of Birmingham in England, or for that matter Birmingham in Alabama in the Southern USA. Within this territory or 'community' of people who have lived in the city for all or most of their lives, sub-groups are identified based on social criteria. This sort of classification isolates, to take a random example, the category of 'young females in Birmingham with working-class jobs', distinguishing them from other social categories. In a second stage, the research samples the speech of the different groups, usually through extended one-to-one sociolinguistic interviews. The researcher then counts how often a particular speech feature is used.

For example, in the English Birmingham, the issue might be how often each speaker pronounces the diphthong vowel in words like *right* and *time* with a phonetically backed and rounded starting point. In this example, the local Birmingham pronunciation [ɔɪ] is in opposition to [aɪ] which is the less localised and more 'standard' variant in England. Phonetic forms occupying intermediate positions between these variants might also be recognised. Variant forms of sociolinguistic variables tend to be influenced by the details of their linguistic placement. For pronunciation variables (linked specifically to a speaker's accent, then), the positions that different pronunciation forms occupy in the stream of speech-sounds, and the sets of words that they occur in, are factors that are likely to impact on the frequency with which they are used. These patterns might affect everyone's speech. A typical finding would then be that most speakers in the sample would in fact use a mixture of different pronunciation forms – e.g. using both 'standard' and 'non-standard' variants of this sociolinguistic variable (ai). But overall frequencies of use would very probably differ across speakers and sub-groups when statistical averages are taken.

At the end of the process of categorising and counting the distribution of various linguistic variants in a body of data, a type of statistical truth would emerge. It might allow us to say that, overall, Birmingham speech does indeed have some distinctive tendencies of pronunciation – different from the speech of other regions and from 'standard English' pronunciation. That is, descriptively speaking, Birmingham speech is a relatively distinctive social style. The descriptive evidence would go some way towards distinguishing the city as a 'speech community', even though the 'standard', less-localised forms of speech crop up in Birmingham too. But people living outside the city would use some of the local or 'non-standard' feature less often than those living in the city, or not at all. Looking at how speech is socially organised within the city, we would probably be able to say that the speech of particular social sub-groups in Birmingham differs in some statistical respects. Perhaps, overall, women in Birmingham use the [ɔɪ] feature in words like *right* and *time* less often than men do. Perhaps women with more prestigious jobs use it less than women with low-prestige jobs. So there are social styles, at least in a quantitative sense, associated with these groups too.

Labov, however, doesn't use the term 'style' in this sense. He refers to what I am calling 'social styles' of speech simply as 'social variation'. He reserves the terms 'style' and 'stylistic variation' for a further sort of language variation that can be detected in sociolinguistic interviews (e.g. Labov 1972b). This is when he is able to show that, again in a statistical sense, individual people speak 'less carefully' at some points in an interview than they do at other points. When they are being 'less careful' or more relaxed they will typically use features of the local style more frequently than in their supposedly normal interview speech. In this way Labov introduced the idea of 'stylistic variation' to refer to 'intra-individual' speech variation – variation 'within the speech of single individuals'. This became a very familiar claim in community-based studies of language variation and change, and we will look at it in much more detail in Chapter 2. But it is important to note that, although Labov is mainly concerned with social style at a community level, his original insight about stylistic processes related to the individual speaker and to particular social contexts of speaking. That is, he was interested in what happens when an individual speaker delivers a version of a social style in a range of particular speaking situations. This proves to have been a seminal insight. As we shall see, however, the survey methods that Labov pioneered tend not to give priority to the local processes through which this happens. They orient much more to styles than they do to styling. The convention of basing variationist research on speech in interviews clearly limits the range of social contexts in which styling can be observed and analysed.

Several other sociolinguistic traditions, beyond variationism, are fully sensitive to contextualisation processes and have been so from the earliest days of sociolinguistics. The 'active contextualisation' perspective on social style that I am arguing for in this book is already established in other parts of sociolinguistics, and was central to Dell Hymes, John Gumperz and others' conception of *the ethnography of speaking* (Hymes 1962, 1996; Bauman and Sherzer 1989; Gumperz and Hymes 1972). The theoretical tension that we have to deal with in later chapters is in fact well summed up by the contrasting implications of the terms 'speech' and 'speaking'. The variationist study of social styles/dialects has oriented to speech and to speech data, when it also needs to orient to speaking and to the styling of meaning in social interaction. This is not an oversight or even a limitation of variationist sociolinguistics in its own terms. Variationism has simply set itself other primary objectives, linked to understanding language systems and how they change, rather than understanding social action and interaction through language. The objectifying priorities of variationist sociolinguistics show through in much of its core terminology. The word 'variation' itself implies an analyst's viewpoint, looking down at arrays of variant forms distributed over some spatial matrix. What 'varies' is the community's or the speaker's language system; more locally, what 'vary' are sociolinguistic variables (linguistic units of variable production) defined in the system. This organisation isn't accessible to, or even directly relevant to, people engaged in speaking and listening, although it is the variationist's main concern. What matters to people is the meaning that language variation might add to their discursive practices – what people are trying to mean and what they hear others to be meaning.

Formal category systems and taxonomies used by researchers in many fields of inquiry often imply equivalence between categorised units, along the lines of 'this item is one of this type and goes here, and that item is one of that type and goes there'. All research that is based on coding and counting will make assumptions of this sort, and variationist sociolinguistics does this too in some respects. Variant forms of sociolinguistic variables are defined as being equivalent in their referential meanings. In the (English) Birmingham example, the phrase *right time* has the same linguistic (referential) meaning however it is pronounced, and [aɪ] and [ɔɪ] are, to that extent, equivalent in their meaning. Whatever the speaker's accent, the utterance seems to convey the same basic information. But this approach reduces the scope of the term 'meaning' and tends to wash out issues of value as they attach to variable language in actual use. When said in a Birmingham accent, the utterance and the speaker might conceivably be held to be less convincing or authoritative, for example. The *social* meaning of the utterance, depending on how it is phonologically styled, might interconnect in significant ways with other social aspects of the speech event in which it is embedded.

Bridging between survey orientations and practice orientations in the sociolinguistics of variation seems an obvious development, even though the objectives and assumptions of (broadly) Labovian and (broadly) Hymesian sociolinguistics have traditionally been quite separate. But the separation of these two agendas is in many ways artificial. There is a certain oddness in *not* addressing social interaction as a medium for variation research, in addition to its commitment to social surveying and to reaching generalisations at that level. There is no inherent clash between 'macro' and 'micro' levels of variation analysis. One important theme in later chapters is that local processes of meaning-making depend on the affordances that socially structured variation in some sense provides, even though we need to be far more precise than this about how levels of analysis inter-relate. Speaking is the basic modality of language, where linguistic meaning potential is realised and where social meanings of different sorts are creatively implemented. If we decide to engage with the idea of social meaning, however we precisely define it, social meaning will not be something separate from the activation and interpretation of meaning in acts of speaking. The term 'discourse' (despite the many different senses in which it can be used – see Jaworski and Coupland 2007) is a useful shorthand for this wider concern. The research agenda around style can therefore also be referred to as the analysis of 'dialect in discourse'.

Quantitative analysis of the distribution of speech variants among groups of speakers is an abstraction away from the social process of speaking and of making meaning in context. It is of course an entirely legitimate research method, suited to its own purposes of generalising about language variation and change. But investigating variation in the context of social interaction is simply looking at language variation in its primary ecosystem of discursive meaning, and it can therefore claim to be a sociolinguistic priority. A more institutional argument is that there should be benefits to any one tradition of sociolinguistic research in reaching out to other traditions. So much of sociolinguistics nowadays is grounded in analyses of discourse and social interaction that, once again, it would be strange for variationism *not* to move into that arena. This move might allow us to find other, more integrative, sorts of sociolinguistic truth.

1.3 STYLE IN SOCIOLINGUISTICS AND IN STYLISTICS

It should already be obvious that the term 'style' has significant but largely different histories in sociolinguistics and in other fields. In the sociolinguistics of variation, style has been a very limited concept and a peripheral concern. In his overview of variationist sociolinguistic research Jack Chambers writes that 'style is an important independent variable but it is never the focal point (Chambers 1995: 6). As we will see in Chapter 2, stylistic variation has been treated quantitatively in sociolinguistic surveys in exactly the same way as social (or social class-related) variation is treated. It has been a matter of demonstrating that 'intra-individual' variation exists and that the nature of such variation can be explained by some simple principle or other. In this section, in order to gain some perspective, we return to some early *non*-sociolinguistic treatments of language style. Naturally enough, there are many points of contact and overlap between early sociolinguistic treatments of style and early stylistics. But those early

emphases and interests have in fact persisted much longer in variationist sociolinguistics than they have in stylistics itself. Modern
stylistics has blended into different forms of discourse analysis, pre-
figuring some of the general arguments I am making in this book.

The discipline label 'stylistics' was popularised in the 1950s, and it
came to be thought of as a discrete field of linguistics or applied
linguistics. 'General stylistics' (Sebeok 1960) was interested in all
forms of language text, spoken and written, distinguished from the
sub-field of literary stylistics. Early stylistics was dominated by linguistic structuralism, which emphasised the structural properties of texts
at different levels of linguistic organisation (phonological, grammatical, lexical, prosodic). It gloried in the technical sophistication of
linguistic description, at a time when linguistics was still developing
momentum. Stylistics was largely based on taxonomies – lists of
language features, levels and functions. For example, a very simple
hierarchical analysis of English style was offered by Martin Joos in
his strangely titled book, *The Five Clocks* (1962). The 'clocks' were levels
of formality in spoken and written English, which Joos labelled 'fro-
zen', 'formal', 'consultative', 'casual' and 'intimate'. It was based on
an intuition about degrees of familiarity/intimacy between people
which, Joos argued, impacted on communicative style. The detail of
how Joos meant these terms to be applied is not particularly important here, but the 'clocks' idea endorses a *linear* scale of 'formality'.
Formality or communicative 'carefulness' is assumed to dictate a
speaker's stylistic choices or designs. As we'll see, this is how Labov
came to operationalise sociolinguistic style too.

Roman Jakobson, in a famous lecture delivered in 1958 (Jakobson
1960, reprinted in Weber 1996a), is often credited with giving the first
coherent formulation of stylistics. Jakobson's theme was the relationship between poetics (aesthetic response to language and text) and
linguistics. His argument was that the investigation of verbal art
or poetics is properly a sub-branch of linguistics. He reached this
position by establishing that the *poetic function* of language, which he
defined as 'the set ... towards the MESSAGE, focus on the message
itself' (Jakobson 1996/1960: 15; reprinted in Weber 1996a: 10–35), is a
general function of all language use. It is not restricted to poetry and
other literary texts. Jakobson argued that, if language always has a
poetic function, linguistics must account for it, and that it could
and should therefore account for poetry and other artistic forms too.
The most original aspect of Jakobson's paper is his attempt to list
all the main functions of language. The poetic function stands alongside the *referential function* (the cognitive ordering of propositional

meaning) and the *emotive function* (affective and expressive meaning). Other functions are the *conative function* (organising meaning relative to an addressee), the *metalingual function* (language 'glossing' or referring to itself) and the *phatic function* (language marking that people are in social contact).

This is a classically structuralist piece of theory, although Jakobson's view of the multi-functional constitution of texts left a long legacy of functional approaches to linguistics as well as to stylistics in particular. In the 1958 lecture Jakobson is in fact quite scathing about 'the poetic incompetence of some bigoted linguists' (1996: 33), and at one point he quotes Martin Joos very disapprovingly for his excessive faith in absolute categories. For the contextual analysis of spoken style, Jakobson's writing is in some ways liberating as well as in other ways constraining. His claim that poetics deals with verbal 'structure' does seem to restrict the remit of stylistic inquiry to what we can read from the surface of language texts – their linguistic forms. He gives us no hint that style has an *inter*actional dimension, or that styling needs to be read and interpreted actively by listeners/readers. Similarly, he doesn't assume that stylistic meaning is produced in the interplay between textual and contextual processes, such as histories of social relationships, ideologies of language or intertextual relationships (echoes of meaning between different texts). His stylistics is to that extent 'technicist' and formalist. It puts too much emphasis on analysts' technical competence to reach analytic conclusions about stylistic effects. It sees linguistic description as an analytic competence and as a self-contained method.

There are echoes of these priorities in variationist sociolinguistics, particularly in its earliest detailing of stylistic variation in relation to accent and dialect. It would be surprising if this wasn't the case, when variationism was being coined in broadly the same structuralist intellectual climate as early stylistics. Even so, in Jakobson we also see seeds of perspectives that came to *challenge* structuralist stylistics. His set of linguistic functions already implied that language style involved meaning-making in different but simultaneously relevant dimensions of a communicative act or event. His 'metalingual' function (nowadays more commonly referred to as *metalanguage* and *metapragmatics*, see Jaworski, Coupland and Galasiński 2004; Richardson 2006) pointed to reflexive and self-referential processes at work in linguistic style. He therefore opened a perspective on language in some ways referring to itself, and speakers speaking through some level of awareness of their own stylistic operations and constructed images and identities. Although Jakobson's main objective was possibly a rather hegemonic one – to incorporate literary research into a fast-growing linguistics – the way he foregrounded the poetic function of language implied that stylistics cannot ultimately be a purely descriptive exercise. He showed that language styling, as I argued in section 1.1, has creative potential in the domain of aesthetics.

Linguistic function had been discussed much earlier, for example by Karl Bühler (1934). It was Bühler who first posited the functional categories of *representational, conative* and *expressive* (see Halliday 1996). Bronislaw Malinowski (1923) wrote about the phatic (ritualised, ceremonial) function of language (Coupland, Coupland and Robinson 1992), and J. R. Firth made important contributions to the development of a theory of language genres, which he called 'types of language'. But it was in Michael Halliday's writing that the multi-functionality of language was theorised in most detail (e.g. Halliday 1978). Halliday modelled linguistic meaning as being organised through three concurrent 'macro-functions', which he labelled *ideational, interpersonal* and *textual*. These macro-functions could be followed through from patterns of social organisation, with increasing detail and delicacy, until they explained speakers' lexico-grammatical and phonological choices at the level of individual utterances. This is Halliday's basic model of 'meaning potential' – what language can mean – and of language in use – how language means. The model has developed into a general semantic theory of language called systemic-functional linguistics. But it could also be applied, Halliday thought, specifically to the analysis of language style (Eggins and Martin 1997, Leckie-Tarry 1995).

Halliday introduced an abstract distinction between *dialect* and *register*. Dialect in this sense is language organised in relation to 'who the speaker is' in a regional or social sense, much as I introduced the term earlier. Register is language organised in relation to 'what use is being made of language'. Halliday treats register, or 'language according to use', as a plane of semantic organisation, which can be specified through the concepts of *field* (the organisation of ideational and experiential meanings), *mode* (the organisation of textual and sequential meanings) and *tenor* (the organisation of interpersonal meanings). So a particular register or way of speaking, if we treat it as a uniform type or design of language use, will have distinctive semantic qualities, reflecting speakers' choices from the whole meaning potential of the language. Ideational selections will show up as topics, things, facts or reports, most obviously in the grammatical structure of nominal groups. Textual selections will relate to choices of communicative mode/manner, sequencing, deixis and so on.

Interpersonal selections will relate to social distance between speakers, expressions of attitude, communicative 'tone' and so on. Register or style, in Halliday's conception, is the semantic organisation of linguistic choices taking account of communicative purposes and circumstances (see the useful review in Gregory and Carol 1978).

In Halliday's functional linguistics we see style emerging from the margins of linguistic theory and description, and being highlighted as an inherent dimension or set of dimensions of language organisation. Style is an inherent part of all communicative activity. Halliday says it is wrong to equate style with 'expressive' function alone:

> Even if we are on our guard against the implication that the regions of language in which style resides are linguistically non-significant, we are still drawing the wrong line. There are no regions of language in which style does not reside. (Halliday 1996 [originally 1965]: 63)

He resists 'an unreal distinction between the "what" and the "how" ... and how they may be incorporated into the linguistic study of style' (1996: 64). Register is as much about the 'what' of language use, such as what gets talked about and in what terms, as it is about the 'how' of language use. There is no act of speaking without a register or style dimension at work within it.

As a theorist of grammar and meaning, Halliday has mainly been interested in explaining the organisation of language texts. Systemic functional grammar (as Halliday's theoretical approach is known) is largely an attempt to model the increasingly detailed meaning choices that speakers make, and how meanings come to be realised in particular utterances. It is in some ways a sociolinguistic theory of language, because it tries to trace meaning choices that are made available in particular social contexts. It is of course true that many meaning choices in discourse reflect the social context of speaking in a rather direct and simple way. Speakers, for example, use technical vocabularies associated with specialist topics, purposes and 'registers'. On many other occasions, the link between context and style is far less direct, less determined and more subject to speakers' and listeners' creative agency. Systemic functional linguistics has not specialised in modelling variable language use at the level of accents and dialects. But its general perspectives on style are useful for sociolinguistics, particularly in stipulating that style is socio-semantically motivated. It emphasises that style is part of the process of meaning-making in discourse.

Halliday's concept of register grew out of a theoretical tradition, mainly in British linguistics, that had for some time been interested in the link between language use and social situations. J. R. Firth (1957) coined the phrase *context of situation*, pointing to local (objective and subjective) norms that constrain linguistic style, as in the simple and often-repeated instance when the environment of a church or mosque might be linked to silence or whispered talk. Firth twinned the term context of situation with the term *context of culture*, suggesting a nested arrangement of stylistic constraints. A culture defines a context for social interaction at a macro level, which is then specified into different social situations.

Despite Halliday's argument that style and register imply a ubiquitous dimension of complex meaning organisation in texts, the term 'register' has usually suggested a fixed relationship between 'a style' and 'a social situation'. An example would be the idea that news reading on television would be delivered in a register or style of news reading. The idea is obviously trite, although it captures a generalisation of sorts about social styles – there certainly are stylistic tendencies in 'news reader speak', even though they would not be unique to news reading, and listing them would be a rather tedious taxonomic exercise. The theoretical limitation is that, if a register is defined by the situation that it accompanies, there is no linguistic work for the concept to do. As Judith Irvine implies (Irvine 2001: 27), defining registers, and therefore styles, as situational varieties may have resulted unfortunately from Halliday's theoretical twinning of dialect and register. If dialects are presumed to be discrete regional varieties of a language, then perhaps it seems reasonable to presume that registers are discrete situational varieties of a language. Irvine again makes the point that social situations are in fact often distinguished by types of speakers populating them, and vice versa, so each dimension implies variation in the other. In fairness, this is just what Halliday stressed – that dialect and register needed to be seen as two sides of the same coin, and *not* as independent dimensions of linguistic organisation and difference. Even so, the 'twin dimensions' approach to dialect and register lowers our analytic expectations in relation to each. It endorses the view that variation can be explained in linear terms, and it points us to simple sets of categories in each dimension. The variationist model maintains these same assumptions.

In fact, the statistical and correlational linking of speech style and social situation has lived on in variationist sociolinguistics, where stylistic stratification is defined as speakers speaking differently in different situations (see Chapter 2). In sociolinguistic interviews the physical situation does not change, but types of speech activity are manufactured to introduce different levels of attention to speech by interviewees, and hence different 'situations', subjectively experienced. In this way of thinking, speech style is predicted on the basis of both dialect (relating to who the speaker socially is) and register (what situational constraints are operative), together. 'Speaking differently' is measured by the quantitative means mentioned in section 1.2 – based on how frequently particular speech variants are used by speakers. It is worth stressing again that this offers a statistical definition of 'a style' or 'a stylistic level'. A particular speaker taking part in a defined speaking activity is said to be using or producing a 'style' which is actually a numerical index of 'overall degree of standardness' on an abstract scale.

While the concept of register has not found much favour in contemporary sociolinguistics, the concept of *genre* is very firmly established (Bakhtin 1986, Macaulay 2001, Swales 1990). Common definitions of genre tell us that genres are culturally recognised, patterned ways of speaking, or structured cognitive frameworks for engaging in discourse. So the most clear-cut instances are institutionalised communicative genres, such as political speeches, lectures, post-match sports interviews or stand-up comedy routines. In these cases quite specific frameworks exist, and indeed there are often partial scripts, for how to fill out the discourse of a genre. People recognise these genres when they come across them, and they can refer to them through fairly simple labels; they appreciate their norms and their discursive demands on people taking part. Once again, this fits into a general definition of social styles. Our socialisation into a cultural group's ways of communicating is partly a matter of learning institutional genres – learning how to 'read' them and sometimes learning how to enact them, and coming to appreciate their social resonances and values.

Other genres are much more diffuse. Should we, for example, consider conversation to be a genre, or is better to think of sub-types of conversation as genres? Is banter a genre, or small talk, or gossip, or verbal play, or argument, or flirting, or story-telling (J. Coupland 2000)? Or is 'flirtatious verbal play' a genre in itself, and is 'gossipy story-telling' another one? But even diffuse, less institutionalised and hard-to-label ways of speaking like these will meet the main criterion for genre. This is the criterion that participants have some significant awareness, as part of their cultural and communicative competence, of how the event-types they are engaging with are socially constituted as ways of speaking. They will, at least to some extent, appreciate the constraints and opportunities that a particular genre brings with it. We will need to build on this core idea of genre in later chapters. For the moment it is enough to emphasise some fundamental points about the relationship between a notion of genre and early notions of style.

First, when we think of speech genres, we are pulling together what otherwise seem to be different levels of 'the social' – cultural salience and local acts of speaking. This is one way in which there is a necessary link between the local organisation of talk and macro-level social structure. To understand speaking and styling as sociolinguistic processes, we have to entertain a notion of social organisation that brings together situational and cultural contexts, much as J. R. Firth had originally suggested. Second, any notion of genre is an *interactional* notion – it specifies social positions, roles and responsibilities for social actors, and usually multiple participants. In the conceptions of style that have come up so far, we have mainly been concerned with the talk or text produced by a single person, or people grouped together in abstract ways (recall the 'young Birmingham women'), speaking under certain conditions (recall 'formal talk in an interview'). Third, genre gives an idea of social context where it is clear that the organisation in question is partly pre-figured in the social environment (culturally recognised and endorsed) and partly constructed by speakers themselves. When we embark on a sequence of gossip, we have an initial understanding that conversation can go this way, that there are specific possibilities and sanctions attached to it, and perhaps that there are specific costs and outcomes. But there is no contextual 'flag' signalling that this is how we *must* now converse. Gossip is often initiated through some subtle process of discursive negotiation whose result may be some sort of consensus that 'we are now gossiping'.

Variationist sociolinguistics, and studies of style in that tradition, have very rarely entertained any notion of genre, although it is a fundamental concept for the analysis of social meaning. I will be arguing later on that even the social meaning of particular sociolinguistic variants depends on a reading of genre and social context in that sense. In fact we will have to go much further into how social contexts are constituted than just asking 'what genre is this?' Styling is part of the process of genre-making, but also part of the process of genre-breaking. Styling can reshape conventional speech genres and how we expect to participate in them. For this sort of analysis we will also have to engage with theoretical ideas like discursive *frame* and discursive *stance*, which describe perceived qualities of social interaction operating more locally than genre.

As I have already mentioned, some sociolinguistic theories of social context have been concerned with active, local meaning-making for a long time. In these approaches it makes less sense to talk about 'styles in contexts' and more sense to talk about processes of *contextualisation* – sociolinguistic style *creating* context as well as responding to context. Arguments of this sort were made as far back as the 1970s when, for example, social psychologists of language argued that speech style should not be approached in a 'static' way but in a 'dynamic' way (Giles and Powesland 1975). Social psychologists were predisposed to seeing contexts as the outcome of subjective processes. As Howard Giles says in a reflective comment about earlier research of his own with colleagues, they were interested in 'how speaker-hearers carve up contexts psychologically and subjectively' (2001: 211). This idea opens up important possibilities, and not least that different people might construe any given social context differently, with the important implication that 'the current context' (or genre or frame, and so on) often has a degree of indeterminacy about it. Context is also amenable to tactical manipulation, and one participant can engineer another's understanding of 'where we stand in this context', perhaps to shock, to amuse or to confuse. This is one of those circumstances where Jakobson's metalinguistic function comes into discursive play. The social psychology of situational construals has not typically tracked local contextual manipulations of this sort, even though it has provided the conceptual apparatus to do this sort of analysis for a long time.

In sociolinguistics, John Gumperz developed a view of active context formation through his notion of *contextualisation cues* (Gumperz 1982: 130–52). In conversation, speakers routinely signal to others how aspects of what they are saying should be heard and analysed. A discourse marker such as *oh* at the head of an utterance, said with a short falling intonation from a high start, perhaps accompanied by a raised eyebrow, can signal that what follows is likely to be a disagreement. Gumperz says that contextualisation cues are links between surface style features and how the content of talk is to be understood and 'what the activity is' (1982: 131). But cues can create contexts in other, less consensual ways too. Accent features, intonation features and so on can lead to inferences, correct or not, about a speaker's social origins or communicative competence. Gumperz calls this process *conversational inferencing* and shows that it is a potentially damaging process of social labelling and attribution. Social attributions – for example associating forms of speech with gender, age, class or racial categories, and inferring competences of personality characteristics to them in turn – are made possible through social stereotypes (Hewstone and Giles 1986). Once again we see a theoretical nexus between local happenings in talk and socially structured beliefs and expectations, and this is the territory in which sociolinguistic styling operates.

This introductory discussion shows that issues of social context are at the heart of any analysis of language style, but also that there are many different ways in which sociolinguistics can address social context. The main distinction is between approaches that pre-determine context, recognising or even consciously setting up 'social contexts' within which to analyse style variation, and approaches that invert this relationship. In that alternative perspective, style lives in a dialogic relationship with context. Context (as in the concept of genre) is in part a socially structured phenomenon that speakers have to subscribe to and that they often live out in their talk. But context is also, in part, the product of their discursive operations. Variationist sociolinguistics has stuck with deterministic formulations of context and not generally explored the implications of social construction. As we shall see, that constructionist impetus has come more from anthropological linguistics and discourse analysis. The active/verbal/agentive sense of the term 'social meaning' becomes important in a constructionist analysis, and we need to review this core concept further, in the next section.

1.4 SOCIAL MEANING

Social meaning has always been a relevant concern in sociolinguistics, but what exactly does it refer to? Sociolinguistics is an exploration of 'the social significance of language', although we can unpack this idea in different ways. Linguists might assume that the domain of meaning belongs to them, but in fact social meaning is a core concern of many disciplines. It can refer to how we impute meaning to, and take meaning from, our cultures, our communities, our personal histories, our social institutions and our social relationships. Cultural values and norms, social power and status, intimacy and distance are all social meanings. Then there are the meanings we invest in our own and other people's social positions and attributes – selfhood, personal and social identities, social stereotypes, prejudices, conflicts and boundaries. These concepts already go a long way towards defining the problems and questions of all forms of social science, sociolinguistics included.

Many of the social sciences are interested in social meaning in a linguistic sense too, because they recognise that language provides the salient fields of action for so much of social and cultural life. A large slice of contemporary sociology, anthropology, social psychology, communication/media studies and other related disciplines is avowedly 'discursive' (and this usually means taking a 'social constructionist' view of the role of language). These disciplines generally recognise the *constitutive* power of language in the structuring of social categories and social life in general. Discursive/interactional sociolinguistics shares these assumptions too. Language-based disciplines are generally better equipped than others to undertake analysis of social meaning when there is an explicitly linguistic analytic focus, but this potential isn't always realised. A first step might be for sociolinguistics to widen its own remit when it comes to social meaning. The range of issues I have just sketched out is massive and daunting. I am not suggesting that an interactional sociolinguistic approach can do adequate service to all of them. But there is a stark contrast between the narrow sense of social meaning that has dominated in variationist sociolinguistics and the extremely broad reach of the concept elsewhere. A social constructionist approach to social meaning cannot avoid reaching into complex territories of cultural, personal, historical and sequential meanings. This is its strength and its weakness. But I will be arguing that sociolinguists *should* go after this sort of complexity of social interpretation, simply because social interaction itself implicates this level of complexity.

It is useful to look at an influential and representative variationist sociolinguistic view of social meaning. Jack Chambers writes that 'the most productive studies in the four decades of sociolinguistic research have emanated from determining the social evaluation of linguistic variants' (Chambers 2004: 3). I am sure Chambers is using the phrase 'social evaluation' as a synonym for 'social meaning', even though it might be preferable keep the term 'social evaluation' for the process of judging speech varieties or speakers. Social meaning is at the core of language variation research because, as Chambers says, 'the variants that occur in everyday speech are linguistically insignificant but socially significant' (2004: 3). His examples in an introductory discussion are these:

Adonis saw himself in the mirror
Adonis seen hisself in the mirror

These examples, and particularly the second one, may not strike us as 'everyday' utterances, even in the hypothetical context, as it might be, of someone talking about a scene they have just watched in a classical play. But the examples clearly make the point that different linguistic forms can express what is referentially the same meaning, while different social nuances are present. (This is broadly the definition of a sociolinguistic variable and its variant forms that we discussed in section 1.2.) Chambers is pointing out that the grammatical meaning of past tense in English can be expressed either by *saw*, which is conventionally called 'standard' linguistic usage, or by *seen*, described as 'non-standard' usage. Different forms of the reflexive pronoun – *himself* versus *hisself* – stand in the same relationship to each other. The linguistic or referential meaning is unchanged whichever form is spoken, but, Chambers points out, the sentences 'convey very different social meanings ... [and] *socio*linguistic significance' (2004: 4).

The second sentence of the contrasting pair is rather captivating, socially and contextually, if we try to analyse it as an act of speaking rather than just as a constructed example of 'non-standard' language. Who could have said this, in what circumstances and why, and what social meaning would we impute to the speaker or to the social arrangements that might have made this a sayable and interpretable utterance? The most striking aspect is the wonderful mis-match – the semantic dissonance – between the utterance's referential or ideational meanings (what its words denote or refer to) and the vernacular (or 'non-standard') dialect forms. We have the classical, mythological, high-culture moment of Adonis seeing his own image in a mirror, voiced through vernacular English dialect grammar. Past-tense *seen* and the reflexive pronoun *hisself* are certainly English dialect forms we can find in common use (see, for example, Cheshire 1998). But a stylistic sociolinguistic analysis (rather than a dialectological analysis) would point to a clash of stereotyped social milieux, not to simple 'variation'. Jenny Cheshire writes about 'non-standard' grammar using features of this sort among young people in Reading (a city to the west of London) indexing 'vernacular culture', and (notwithstanding the fact that the language code is English) Adonis and his mirror can be assumed to reside in a different cultural field. So we might reach for social explanations in terms of genre or register. Is the utterance *Adonis seen hisself in the mirror* said in parody? Or might it actually be a moment from classroom discourse in Reading where some school kids have been required to sum up the action of a play? Is it a studiedly anomalous bit of meaning-making of the sort that attracts attention and humour? (I suspect we have hit upon Jack Chambers's own motivation.)

Chambers is certainly not seeking to make points like these. His objective is simply to introduce the concept of social meaning in a discussion of language variation. But I think his discussion of these examples hints at what does and does not generally matter about social meaning to variationists. Chambers says that the first sentence 'is emblematic of middle-class, educated or relatively formal speech, while the second is emblematic of working-class, uneducated or highly colloquial (vernacular) speech' (2004: 4). Firstly, this view assumes that a direct indexical relationship exists between a socio-linguistic variant and a social meaning. And secondly, it reads social meaning mainly in terms of social group membership and social identity in that category-bound sense. Chambers uses the idea of 'emblematic' status to express the direct link between grammatical 'standardness' (my scare-quotes) and 'middle-class, educated or relatively formal speech' (Chambers's words). (In fact, he might mean that grammatical 'standardness' is emblematic of middle-class-ness and educated-ness, because grammatical 'standardness' *is* a way of speaking, not an emblem of a way of speaking.) The main assumption here is that the grammatical 'standardness' of past tense *saw* stands for (connotes, implicates, signals, evokes, indexes) being a member of the social group we know as 'educated middle-class', and so on. Later in the same source Chambers in fact says that the social significance of linguistic variants is very often *not* an attribute of their presence or absence in a person's speech, but rather of their frequency in that person's speech compared to someone else's speech (2004: 115). But we can come back to the complicating issue of statistical frequencies and their connection to social meaning in Chapter 2.

So does 'standard grammar' – always and necessarily – emblematically signal that a speaker is a member of the 'educated middle-class'? Apart from the severe difficulties of defining these sociological terms, we have not yet taken account of contextualisation. A key problem with the terms 'standard' and 'non-standard' (and one of my reasons for scare-quoting them) is that we can really only understand one of them in relation to the other. There might be some social shadow of 'educatedness' around 'standard' grammar if we are made aware of there being a shadow of 'uneducatedness' around a 'non-standard' or vernacular alternative grammatical form. The social meaning that Chambers posits seems to be an effect of putting the two utterances next to each other as examples, more than a result of the inherently 'emblematic' status of either. Following Irvine (2001), Ben Rampton stresses 'the indelible relationality of styles' (2006: 379, note 5). This is the same point that I made earlier, that styles achieve their meaning through contrast and difference. If we take the view that 'standard' grammar is 'least exceptional' language – a moot point, but *Adonis seen hisself in the mirror* isn't an unexceptional utterance form – then the grammar of the 'standard' equivalent sentence isn't truly emblematic of anything; it is unexceptional.

There is obviously some need for further clarity in this sort of discussion, and it will be useful to look back to early semiotic theory where concepts in the general area of 'standing for' relationships were first developed. The link between an expression or form and what it meaningfully stands for is usually referred to by the term *indexicality* that has already come up in the discussion (but see also Milroy 2004, Silverstein 1976). The formal definition of an *index* was conceived by Charles Peirce (1931–58). Peirce said that an index is a relationship between a sign and a referent (the object that it is linked to) which is based on a physical or in some other way objective or 'real' association. For example, a bullet hole 'indexes' the fact that a bullet has penetrated a surface. An index can in theory be distinguished from an *icon*, which is where we perceive some sort of natural resemblance between the sign and the object that it signifies, such as when a photograph provides an iconic 'likeness' of a person. A third type of relationship occurs with *symbols*, where societies forge links that are originally arbitrary between signs and meanings, such as an eagle being taken to stand symbolically for authority. Using these terms carefully, following Peirce, we would have to say that a grammatically 'standard' variant, treated as a sign in semiotic theory, has *symbolic* meaning, because the link between it and being middle-class is arbitrary rather than natural or objective.

The study of *language ideologies* – the study of how languages and linguistic styles or features come to have given social and ideological meanings – suggests ways in which links of this sort can in fact be reshaped (Gal and Irvine 1995, Irvine 2001). There is the process of *naturalisation*, when arbitrary signs that we would technically call symbols are treated *as if* they were (natural) icons or (objective) indexes. We can see that technically arbitrary or meaningless bits of sound and linguistic form, like features of accent and dialect, very frequently come to have indexical-type meaning. People come to believe that using a particular accent caries the 'objective' or 'natural' meaning of 'low social class' or 'uneducated speaker'. The process called *recursion* refers to the expanding of a meaning relation, for example when the meaning 'uneducated speaker' gets attached to a single speech feature. This might be the grammatical feature 'non-standard past-tense *seen*' as in Chambers's example, or the phonological feature often referred to as 'G dropping' – using alveolar [n] instead of velar [ŋ] in words like *waiting, seeing, something* and *nothing*. The ideological process of *erasure* is when a pattern of meaning associations is simplified, and one part of the meaning complex is forgotten about or elided (Gal and Irvine 1995, Manning 2004).

These ideas about language-ideological processes help us to see that indexical relationships (using this now as a general term) are not entirely stable over time. Recursion and erasure might come about through slow historical processes of change, as the social meanings of a linguistic form or pattern gradually shift. But it is quite feasible for speakers to bring about similar shifts locally in their talk. They can, for example, creatively forge a new association between a linguistic form and an individual or group not previously linked to it. Other sorts of shift are also possible. Penelope Eckert writes about the process of stylistic *objectification* in young people's social development:

> social development involves a process of objectification, as one comes to see oneself as having value in a marketplace (Eckert 2000: 14).

She argues that 'at this point, speakers can point to social meaning – they can identify others as jocks or burnouts [group labels that young people use to mark their pro-school or anti-school orientations – see section 2.5], as elite or working-class, educated or not, prissy or tough' (2000: 43). Therefore, sociolinguistic indexicalities are sometimes matters of social attribution, and they become amenable to being discussed, argued over and renegotiated, metalinguistically.

So, even when we are dealing with social meaning in terms of the indexical potential of social styles such as accent/dialect features, individually or in bunches, we have to be aware of complexities and possible instabilities in meaning relationships. We should not expect linguistic features to have unique social meanings, even in the same socio-cultural settings. Scott Fabius Kiesling's (1998) study of the complex social meanings of the 'G-dropping' variable used by young men in college fraternities in the USA is an excellent case in point. Kiesling suggests that the 'non-standard' [n] form of the (ing) variable among male students can index the social attribute of being 'hardworking', or having a 'casual' approach or being 'confrontational'. In Kiesling's view the [n] feature has no meaning as such, and acquires meaning 'only when an identity takes shape through the tension between the text and content and the negotiation between speaker and hearer' (Kiesling 1998: 94).

In later discussions we will need to return to these active contextualisation approaches to indexicality. They clearly undermine the assumption of 'one form, one social meaning'. But they also imply that we should look for social meaning in different places. It is not the case – or at least it is not *only* the case – that language forms are allocated meanings by the sociolinguistic system and then 'selected' locally. We will need to think in terms of social *meaning potential* (to use Halliday's phrase) being called up or activated or validated, or undermined or challenged or parodied, in particular discursive frames for particular local effects. This would imply, once again, that social meaning doesn't exclusively reside in linguistic forms, or even in so-called speech communities or in speakers' sociolinguistic histories and experiences. It is partly a situated achievement in acts of speaking.

1.5 METHODS AND DATA FOR RESEARCHING SOCIOLINGUISTIC STYLE

Discussions of sociolinguistic research methods and data have usually focused on one main contrast. This is the contrast between the use of intuited or 'made-up' linguistic data and the use of observed or authentic or naturally occurring data. These terms and distinctions are actually not as straightforward as they appear. Sociolinguistics has always committed itself to the principle of linguistic *observation* (Labov 1972c) because it has been assumed that unforeseeable regularities of language variation can be found only through careful surveys and their analyses of real speech data. Variationist sociolinguistics is self-consciously bullish about its empirical discovery procedures. It is clearly an empiric*ist* research tradition. Its epistemology – its research philosophy – is grounded in neutral observation, minimising observer-effects, and objective analysis of data through precise and replicable quantitative procedures. William Labov outlined what he called the *observer's paradox* (1972b: 61ff.). This is the tension implied in needing to observe speech data of the sort that is produced when speakers are *not* being observed. Labov reasoned that the process of observing speech would make a speaker speak self-consciously and therefore unnaturally. This was the basis of his method for eliciting style-shifts in interviews (see Chapter 2). This line of argument represents communicative reflexivity as a methodological problem.

The standard procedures of the sociolinguistic survey interview were developed as a way of getting round the apparent problem of the observer's paradox. Observation remains the key method for variationist sociolinguistics, and sociolinguists often feel that need to 'leave the laboratory' and 'get out there' into the 'real world' of language use. Crawford Feagin (2004), for example, writes about the need to 'enter the community' to solve the observer's paradox.

Technical research apparatus to do with sampling, recording, transcription and formal analysis follows on from this. A concept of 'good data' exists in variationist sociolinguistic surveying and it relates to criteria of naturalness, untaintedness and representativeness, as well as to the need to get excellent acoustic quality in audio-recording. These priorities follow from the primary objective of discovering how linguistic systems are structured and how they might be changing.

Any study of speech style, including research targeted at linguistic variation's role in the construction of social meaning, has to engage with these classical problems of sociolinguistic method. All sociolinguistic studies need 'good data', even though they will interpret this idea differently. But the empiricist assumptions driving sociolinguistic observations introduce their own problems of theory and method. One of these problems is the basic assumption that speaking is 'real' or 'natural', provided it is not observed. As we will see, it is well worth exploring what lies behind these assumptions and behind the general appeal to 'sociolinguistic authenticities' and 'the authentic speaker'(see section 7.2). *Is* it in fact possible to define naturalness in speaking, and to determine when speaking is and is not natural? *Is* it enough to rely on sampling procedures and clever devices in the design of interviews to gain access to the 'ordinary' or 'everyday' usage that variationists value? What is 'authentic speech' and what defines authentic speaking (Bucholtz 2003, Coupland 2003, Eckert 2003)?

As we will see later, these may not even be the most profitable questions to ask. Instead of either glorifying authenticity or dismissing it out of hand, we can approach it in other ways. Authenticity could be a powerful concept to use *within* the analysis of style. Styling, for example, creates social meanings around personal authenticity and inauthenticity, when speakers parody themselves or present themselves as 'not being themselves'. Erving Goffman (e.g. 1981) has given us intriguing insights into how performance and theatricality intrude into everyday social practices, and sociolinguistic variation gives us resources to 'stage' our identities in many different ways. We can think about 'self-authentication' and 'other-authentication', but also 'de-authentication', as strategic possibilities for how we construct identities in talk.

The conventional wisdom around authenticity has been far more straightforward. Sociolinguistic surveys have tended to assume that speakers are, in themselves, authentic members of the groups and the 'speech communities' that they inhabit – recall our Birmingham women, once again. This assumption is part of the political ideology of variationism, dignifying 'ordinary people' and vernacular speech as issues of community entitlement. The empiricist approach puts speakers into fixed social categories and assumes that being a member of one rather than another social group has consequences at the level of language use. But we can alternatively ask how people align themselves with social groups, for different purposes at different times. How is language variation implicated in these acts of social construction? There may well be times when speakers style themselves as 'authentic Birmingham speakers' or 'authentically female', or both simultaneously, or neither. So authenticity is not so much a condition of a research design; it is a social meaning.

For the sociolinguistic analysis of style, where the emphasis is on local contextualisation as well as on socially contextualised speech, it is actually difficult to define the 'best' data to use. There is certainly no need to prioritise the use of interview data, nor any need to rule out interviews either. Conventional sociolinguistic interviews are quite strongly shaped in advance, setting out different types of speech activity for interviewees to engage in, such as answering questions, telling stories, reading written text aloud and reading word-lists. But most social situations will have a pre-existing social architecture and a genre structure within which social meanings can be negotiated. What matters for a stylistic analysis is that the analyst should understand these contexts and be able to appreciate social actors' own understandings of them. That is, there is a greater demand for *ethnographic* understanding of social context in stylistic research, because we cannot assume that the research design itself has defined social contexts as they are relevant to the data. For example, gender identity is not accounted for in advance by establishing groups of speakers that we label male and female. What we need is a nuanced understanding of how gender provides part of the historical and ideological backdrop to a particular interaction. This might then give us the chance to read stylistic, discursive processes in which gender is negotiated. Social class is perhaps the most telling example, since the meanings of class have shifted so radically over recent decades in the West and social status is so clearly a matter of local contextualisation – a matter of being able to perform the role.

Ethnographic understanding can itself be gained in different ways (Hammersley and Atkinson 1995). The primary resource is the researcher's own understandings of particular social histories and norms, of habitual modes of speech and genres, and of how forms of speech and social contexts generally work meaningfully into each

other. Stylistic analysis, and interpretive sociolinguistic research generally, are often difficult to do outside a familiar ecosystem. It is also
useful, where possible, to use different techniques and approaches
to answer sociolinguistic questions. For example, style analysis can
be very usefully informed by earlier variationist surveys, where the
quantitative distribution of sociolinguistic variables gives us a generalised appreciation of which speech variants are symbolically active,
and in what general ways. A good example (see section 5.8) is Ben
Rampton's distributional analysis of the UK varieties and features he
calls 'posh' (or 'standard' or Received Pronunciation) and 'Cockney'
(London-accented speech). Attitude surveys are a different sort of
resource again (see section 4.4). They can fill out our understanding
of general ideological beliefs about language variation. So, multiple
research methods can be combined in the analysis of sociolinguistic
style, even though the main challenge is to build local analyses of
styling *in situ*, and this will probably involve qualitative rather than
quantitative analysis, and interpretive rather than empiricist research
designs.

Case studies and the speech of particular individuals or interactional clusters of people will be the main focus in style research. This
will sometimes be because we have good reason to be interested in
those individuals *as individuals*, as Barbara Johnstone has argued
(Johnstone 1996). I have already mentioned that sociolinguistic
studies of variation usually play down the individuality of speakers,
because researchers are more interested in statistical patterns when
speakers are grouped together. When sociolinguistic studies of style
variation have done this, the results have often been important and
revealing. Conversation analysts too talk about 'mundane data' –
a celebration of the ordinary, which sociolinguistics has also
contributed to – and it is true that 'ordinary speech' is often remarkable when it is closely analysed. Ordinariness also has powerful
democratic associations. On the other hand, speakers can be socio-
linguistically interesting for their unique and non-ordinary characteristics. There are sometimes relevant cultural-historical factors for
studying key individuals, for example in my considering of a famous
Welsh politician's public oratory (section 6.4). Styling is part of the
make-up of public as well as private discourses, and there is no over-
arching need to restrict sociolinguistics to sampling the speech of
'ordinary folk'. Whichever speakers we settle on as informants – for a
wide variety of reasons – the individual case needs to be addressed as
well as the general tendency. This is because aggregation *rounds down*
our understanding of stylistic processes. It often blurs the potential

for analytic insight. Single-case analyses are more likely to allow an adequate sensitivity to context and contextualisation, where we can come to understand what the styling of variation can achieve. There *is* the possibility of generalising from single-case analyses, but it involves generalising to what is stylistically possible, rather than to 'what people typically do'.

Some of the case studies I summarise, especially in Chapter 6, derive from mass media sources. This way of working seems to infringe socio-linguistic norms for variation research, because language 'in the community' has not usually been taken to include mediated language. But the reach and impact of media language in contemporary social life are indisputable. The boundary between private and public life-domains is less clear than it was previously, and mass-mediated language is often based on informality and intimacy as well as formality and distance. Norman Fairclough (1995a) makes the point that public discourse is in many ways being *conversationalised*, even if he is suspicious of the motives behind this sort of realignment. But equally we can say that 'everyday talk' is taking on qualities of performance and reflexivity that we would formerly have associated with mass-media rather than interpersonal domains. The media are increasingly inside us and us in them. This is not a simple claim about how the mass media might be causally involved in language change, which has been a controversial issue in sociolinguistics. It is more a matter of how footings for social interaction and stylistic designs for talk seem to be crossing over, as between on-air and off-air contexts (see section 7.3).

At the same time, it is probably true that institutionally framed talk media (TV and radio) provide stronger and more interpretable frames for spoken performance, and this relative clarity sometimes helps us analyse style at work in spoken performances. Media talk, with its typically very strong reflexive design, its transparent genre structures and its repeated formats, is in many ways a more vivid representation of more 'everyday' social interaction. It is not different in kind, and it does not necessarily demand more specialist analytic concepts. Ethnography is often understood to involve close participant observation done over extended periods of time spent with the people and contexts we are researching. As I mentioned earlier, this is a key resource for understanding cultural norms and conventions of social meaning. But mass media are of course a constitutive part of our cultures, and most of us can't avoid being ethnographers of mediated talk and relationships, as well as ethnographers of non-media discourses in our own environments.

1.6 STYLE IN LATE-MODERNITY

I have organised most of my introductory comments around the relationship between survey research on linguistic variation inspired by William Labov and alternative approaches to language in context. This relationship also has an important historical dimension. No-one can doubt that the social worlds to be described, in 1960 (when variationist research was formalised by William Labov) and today, are very different. There are good reasons to use different labels for these time-periods, although labelling epochs and seeming to claim that an epoch is summed up by its label are risky strategies. The terms 'modernity' and 'late-modernity' (or 'high modernity') (Beck, Giddens and Lash 1996, Giddens 1991) have at least some potential to point to social changes in the West since 1960. The term 'late-modernity' might be preferred to 'post-modernity' because it suggests a capitalist modernity that is moving out of its 'early' phases of developing global economic markets and reaching into new cultural spheres. It suggests that modernist social arrangements have not in any simple sense lapsed. Modernity was the condition of the so-called 'developed world' as it had emerged from the Second World War, quite hierarchically structured through social class and region, with rather rigid gender, race and age norms. Modernity tended to keep people in their allotted places. It generated relatively clear social styles. The decade of the 1960s is often associated with the beginnings of a rethinking of the normative basis of social structure. Popular culture and mass communication technologies began to accelerate, and are accelerating ever faster now. Culture has become increasingly commodified (see for example Schilling-Estes (1998) on the performance of 'quaint' dialect in Ocracoke in the USA) and 'choice' has become a buzz word in most dimensions of social life. Society today is characterised by high levels of mobility (geographical and social), complexity, fragmentation, contradiction, risk and disembedding. Social life seems increasingly to come packaged as a set of lifestyle options able to be picked up and dropped, though always against a social backdrop of economic possibilities and constraints. Anthony Giddens theorises late-modernity as a 'runaway world' (Giddens 2002); Ulrich Beck theorises it as 'the risk society' (Beck 1992). Late-modernity offers new opportunities for social change and for release from old structures and strictures. But it also complicates social identities, social relationships and social institutions as it detraditionalises and destabilises life.

There is a debate in social theory around whether these are 'real' changes or changes in how we look at and interpret the social world. For example, people could, and of course did, move geographically and socially in earlier times. Through the centuries the social categories of gender, age, class and even race were never totally constraining and determining. We will certainly see more social complexity if we look for it. However, in terms of degree, mobility is obviously far more characteristic of the twenty-first century than forty or even twenty years ago. Flow is a key quality of globalisation (Hannerz 1996). Late-modernity is not only a set of changes within particular parts of the world but also a new set of global inter-relationships. In fact the idea of 'community' is further complicated by globalising tendencies in late-modernity, including the relentless drive towards consumer culture and the spread of genres and styles associated principally with the USA, particularly in popular culture. Social class and racial inequalities persist stubbornly, but class membership in the West is not the straitjacket that it was. Within limits, some people can make choices in their patterns of consumption and take on the social attributes of different social classes. In turn, the meaning of class is shifted.

It would be wrong to treat late-modernity as a clearly definable social climate in which social action now happens. Late-modernity makes social life more contingent and unpredictable, and the epistemology of social construction is a response to it. We might say that social life is *more obviously amenable to being socially constructed* in late-modernity, and this brings language and discourse more clearly into perspective. Language is a major resource through which we construct our social worlds and sociolinguistic approaches to local contextualisations of meaning are well attuned to this perspective. But style, in the sense in which I am dealing with it in this book, is *generally* well attuned to the nature of language use in late-modernity. The word 'style' itself, dated in some of its uses, is also a buzz word of late-modernity. It refers to short-lived fashion and to adoptive ways of dressing and behaving. It is oriented to consumption. Style is treated as an agentive possibility for social identification – how we can style ourselves. *Lifestyle*, as mentioned above, is often said to be supplanting social structure (e.g. class) as an organising principle of late-modern living (Machin and Van Leeuwen 2005). Studying social meaning through sociolinguistic styling gives us a way of under-standing social identities and social relationships with sufficient flexibility and dynamism to capture some of the qualities of late-modern social life.

1.7 LATER CHAPTERS

Chapter 2 returns us to the earliest days of style research within the variationist paradigm. I assess the value of the structural model of variation that Labov introduced, specifically as a basis for understanding style in speech. Chapter 3 reviews the best-developed and most coherent sociolinguistic theories of style – audience design and speech accommodation theory. These are the approaches that opened up our appreciation of the socially constructive potential of style-shifting. They deal with the relational designs in styling, where style follows specific motives and delivers specific communicative effects. Chapter 4 then stands back to consider the idea of sociolinguistic resources for meaning-making through style. Where do social meanings come from, and what affordances do they bring to styling?

Chapters 5 and 6 deal with qualitative and interactional approaches to style, with an emphasis on the creative contextualisation of social meanings. Chapter 5 examines person-centred stylistic constructions where speakers perform 'acts of identity', breaking as well as keeping to sociolinguistic norms, in different communicative genres and keys. Chapter 6 focuses more closely on stylistic performance, and indeed on what we can call 'high performance' events, when stylised and sometimes extravagant identities are brought into play. In the final chapter I attempt to consolidate a few of the key arguments and positions that emerge in the book, specifically arguments around authenticity and mediatisation in late-modernity.

It should therefore be possible to read Chapters 2 to 6 as a progressive funnelling down of critical attention, from the broad sweep of survey research in Chapter 2 to the contingencies of local construction and performance in particular communicative events in the later chapters. This rhetorical structure is intended to mimic the sharpening and specifying of analytic concerns that, I am suggesting, sociolinguistics needs to adopt under the rubric of style and styling.

2 Style and meaning in sociolinguistic structure

2.1 STYLISTIC STRATIFICATION

The idea of organised difference, structured heterogeneity, in language is fundamental to variationist sociolinguistics (Weinreich, Labov and Herzog 1968: 99–100; Bayley 2004: 117). Understanding linguistic diversity in one sense or another is a key concern of all sociolinguistic approaches, but being able to demonstrate general principles at work in the *structuring* of linguistic differences linked to language change has been the great achievement of variationism. Finding order where randomness was thought to prevail is a classical quest in empirical science. In Chapter 1 I noted the empiricist leanings of the language variation and change paradigm. It has developed tight specifications for how language use should be observed in what have been called 'speech communities'. The approach has demonstrated statistical regularities of 'sociolinguistic structure'. In this chapter the point I want to return to is that these priorities, which are admirable for understanding linguistic systems, have supported only a very narrow conception of stylistic variation. The sociolinguistic study of style was born in these circumstances and has delivered several important general findings. But I will emphasise what is left *un*addressed in a structural model of style.

We have already touched on some of the political issues behind variationism. Demonstrating orderliness across the social class spectrum of language variation certainly has political implications. Social elites and elite institutions – or somewhat wider forces that we might call 'the establishment' – have always held strong views about social propriety and linguistic properness (Mugglestone 2003). The establishment was never in doubt that orderliness, according to its own definition, was its own proper concern, and that part of its duty was to conserve linguistic orderliness in social affairs. Acting concertedly *against* establishment values, the sociolinguistics of variation took

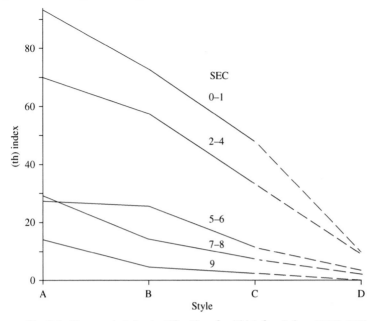

Fig. 2.1. Class and style stratification for (th) (after Labov 2006: 167)

on the task of showing orderliness in so-called 'non-standard' or 'stigmatised' speech, especially in urban contexts. William Labov's survey methods were brilliantly able to demonstrate forms of social orderliness in linguistic distributions that could only be identified if researchers looked beyond elite speech. This involved detailed scrutiny of the speech of all social classes. The result was a layered pattern – a form of sociolinguistic structure that Labov called *social stratification*.

Labov's classical mapping of linguistic variation in New York City's Lower East Side (Labov 1966, 1972a, 1972b) took the form of tables and charts which organised variation in two principal dimensions, referred to as social variation and stylistic variation. Social and stylistic factors were thought of as constraints on variation, alongside 'linguistic' or 'internal' constraints imposed by the linguistic contexts in which particular variable features operate. Figures 2.1 and 2.2 are probably the most widely discussed representations of Labov's striking findings. Labov (2001a: 36) notes that the Lower East Side study was methodologically less complete than his later research in Philadelphia, and that the earlier study is perhaps over-exposed in general reviews (like my own here). On the other hand, it was the Lower East Side study in New York that established the main

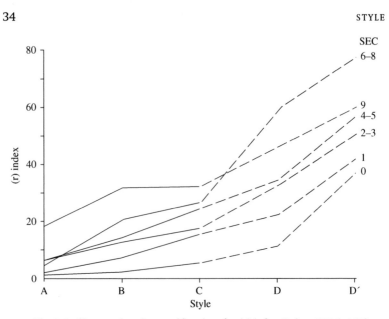

Fig. 2.2. Class and style stratification for (r) (after Labov 2006: 152)

parameters and principles of urban variationism. (See Labov 2001a, Chapter 2 for a detailed account of his Philadelphia research.)

Each figure shows that, in respect of one particular pronunciation variable and in a statistical sense, speech variation in New York City patterns according to social class – the vertical dimension of each figure – and simultaneously patterns according to 'style' – the horizontal dimension. The data set comprised 151 interviews, 50 of them when the researcher interviewed a single adult alone. In this study the phonetic detail was coded impressionistically and numerical results were not analysed through formal statistics (Labov 2001a: 36–7), although Labov's later research was far more robust in these regards.

The sociolinguistic variable (th) in Figure 2.1 refers to variation in the choice of consonants when speakers pronounce written 'th' at the beginning of words like *thing* and *through*. The variable is analysed in terms of the frequency of occurrence of its 'stigmatized' or 'non-standard' variant – how often speakers in a particular group and in a particular speech activity pronounce a [t]-like sound in place of the 'standard' [θ] variant. The index scores for (th) represent actual amounts of [t] pronunciation relative to the maximum potential occurrence. Comparably, variable (r) in Figure 2.2 relates to pronunciation corresponding to written 'r' after vowels, in words like *guard* and *four*.

It is, once again, analysed in terms of the frequency of occurrence of its less prestigious variable, which is zero (no [r] sound), as opposed to audible [r]-coloured or '[r]-ful' realisations. (As Labov does, I use the [r] symbol here to represent a generic [r] sound; the feature is actually continuant [ɹ] in IPA terms.) In each case, numerical values are obtained for each variable at each point on the graph, where data can be calculated for a particular social class group speaking in a particular 'style' during the interview.

Values for five social class groups (called 'SEC' groups in the figures, referring to socio-economic classes) are marked in Figure 2.1 and for six social class groups in Figure 2.2 – the lines running left to right across the graphs. SEC group 0–1 is the lowest social class, through to SEC 9, which is the highest social class. The data for (th) is from interviews with 81 adults; Labov does not clearly describe the sample for the (r) results although it must be comparable. Figure 2.1 shows values for four 'contextual styles', and Figure 2.2 has these same four, labelled A, B, C and D, plus a fifth labelled D'. Definitions of the 'contextual styles' are given below each figure. Category A is so-called 'casual speech', which was contextually engineered in the socio-linguistic interview, for example by getting speakers to become emotionally absorbed in narratives they were telling the interviewer. B is 'careful speech', taken to reflect the usual level of formality in interview exchanges. C, D and D' are different sorts of read-aloud speech, based on reading out a passage of continuous written text (C), lists of words (D), or lists of 'minimal pairs' (D', words differing minimally from each other in some limited phonetic respect).

Labov offers the metaphor of stratification to describe variation in each dimension – social stratification and, the main interest for present purposes, *stylistic stratification*. The metaphor of social stratification picks up on the familiar way of referring to social class arrangements as being a 'vertical' form of social structure. It is entirely conventional, but ideologically very significant, to refer to 'high' versus 'low' social class. But note that Figure 2.1 places data for the 'lowest' social classes nearest the top of the figure, while Figure 2.2 has them the other way round. Labov's sociological formula for measuring social class combines indicators of occupation (of the family 'bread-winner'), education (of the speaker) and income (of the family). This results in the numbered groups in each figure which are then labelled 'lower class' through to 'upper middle class'.

The (th) variable is an example of what Labov calls a stable sociolinguistic variable, whose distribution and value has not changed in the community for many decades. Figure 2.1 shows that it sharply ranks or stratifies the social classes 'vertically' in their 'casual' and 'careful' speech modes, and also (though less dramatically) in the read-aloud speech, based on averaged numerical values. In fact, as Labov says, there seem to be two main bands or strata according to social class. As the 'styles' change from less formal to more formal (from left to right in the figure), we get an impression of speakers 'editing out' the stigmatised [t]-like feature from their pronunciation. According to the graph this is particularly true of the lowest social classes – the ones that have the highest frequencies of the feature in their 'casual' speech. Note that the extent of difference between the social class strata decreases as formality increases. That is, the 'editing out' effect reduces the social class differences between the groups in respect of the (th) variable.

With the (postvocalic r) variable, audible [r]-colouring after vowels, produced by forming an articulatory constriction with the tongue behind the teeth ridge, was an increasingly common prestige feature at the time of the research, one that Labov showed was a change in progress in New York City. In the Figure 2.2 data, although most social class groups use quite modest frequencies of the [r] feature in their 'casual' speech, they progressively use more of the feature as the formality of the speech activity increases (again, moving from left to right in Figure 2.2). A 'cross-over' pattern for social class groups 6–8 emerges in these results. Groups 6–8 are usually referred to as the 'lower middle classes'. They outstrip the highest social class group in their very high frequencies of [r] use in the most formal (read-aloud) speech activities. Labov suggests that the pattern gives us evidence of linguistic change under social pressure:

> the hypercorrect behavior of the lower middle class is seen as a synchronic indicator of linguistic change in progress (Labov 1972b: 115).

Stylistic variation in this seminal study was therefore introduced as a pattern of numerical ordering according to a linear scale of formality, not unlike Martin Joos's 'five clocks' discussed in Chapter 1. (Labov in fact cites Joos – 1972b: 80.) Labov's terminology – 'careful' versus 'casual' styles – reflected the underlying theory that stylistic variation was a consequence of differential *degrees of attention to speech*. That is, he argued that his speakers became more aware of their own ways of speaking as the interview activities moved along a notional scale towards greater formality. They were less attentive to their speech in 'casual' style, more attentive in 'careful' style, and, by implication, even more so in the read-aloud styles. Many sociolinguists have challenged or even rejected the attention-to-speech theory. As we will see later, other explanations for the same patterns of variation can be suggested. But the general idea of stylistic variation as 'structured' and systemic is less often challenged. Labov confirms his early perspective on stylistic stratification in a more recent chapter. He says that:

> communities display both social stratification and stylistic stratification with the same variable. For a stable sociolinguistic variable, regular stratification is found for each contextual style; and conversely, all groups shift along the same stylistic dimension in the same direction with roughly [similar] slopes of style-shifting (Labov 2001b: 86).

We need to look more critically at what Labov's approach implies and assumes, and at what it excludes. All the same, it is important to stress that empirical research on stylistic variation, at least within the variationist canon, has been relatively rare since Labov's groundbreaking early studies. Recall Jack Chambers's comment that style is never of central importance in variationist sociolinguistics. In this tradition, the idea of style has been mainly taken over into Allan Bell's audience design framework (see Chapter 3), followed by less methodologically rigid and more ethnographic approaches that are the focus of later chapters. Peter Trudgill's early replication of Labov's New York City survey in Norwich in the east of England (Trudgill 1974) matches the Labovian design point for point. Trudgill found very similar distribution tendencies across the same categories of 'style' that Labov introduced, for example in the (ing) variable (alveolar [n] versus velar [ŋ] in '-ing' suffixed verbs). Walt Wolfram's (1969) study of African American English in Detroit showed style differences among his working-class speakers. For example, they had far higher rates of deleting third-person singular present tense -s endings (*he go* versus *he goes*) in their interview speech than in read-aloud styles. Similarly with variation in presence/absence of the copula (verbal 'be' – *he mine* versus *he's mine*). Reid (1978) and Romaine (1984a) are examples of other variationist studies producing comparable findings of orderly stylistic variation.

2.2   LIMITS OF THE STRATIFICATION MODEL FOR STYLE

First we should return to a point made in Chapter 1. Figures 2.1 and 2.2 visually express the assumption of social and stylistic variation operating in two closely related but separate dimensions. This is directly reminiscent of Michael Halliday's discussion of 'dialect' and 'register',

as 'two sides of the same coin'. Labov's statistical treatment of variation is based on a particularly strong interpretation of the 'two sides of
a coin' idea. The two-dimensional display of variation assumes that
style is a contextual re-ordering of precisely the same form of speech
variation that distinguishes social (i.e. social class) groups. Social and
stylistic 'planes of variation' are two different abstractions from the
same data. Formality or carefulness is assumed to be a matter of
speakers modifying their speech in respect of those same features
that define their place in a social hierarchy. We might say that 'speaking carefully', in this model, is no different from speaking in the
person of a socially more prestigious speaker – it is assumed to be a
re-voicing of social class, or a modification of a speaker's social class
self-projection.

Labov suggested that 'The same sociolinguistic variable is used to
signal social and stylistic stratification. It may therefore be difficult to
interpret any signal by itself – to distinguish, for example, a casual
salesman from a careful pipe-fitter' (1972b: 240). It has always been
tempting to suggest a rebuttal to this claim – that, if you really needed
a pipe-fitter and not a salesman, you would find ways to tell the
difference. The more serious point is, though, that social and stylistic
dimensions are only *made to seem* related in this intimate way by virtue
of the method of analysis and the method of displaying findings.
Social meanings made around class and social meanings based around
formality/carefulness (even if for a moment we accept that style is
variation in a dimension of formality) *can* be quite unrelated, and they
can be articulated through *different* linguistic resources. For example,
speaking slowly is not an obvious correlate of higher social class,
although it sometimes marks or implies a careful approach to communicating. Speaking through a low prestige dialect doesn't in itself
attract attributions that one is always being 'casual'. Stylistic projections of self often *do* entail social class semiosis, especially in those
societies where class is deeply ingrained in the social fabric. But it is
reductive to limit a theory of style in speaking to speakers playing
with class identities.

In later work Labov adds some detail to his theorising of stylistic
variation but without modifying his original assumptions. For example, in comparing his Lower East Side New York study and the later
Philadelphia study he says that methodological advances in the later
research allowed researchers to record data that were closer to community norms for vernacular speech. Even in 'first time' recording
sessions in Philadelphia, researchers were more familiar to, and more
accepted by, informants. As a result, '"casual" and "careful" speech are

relative terms' (Labov 2001a: 105, with original quote-marks). This is an important caveat, possibly recognising that stylistic 'strata' are to some extent artefacts of the empirical methods used. On another occasion Labov provides an interesting break-down of the categories 'careful speech' and 'casual speech' in terms of sub-genres of talk that sociolinguistic interviews allow (Labov 2001b). 'Careful speech' is filled out partly by the category 'response', which he defines as the first part of an informant's speech following speech by the interviewer. If the informant then develops a response into a personal narrative, that 'narrative' becomes a category in 'casual speech'. Talk about 'language' (that is, metalinguistic discourse) is assigned to 'careful speech', while most speech about 'kids', particularly when it takes kids' point of view, is assigned to 'casual speech', and so on. Labov argues that this refinement confirms the validity of the two main types of speech, but lets us 'register the dynamic component of sociolinguistic behavior' (2001b: 108).

Ben Rampton has a positive critical reading of Labov's way of handling the class/style relationship. The idea that social class positions can be 'carried into' or 'realised in practice as' some form of variation by each individual speaker is, Rampton suggests, theoretically liberating (Rampton 2006: 229). It is certainly true that, if we read Labov's method as a moral argument, it might seem to 'free' speakers from the tightest strictures of their apparent class position. They can style-shift out of class. But the uniform directionality of style-shifting that emerges from Labov's graphs is not really liberation. It seems more like a claim about a 'pattern of the culture' where speakers who attend more closely to their speech regularly shift in the direction of the establishment norm. To me, Labov's style-shifting speakers suggest a shoal of swimming fish, grouped together in a social bundle, who suddenly veer away together in a single new direction when they recognise the presence of a predator. If the shoal of fish is an aggregation of working-class speakers, their style-shifting might be a culturally predictable veering towards 'safer waters', when threatened by the ideological predator – the establishment's demand that public speech should be 'more correct'.

Variationist sociolinguistics has sometimes been criticised for overplaying and presupposing the importance of social class in its sociology. This is most obviously so in its interpretation of gender differences, where once again the dominant approach has been to establish gender-related variation in terms of class-related variables (see Chapter 5). So, the assumption has appeared to be that the class order is to some extent replicated in the statistical patterning of men and women's speech. Men, that is, are 'less posh' (where 'posh' is a rather disapproving representation of 'standard' establishment demeanour). As a descriptive fact of variation, men *do* regularly emerge with higher index scores than women in their use of vernacular speech variants, when they are surveyed speaking in similar social circumstances. But the question of more relevance to this debate is what the research design, and what the way of displaying findings, allow us to know about sociolinguistic style and styling. It is evident that the survey techniques we have been looking at allow very little discretion in social interpretation. The simple categories of 'careful' and 'casual' are intended to account for the full range of stylistic variation in unscripted speech, bearing in mind that the 'most careful' contexts in sociolinguistic interviews are read-aloud styles. Others have objected that read-aloud styles and spontaneous speaking styles can hardly be considered parts of the same scale continuum (Milroy 1987: 173–8, Schilling-Estes 2004a: 382).

Variationist surveys have been enormously successful, if the quest is to demonstrate statistical orderliness in the co-variation of particular social and linguistic distributions – that is, in the description of social styles of speech. Labov makes it clear that he values precision, accuracy, objectivity and power of generalisation in research. He comments as follows on stylistic research of the sort that was done before his own:

> I would say that stylistic variation has not been treated by techniques accurate enough to measure the extent of regularity [in stylistic variation] which does prevail. (Labov 1972b: 81)

In the same place he writes of 'discovering the system within the variation', and there is no doubt that it is the systematicity of stylistic variation that is important in this perspective. This is in turn because, as we saw in connection with (postvocalic r), a regular and uniform shift towards a prestige norm in 'careful speech' can be taken as evidence of a linguistic change in progress. But style is not only of interest when it is ordered and systematic. The agenda we began to develop for a stylistics of variation in Chapter 1 – including understanding what variation can mean for speakers, and entertaining complex and contingent contextualisations of meaning – are not part of the remit of canonical variationist stylistics.

The treatment of style, and of variation generally, through *linear scales* of different sorts is the most constraining aspect of Labov's method. The next section opens up the assumptions made about 'standard' and 'non-standard' speech, and linearity is strongly implied there too. But linearity dominates social as well as linguistic aspects of variationism. We have seen that social class is characterised as a linear (vertical) scale, and that formality is characterised as linear (horizontal) scale that reinterprets the scale of social class. The underlying principle, which forces social (including situational) variables into linear arrays, is mathematical. If speech variation is captured in terms of different frequencies of occurrence of speech variants, and if the fundamental design of the research is correlational, it follows that social variables have to take a comparable linear shape in order to be entered into statistical procedures. Correlation analysis is the statistical assessment of degrees of co-variation, and variationist analysis examines correlations between numerical arrays. But the important point here is that social data and linguistic data have to be *shaped* into linear strings, to meet the demands of this design.

Acts of speaking and the meaningful variation that they articulate are *not* inherently linear. It can be argued that the basic unit of analysis for language variation is the individual occurrence of the individual linguistic variant, for example the single occasion when a grammatical form like *seen* is used as the simple past tense of 'see' in Reading, or when a single audible [r] is pronounced postvocalically in New York. A single use of a single sociolinguistic variant *can* be socially meaningful, even though the value of aggregating much larger amounts of sociolinguistic data and looking for general statistical tendencies can be easily appreciated. But variationists are adamant that stylistics needs to be done quantitatively:

> whether or not we consider stylistic variation to be a continuum of expressive behavior, or a subtle type of discrete alternation, it is clear that it must be approached through quantitative methods ... The remarkable fact is that the basic unit of stylistic contrast is a frequency set up by as few as ten occurrences of a particular variable. (Labov 1972b: 109)

Labov's methods successfully manipulate 'style' quantitatively, under certain constraints of design and interpretation, but it does not follow that style analysis can only be done quantitatively. Reliance on frequency as the main criterion of sociolinguistic difference introduces a considerable level of abstraction into the account of variation. An individual speaker's speech is characterised as a numerical array for a given sociolinguistic variable in a given social situation or speech activity. Then arrays for individuals are aggregates into even more abstract statistical indices representing a group's 'style' in a contextual type. These methods keep us at a considerable distance from the primary contextual operations of speaking and from a 'dynamic' account of sociolinguistic styling.

In survey research, abstractions and idealisations of this sort are inevitable. The research needs to round down its social and linguistic coding into manageable formats, to make them amenable to statistical treatment. Strong generalisations have been produced by these methods, and I am in no sense trying to invalidate them. The point for an analysis of contextual styling, however (as opposed to a distributional analysis of social styles), is that a reductive, survey-type approach risks vitiating the entire enterprise. If we want to move beyond demonstrating certain gross tendencies in the co-variation of speech and social situation – to go beyond a simple predictive account of 'speech registers', in fact – we need to loosen some dominant assumptions about linear variables and correlational explanation. One fundamental obstacle to this is sociolinguistic convention in the handling of 'standardness'.

2.3 'STANDARD' AND 'NON-STANDARD'

I have persisted in using quote-marks around the terms 'standard' and 'non-standard' in order to achieve some critical distance from them. Once again though, they are entirely familiar sociolinguistic concepts. It is 'standard practice' to identify particular variants of sociolinguistic variables as being 'standard', for example the velar [ŋ] nasal forms of '-ing' in words such as 'jumping', 'rapping' and 'something' that I have referred to on a couple of occasions already, or single negation, as in *I didn't see any spaceships*. Contrasting variants are therefore called 'non-standard': alveolar [n] forms of '-ing' or multiple negation forms like *I didn't see no spaceships*. In many English first-language speaking contexts, with English being such a heavily standardised language and with the cultures themselves arguably being 'standard language cultures' (J. Milroy 2001: 530), these ways of referring to linguistic variants seem natural.

But 'standard' does not simply refer to a completed history of linguistic standardisation. It refers to an ideological contest and it articulates a position or point or view in relation to that contest (Coupland 2000). As James Milroy and Lesley Milroy (1997) point out, standardisation is an on-going process of suppressing variation and a drive towards uniformity, in speech and in some other forms of social practice. It is countered by a process Milroy and Milroy call 'vernacular maintenance' (1997: 53). The drive to maintain vernacular speech is equally ideological, and as a process it is not dissimilar to the process of standardisation. The difference between the two processes, they argue, is that the former is institutionally endorsed while the latter is not. Vernacular maintenance is an ideology worked up within social networks, usually operating in tight communities. One problem with the term 'standard' is therefore that it forecloses on ideological conflict and on its outcomes. It presupposes that there is a set of linguistic forms whose social value is known and uniform – they have an establishment-endorsed value, often called 'prestige'. 'Non-standard' forms carry an expectation of being 'stigmatised' and of having 'low prestige'. They might (in addition) have what has been called 'covert prestige' (Trudgill 1974, Labov 2001a: 24) – prestige that is somehow endorsed below the surface of public discourse, but which leaves their 'overt' stigmatisation untouched.

There are several problems here. One is that social judgements of ways of speaking usually attach to sociolinguistic varieties or speaker prototypes rather than to individual linguistic features. (In Chapter 4 we will briefly consider a study in which several major varieties of spoken English are evaluated by large groups of people.) Individual linguistic variants pattern in complex ways to make up regional or social varieties (accents and dialects) and it is not obviously true that a single feature will carry the same social meaning in the context of different varieties. For example, 'non-standard' Liverpool English in the UK has central [ə]-type onset to the (ou) variable (Newbrook 1999). It is a distinctive part of the local vernacular speech, mainly associated with working-class people. But it is very similar to the Received Pronunciation form of (ou), [əʊ] which in other UK dialects is realised with a more open start-point to the diphthong, or indeed with a monophthongal [oː]. So Liverpool (ou) (which might historically have been a hypercorrect form, produced when speakers tried to eradicate this aspect of their regional identity) shares a phonetic shape with sounds that are elsewhere considered posh. This is a particularly problematic case for the 'standard–non-standard' opposition to handle. But it is more generally true that it is unsafe to assume that features that happen to appear in the variety conceived to be 'standard' (such as 'Received Pronunciation' in Britain) somehow *are themselves* 'standard', and vice versa.

The simple linearity that is presumed to underlie 'standard' versus 'non-standard' usage is also badly suited to many sociolinguistic settings. Tore Kristiansen describes a sociolinguistic situation in the town of Naestved in Denmark where variation orients to three targets, which he calls 'norm-ideals' (Kristiansen 2004). The speech of individuals is more or less Zealand (the regional dialect norm of the island called 'Sjælland' in Danish), more or less Copenhagen (the capital city norm) and more or less 'standard' (which in this case refers to an urban but modern variety). English language variation in Wales, to take another example, is again subject to competing forces and competing 'standard' varieties, although to use this terminology is always reductive. Received Pronunication has establishment value only in very limited domains in Wales, and a loose idea of 'Educated Welsh speech in English' competes with it (Garrett, Coupland and Williams 1999; Garrett, Coupland and Williams 2003). Correspondingly, the most localised regional speech forms of English in Wales differ considerably in the extent of acceptance/'stigmatisation' they attract. The rural south-western variety stands as a recognisable social style but is held by many to be quite prestigious and 'truly Welsh', in contrast with several other southern varieties, some of which are much more punitively judged.

Much more generally still, however, it is by no means true that 'prestige' uniformly and definitively attaches to varieties that the establishment treats as 'standard' ones. Complex patterns of social judgement are made in people's social evaluations of different varieties. There can be systematic differences between how one group of people and another group evaluate particular ways of speaking. There is evidence (see section 4.4) that some people judge establishment voices to have less prestige than some regionally marked voices. Even if the term 'standard' catches a generalisation such as 'many people in the UK find a Received Pronunciation accent to be relatively high in prestige' (which is still largely the case), it is an extremely loose generalisation. A way of speaking that we are socialised into will in many circumstances strike us as unexceptional or 'unmarked'. It becomes part of the ambient sociolinguistic climate. The well-known semantic ambiguity of the word 'standard' becomes worrying here, because we can plausibly say that what is sociolinguistically unmarked is what we should consider to be 'standard' in one of the term's senses. Alternative terms like 'local' and 'supra-local' are sometimes used, but these introduce their own complications. Cheshire points out, for example, that the spreading glottal stop – [?], T-glottaling in word-final and word-medial position in words like *but* and *butter* in Britain – has partially left behind its quality of being stigmatised. It has become a supra-local feature in Britain, even though we generally associate non-regionality with 'standard' forms and varieties.

For the study of style, there is a dangerous circularity in pre-defining the social meanings of sociolinguistic variants in terms of 'standardness', even though the concept is hard to avoid, or indeed in terms of any other simple social-semantic contrast. Once again the linearity entailed in this is troublesome. It suggests that social meanings for speech are principally ordered along a culturally fixed single continuum of perceived social prestige. In fact we judge linguistic varieties on many dimensions simultaneously, and they often work against each other in complex profiles. But even if prestige *were* linear and straightforward, we would need to allow for the fact – to be demonstrated in later chapters – that social meanings are ultimately constructed in and through their contextualisation in acts of speaking. The use of 'standard' features of speech is *not* limited to marking the speaker's alignment with the establishment, and 'non-standard' speech can be used and voiced with very different pragmatic goals and effects. The contextualisation of variation makes meaning in the interplay between sociolinguistic resources and local performance.

2.4 'NON-STANDARD' SPEECH AS 'DEVIATION'

The history of the core idea of linguistic variability in general stylistics, and of standardness in relation to it, is informative. The Labovian concept of a sociolinguistic variable with different variants – alternative forms of realisation which are not 'meaningfully' distinguished – was an established idea in the early days of stylistics. Stephen Ullman, for example, writing in 1961, offered this definition of stylistic 'expressiveness':

> For the student of style, "expressiveness" covers a wide range of linguistic features which have one thing in common: they do not directly affect the meaning of the utterance, the actual information which it conveys. Everything that transcends the purely referential and communicative side of language belongs to the province of expressiveness: emotive overtones, emphasis, rhythm, symmetry, euphony, and also the so-called *"evocative"* elements which place our style in a particular register (literary, colloquial, slangy, etc.) or associate it with a particular milieu (historical, foreign, provincial, professional, etc.). (Ullman 1966: 101, with original emphasis)

Ullman then links the notion of expressiveness to that of *choice* – choice between '"stylistic variants", as they have been called – which mean the same thing but do not put it in the same way' (1966: 102). One of Ullman's examples of a stylistic effect, resulting from speaker 'choice', is inversion of a grammatical subject phrase in French, as in *le scandale que provoqua sa réaction* and *le scandale que sa réaction provoqua* – both expressions translate into English as 'the scandal which his/her reaction caused'.

Ullman also specifies a 'stylistics of the sound', what he calls 'phono-stylistics' (Ullman 1966: 111). His commentary on speech differences is altogether elitist, centring on what is most 'satisfying', 'successful', 'elegant' and so on. Onomatopoeia as an expressive sound-stylistic process is one example. Another is 'the faulty pronunciation of foreigners' and the 'more serious problems' raised 'when native speakers have an accent which differs from the Received Standard' (same source). Ullman even countenances a form of stylistic 'hypercorrection', which he interprets as the over-application of a rule of 'correction':

> Such speakers will overcompensate their sense of linguistic
> insecurity by using "hypercorrect" forms; the Cockney who, for fear
> of "dropping his aitches", inserts an [h] where there is no need for one
> (1966: 112).

Ullman mentions that aitch-dropping is used not only in George Bernard Shaw's adaptation of *Pygmalion* (where Professor Henry Higgins schools Eliza Doolittle to 'speak like a duchess') but by the Roman poet Catullus who ridiculed his character Arrius, as Ullman says, 'because he would pronounce *insidias* as *hinsidias* and *Ionios* as *Hionios* in order to impress people with his superior education' (1966: 112). Ullman also foresaw a role for statistical treatments of style, writing that such methods were to be welcomed 'though it would be wrong to erect them into a fetish' (1966: 118). One value, he thought, was that 'numerical data may in some cases reveal a striking anomaly in the *distribution* of stylistic interpretation, and may thus raise important problems of aesthetic interpretation' (1966: 120–21).

With hindsight it is easy to see the continuity between Labov's structuralist take on dialect style and Ullman's theorising of style in general stylistics. What Labov brought to stylistics was firstly a comprehensive survey method, which could put some received principles about style variation into practice and reach quantitative generalisations. Secondly, he introduced a progressive ideology, radically different from Ullman's ideas of 'faulty pronunciation' and so on. But the conceptual basis of Labov's approach, centred on a normative standard language and orderly deviation from it, had already been conventionalised. Ullman's politics of language seem altogether reactionary and repressive today, and it is important to bear in mind that Labov's early work was introduced into academic and popular cultures where we can assume there were strong assumptions in place about social life – about fixed social structures dominated by social class. If we consider the history of standard language ideology, for example in Lynda Mugglestone's (2003) illuminating study of Received Pronunciation in England, we can see how those assumptions rapidly became less tenable as the twentieth century progressed. Social change, at least in Britain, has begun to pull the rug from under the sociolinguistics of social class. Social inequalities of course persist, and the distribution of speech forms, as a descriptive fact, continues to co-vary quantitatively with levels of social privilege/ disadvantage. But it is no longer safe to pre-define 'standard' speech and 'non-standard' speech as the voices of the establishment and the working people, respectively. We discuss these social changes more in Chapter 4, under the heading of sociolinguistic resources for styling.

2.5 SOCIAL STRUCTURE AND SOCIAL PRACTICE

Variationists are very clear about where we can find social structure. Jack Chambers says that age, social class and sex are the 'three over-riding social categories in modern industrialized societies' (Chambers 2004: 349). Peter Trudgill says that 'The four major forms of social differentiation which have figured in our research from the very beginning are: social context, social class, sex and gender, and ethnicity' (Trudgill 2004: 373). The principle of stylistic stratification, as we discussed it above, adds a further structural 'form of social differentiation' for variationists. Contemporary sociolinguistic research on variation continues to work with these categories.

This structural model of language variation in urban communities is a cornerstone of what has been called 'a linguistics of community' (see Rampton 2006: 14). Social lives led in 'speech communities' have appeared to order how we speak and how we evaluate speech, although Labov made the reverse assumption – that the speech community was held in place by shared perceptions and understandings about language variation. He took the pattern of regular stylistic stratification that survey methods showed to be evidence of shared perceptual norms. The model seems to imply that speakers 'know their place' in social and linguistic systems, although variationism, as I have stressed, was driven by liberal ideology. All the same, the structural variationist model has repeatedly been criticised for its *essentialism*, defined by Norma Mendoza-Denton as follows:

> [It is] the reductive tendency by analysts to designate a particular aspect of a person or group as explanations for their behavior: the "essence" of what it means, for instance, to be Asian, or Indian, or female … Essentialism in sociolinguistics includes the analytic practice of using categories to divide up subjects and sort their

linguistic behavior, and then linking the quantitative differences in
linguistic production to explanations based on those very same
categories provided by the analyst. (Mendoza-Denton 2004: 476–477)

This sounds like a technical and methodological objection, but
Mendoza-Denton also makes the crucial point that the structural
model is uncritical and relatively atheoretical. It draws its social categories in an ad hoc way, for example ignoring political and power-related
issues in social class and gender and giving priority to distributional
description over social interpretation. These points have been made
for some time, for example by Deborah Cameron (1990), Suzanne
Romaine (1984b) and myself (Coupland 1980, 1988). Methodological
critique remains important, though, because the appearance of sociolinguistic structure in variationist soicolinguistic descriptions is at
least to some extent an artefact. As we saw, the approach sets out to
find structure and orderliness. Methodological choices (examining
selected sociolinguistic variables, grouping speakers in particular
ways, designing the structure of the sociolinguistic interview and so
on) are made in order to maximise the discoverable orderliness of
sociolinguistic structure.

The variationist method is not primarily designed to capture the
meaningful social experience or projection of class, race, age or gender, or of situational formality, through language. Not surprisingly,
when researchers have tried to read quantitative data this way, more
questions than answers have arisen. We can take the example of sex/
gender variation, which has been a core theme of variationist research
for many decades (see also section 5.7). As Jenny Cheshire notes
(Cheshire 2004), Labov emphasises the regular finding that men use
a higher frequency of 'non-standard' forms than women do, in a given
social setting (Labov 1990). Also that women favour incoming prestige
forms more than men do. In her review of this area of research,
Cheshire draws together many of the extrapolations that have been
made, interpreting women's favouring of 'standard' speech. Are
women talking back against their imposed social inferiority by claiming 'standard' speech as their own? Are women seeking to claim
denied social status? Are they avoiding the charge of promiscuity,
which might be a stereotype of 'non-standard speech'? Are men buying into the ideology and 'covert prestige' of working-class life?

These speculations are interesting, but they seem to bear little relation to the data that they seek to interpret. As Cheshire says, 'As it
stands, this stark generalization [that there are reliable differences
between men's and women's speech in relation to dialect variation]
does not tell us much, if anything, about the relation between language

and gender in social life' (Cheshire 2004: 428). We have to keep remembering that the differences in question are probabilistic, based on relative frequencies of use of very selective speech features. As Cheshire also says, there is a lack of research on how the measurable differences are actually perceived. It might even be true that, despite variationists' claims to the contrary, quantitative differences in frequencies of use of particular variable speech features are *not* reliably distinguishable by speakers themselves. Even if they are, we do not have evidence that such differences are understood in terms of the social categories in which they surface – for example that 40% versus 80% use of a 'nonstandard' feature is heard as a marker of femaleness. The issue is equally important in relation to stylistic variation, which of course complicates social group-linked interpretations. Do speakers in fact 'leave behind' their sexual or social class identities when they style-shift? We clearly need a different perspective in order to begin to open up the account of social meaning-making through variation.

Many sociolinguists have distanced themselves from the idea of 'speech community' and taken up the idea of *community of practice* formulated by Lave and Wenger (1991) and Wenger (1998). (See also Eckert 2000: 34ff, 2005; Eckert and McConnell-Ginet 1992; Holmes and Meyerhoff 1999; Rampton 2000; also the extended discussion in *Journal of Sociolinguistics*, volume 9 issue 4, 2005.) A practice perspective reworks the assumptions underlying the structural variationist model. It attends to social 'doing' in place of structural 'being'. It undermines, for example, the idea of sex/gender as a pre-defined dimension or element of social and sociolinguistic structure. Penelope Eckert describes communities of practice as follows, in the introduction to her rich ethnography of jocks and burnouts as adolescent style-groups at Belten High in the Detroit suburbs:

> Meaning is made as people jointly construct relations through the development of a mutual view of, and in relation to, the communities and people around them. This meaning-making takes place in myriad contacts and associations both with and beyond dense networks. To capture the process of meaning-making, we need to focus on a level of social organization at which individual and group identities are being constructed, and in which we can observe the emergence of symbolic processes that tie individuals to groups, and groups to the social context in which they gain meaning. (Eckert 2000: 34–35)

Eckert analyses how jocks and burnouts manufacture and live out styles – styles of dress, activity and speech – which define themselves and separate them from other groups such as punk kids and teachers. Individuals can import new symbolic features into their own interpretations of group-style. Indeed Eckert says that 'both individual and group identities are in continual construction, continual change, continual refinement' (2000: 43).

The community of practice, as it was proposed by Lave and Wenger, is principally a model of social learning and development, an account of how people progressively acculturate to new social environments. The concept is particularly suggestive when we are dealing with social settings, such as high schools and their students, where social and linguistic change, and identity change, are in the air. But it need not be restricted to learning situations as we generally think of them. Eckert says that the community of practice concept 'focuses on the day-to-day social membership and mobility of the individual, and on the co-construction of individual and community identity' (2000: 40), and we can assume that this sort of co-construction is on-going in all aspects of our social lives.

For the study of language variation, a practice perspective breaks the apparent tyranny of pre-formed sociolinguistic structure. But it *maintains* a perspective on structure as a potential achievement of language and discourse. It emphasises social meaning, which, as we've already seen, is to a large extent obscured in classical variation-ist research. More particularly, it emphasises the contextual construc-tion of social meaning:

> Variation does not simply reflect a ready-made social meaning; it is part of the means by which that meaning emerges. A study of social meaning in variation, then, cannot view speakers as incidental users of a linguistic system, but must view them as agents in the continual construction and reproduction of that system. Social meaning in variation is not a static set of associations between internal linguistic variables and external social variables; it is continually created through the joint linguistics and social engagement of speakers as they navigate their ways through life (Eckert 2000: 43).

Agentivity, making and inferring meaning in variation, social identifi-cation and social construction are themes we take up in later chapters, and Penelope Eckert's research and theoretical reinterpretation of var-iation are a major landmark, opening up new analytic possibilities.

Eckert herself, but also Robert Bayley (2004: 135), make it clear that William Labov's own research, from very early on and indeed in the first-ever quantitative study of variation, was alert to how sociolinguistic variation can make meaning in relation to local contexts and issues. Labov's study of the pronunciation of variable (ai) on the island of Martha's Vineyard in Massachusetts, USA (Labov 1972b, Chapter 1) showed how linguistic variation can function as a form of resistance to social pressure. Centralised diphthongs, he showed, were more commonly found in the speech of fishermen in the area of Chilmark on Martha's Vineyard, presumably iconising emotional resistance to the mainland holiday-makers who they felt threatened the island's cultural distinctiveness. Eckert's view is that 'the study of variation' (and she might mean *all* variation research, not merely the Martha's Vineyard study) 'is implicitly a study of social practice, but is built on a theory of structure' (2000: 44).

We could disagree with Eckert to the extent that 'a study of social practice' cannot be quite that unless it engages with discursive practice as its data. When we turn (in Chapter 5) to research on language variation and the management of social identities, I will make the case that we need to put practice itself under the microscope. The Martha's Vineyard study, and much more so Eckert's research at Belten High, attach theoretical weight to constructive social practice, and they discuss the importance of local networks and sensitivities as driving forces behind variation at the level of group usage. But they do their variation analysis in terms of statistical correlations between speech-variant frequencies and social categories, as in the classical paradigm of variation surveys. Eckert gives us revealing transcripts of moments of social interaction involving her adolescent informants, helping to fill out the ethnographic contexts in which value systems and routines are constructed. An example is the practice of urban cruising, which is a geographically and culturally quite specific practice for the kids who do it, full of group-level social significance.

But Eckert's variation analysis in her highly influential (2000) study is to show differential levels of positive statistical correlation between certain speech variants and, for example, the groups of cruisers (male and female) and non-cruisers, or the groups of jocks and burnouts, as in Figure 2.3.

These urban phonological variants, particularly backing of the (wedge) vowel, but to some extent also backing of (e) ([ε] in its IPA symbol) and raising of the nucleus in (ay) ([ai] in IPA) correlate most strongly with membership of the burnout group.

Eckert draws attention to how particular discursive moments are highly salient loci for highly styled socio-phonetic features. She mentions familiar communicative routines such as flirting, teasing and arguing, and particular lexical items such as *dude* and *cool, right, excellent, damn* and *fuck* (Eckert 2000: 218). She notes how socio-phonetically extreme variants add meaning to the utterances in which they feature – such as the word *right* said with a very high nucleus of [ai], *excellent* with backed [ε], *damn* with raised [æ] and *fucked* with backed

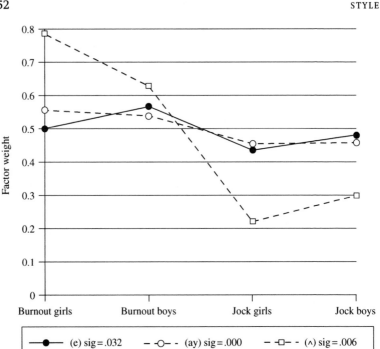

Fig. 2.3. Distributions of variants of (e), (ay) and (wedge) among jocks and burnouts, boys and girls

[ʌ]. The statistical analysis can usefully be complemented by more detailed interactional analysis of the same phonetic resources being meaningfully employed.

For the moment, the key point is one that Eckert's research brings out very forcefully and persuasively. The alternative to a structural model of sociolinguistic variation is *not* one where social structure is out of the picture. A 'communities of practice' perspective stresses how social structures are often emergent phenomena. Social actors, through their association around practical activity and through their discourse practices, can 'work up' social meanings around their own and others' group-level distinctiveness. But even in social situations where this emergence of new identities and new social styles is less in evidence, there is a severe risk of polarising perspectives on pragmatic agency and social structure. Notwithstanding the constructive power of practice, social structure and socially structured meanings for language variation have not disappeared. It may well be true, as many have speculated, that people's agentive potential to rework or 'go beyond' social class, gender, age and ethnicity is greater than under the regime of modernity, and that new and more local social categories are coming to the fore in late-modernity. Perhaps class in particular is generally less attended to, and perhaps its signifiers have become less reliable or less salient. Perhaps there is a general attenuation of class as the dominant system of social meaning, implying that variationism's primary focus on class meanings for variation needs to be extended. But the historical meanings for class, ethnicity and so on circulate as meaning potential for sociolinguistic styling. What we have to be alert to is how these structured social styles can be creatively transformed, rather than expecting them to be empty or irrelevant.

The variationist paradigm set out the structural parameters within which some basic sets of stylistic meaning can function. What was needed as a next theoretical and empirical stage was to broaden the meaning remit for style. It was in the domain of social relationships that sociolinguistic style was reworked, and this literature is the focus of Chapter 3.

3 Style for audiences

3.1 TALKING HEADS VERSUS SOCIAL INTERACTION

The principle of attention to speech – the explanatory idea that stylistic variation is a response to different amounts of attention paid by a speaker to his or her speech – theoretically complements the structuralist approach discussed in Chapter 2. As I suggested there, in a conceptual world of linear variables, a simple linear principle was needed to explain stylistic variation. This chapter examines an alternative approach – in fact two closely related approaches – which very largely supplanted the attention to speech explanation as the mainstream variationist approach to style. One of them, the *audience design* paradigm associated with Allan Bell's research, was very much a development within variationist sociolinguistics. The other approach, *accommodation theory*, associated with Howard Giles and his colleagues' research, was originally a perspective from social psychology, although the general idea of accommodation is a common one in modern sociolinguistics.

The main idea in each of these approaches, shared between them, is that variation in speech style can be explained as speakers/communicators designing their speech/communicative output *in relation to their audiences*. The principle of attention to speech implies a 'talking heads' perspective on language. Although William Labov certainly showed that speakers are connected into the social structures of their 'speech communities', he proposed explaining their stylistic shifts through speakers' internal perceptual processes, psycholinguistically. A psycholinguistic model fits well with the idea of style as intra-individual variation – variation 'within a single speaker', as opposed to variation between speakers and groups. But the early life of sociolinguistics, outside of variationist research, had plenty of proponents of a fundamentally *relational* or *interactional* perspective on style. Many influential approaches to language variation, though not to accent/dialect variation, explained linguistic 'choices' in terms of speaker–listener relationships. Roger Brown's research was particularly important in this regard.

Research on *forms of address* (Brown and Ford 1961; Ervin-Tripp 1973) set out to explain variation in how we typically select different address forms in speaking to different categories of people. In English there is a general tendency to address adults we are unfamiliar with using a title and last name, such as 'Dr James' or 'Miss (or Ms) Harris'. First-naming is a 'less formal' form of address, associated with closer acquaintance or address to people much younger than an adult speaker. Early socio-linguistic research set out to write rules governing address systems, trying to predict which forms would be used in which relational contexts. Even so, the ambition was quite limited, in that context was thinly characterised and the range of address forms included was restricted. Abbreviated names or name-surrogates, not included in the early studies, are a rich sociolinguistic territory. Dated though they seem in print, British males do often still address each other as *mate*. The forms *pal* and *butt* have restricted regional currency, including Liverpool and the South Wales Valleys, respectively. *Guys* as a plural, non-specific form of address is common and seems 'informal', although it is often truer to say that using it constructs a speaking situation as non-institutional and offers a sense of commonality between speaker and listeners. Last-name-only address has mainly died out, or is a relic associated with private schools and the armed forces, and so on.

Forms of address and *forms of reference* (how we refer to non-present others) are selected from similar repertoires, but different norms and conventions can apply in each mode. How we address someone and how we refer to him or her out of their hearing are of course subject to very different design characteristics and considerations. The relational effect of referring to one's mother, for example, as *Mum* or *Mom* when speaking to a third person brings relational meaning sharply into focus. The familial intimacy that is marked by using the form *Mum* or *Mom* to one's mother carries over into the new context of speaking, as in *I took Mom to the beach last week*. But the person listening in the new context is likely to wonder what it implies about the current relationship between speaker and listener – that the speaker is prepared to open this small window onto her or his family relationships. (See Dickey 1997 for a more recent discussion of address and reference forms.)

Another early and closely related sociolinguistic paradigm dealt with *pronoun choices* in face-to-face talk (Brown and Gilman 1960). These sets of alternatives are particularly salient in many Romance languages like French, Italian and Spanish, but also in German, Russian, Greek and other languages. In general, variation in pronoun address was more salient in earlier times than it is today. The relational implications of addressing someone with the *tu* versus the *vous* personal pronoun in French, or the *tú* versus the *usted* (or third-singular verb morphology without the third-person pronoun itself) in Spanish, are usually fairly clear. French, for example, has the verb 'tutoyer', meaning 'to address someone using the *tu* form', and therefore by implication 'to be socio-linguistically intimate with'. Brown and Gilman analysed pronoun 'choice' in terms of relational power and solidarity. More powerful people would tend to 'send *tu* downwards' in a social status or power hierarchy, and 'less powerful people' would 'send *vous* upwards'. Symmetrical pronoun use would mark equal power or status, and therefore became the general 'polite' convention. Among equals, a shift from *vous* to *tu* over time would mark a change of relational footing between them, as they become more intimately acquainted. Brown and Gilman tracked a progressive historical shift away from a period when the power semantic was dominant to one when the soli-darity semantic took over. We are reputedly living in an era when intimacy (or purported intimacy – see Fairclough 1995a) generally pervades social arrangements. Relational politics are largely negotiated through language, so the issues introduced by Roger Brown and others in the 1960s are thoroughly contemporary, even though patterns of usage have clearly changed over the intervening decades.

The point for the moment, however, is that 'relationality' and the stylistic negotiation of relational meaning were strongly represented in early sociolinguistics. The sociolinguistics of address was generally conceived (but not generally expressed) in very similar ways to the analysis of dialect variation. We can think of French *tu* versus *vous*, and first-name address versus title-plus-last-name address, as socially meaningful variants of sociolinguistic variables. Variation among var-iants is 'stylistic' in the general sense of being associated with differ-ent contexts of use. But in this case the variants are associated with different relational categories or configurations. We might say that the 'choice' of stylistic variants in these paradigms is relationally sensitive. It either reflects or constructs qualities of social relations between speakers and listeners.

Politeness research (Watts 2003) was originally stimulated by Erving Goffman's writing on the presentation of self in everyday life (Goffman 1959). In its full formulation as a sociolinguistic model by Penelope Brown and Stephen Levinson (1987) it too was presented as an explanation of how some key aspects of social relationships are managed through discourse. The central concept is *face*, which is theoretically split into positive face (a person's reputation or good standing) and negative face (a person's entitlement to maintain personal freedom or autonomy). Both positive and negative face are relevant to speakers and listeners alike. Talk is modelled as the management of speakers' and listeners' face-needs, and as the management of threats to face. A command, for example, will most obviously threaten a listener's negative face (his or her freedom from intrusion), while an insult will generally threaten the listener's positive face (her or his good standing). The theoretical notion of politeness goes beyond everyday uses of the term and covers all the discourse routines and devices by which speakers do facework relative to their listeners. For example, a request such as asking someone for a lift to work is likely to be expressed in ways that attend to the listener's negative face. We say *would it be OK if you gave me* ... or *is there any chance of* ... or *might it be possible for you to give me* ... a lift. Our culturally learned sensitivity to norms of politeness makes us avoid using 'bald', unmitigated expressions and more face-threatening utterances such as *give me a lift* or even the conventionally polite *please give me a lift*. Although we are well beyond the field of dialect variation, it is once again wholly appropriate to see these 'choices' as stylistic ones, encoding social meaning at the level of interpersonal relationships.

Early sociolinguistics, as I mentioned in Chapter 1, made regular use of the concept of register – a way of speaking linked to a situational type or genre. Many of the most commonly described registers can be called *addressee registers* – ways of speaking that are defined principally by who speakers are addressing. So, for example, we find literatures on 'baby talk' (talk to babies and young children – see Snow and Ferguson 1977, Ochs and Schieffelin 1986) and 'foreigner talk' (talk to foreigners – see Ferguson 1996). A substantial literature also exists on what is sometimes called 'elderspeak' (talk to older people – see Coupland, Coupland and Giles 1991). This is not the place to review these approaches, but they generally deal with wide arrays of stylistic and discursive features that can be shown to arise in talk addressed to these particular listener groups. Some of them, particularly research in the sociolinguistics of ageing and later life, have been heavily dependent on Howard Giles's accommodation framework that we consider below. These frameworks were further parts of a sociolinguistic climate in which issues of relational design in talk were very firmly and widely established from at least the 1970s.

We should add to this the phenomenal growth of discourse analysis and conversation analysis from the same period. These approaches, diverse as they were and are, share the premise that meaning in discourse/conversation has to be analysed relationally. Meaning, in the familiar phrase, is *co-constructed* through dyadic or multi-party involvement in talk. In later chapters, in line with the wider priorities of discourse analysis and interactional approaches in sociolinguistics, we will have to think *beyond* relational issues in talk. But it is worth reflecting on how inadequate any approach to discourse and communication is if we *exclude* considerations of social relationships. Commonplace definitions of 'communication' and even of 'language' appeal to ideas like 'sharing of meaning', 'mutuality of understanding' and 'engagement with others'. It is not at all surprising then, in view of these many developments, that the most sustained and convincing alternative to William Labov's approach to style-in-variation came from a perspective that stressed the relational meanings of style and the general idea of *recipiency*. This is what Allan Bell's audience design paradigm provided.

3.2 AUDIENCE DESIGN

Bell conceived the *audience design* framework to account for variation he was finding in his research on broadcast news in New Zealand. A ground-breaking paper set out the main tenets of the approach (Bell 1984), which Bell himself reviews in a more recent chapter (Bell 2001). Two of the several radio stations that Bell was recording in the 1970s happened to be broadcast from the same suite of studios and to involve the same individual newsreaders. This allowed him to compare the newsreaders' speech styles in two different broadcasting modes – when they were working for National Radio (station YA), as opposed to a community station (ZB). Both stations were government owned at that time.

Using Labovian quantitative methods, Bell was able to show that there was systematic variation in some aspects of the newsreaders' speech across the two contexts of broadcasting. Several linguistic variables were studied, although results for one variable were particularly striking. The variable (intervocalic t) has two salient variants. The voiceless stop consonant [t] is generally associated with 'standard' usage, certainly in the UK but tending that way in New Zealand too. An alternative variant is a voiced stop or flap [ɾ], auditorily close to [d] – the variant that is in fact 'standard' in most USA English. This is Bell's summary:

> The newsreaders shifted on average 20 percent in each linguistic environment between stations YA and ZB. Single newsreaders heard

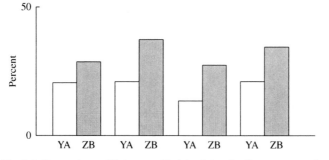

Fig. 3.1. Percentage of intervocalic /t/ voicing by four newsreaders on two New Zealand radio stations, YA and ZB (after Bell 2001: 140)

on two different stations showed a consistent ability to make considerable style-shifts *to suit the audience* (2001: 140, my emphasis).

Figure 3.1 shows this variation graphically.

Bell's justification for this interpretation – that audience design produces the variation effect – is the result of attempts to positively correlate various factors. He says that 'only the audience correlated with the shifts evident here' (same source), because the speakers, the institutional context, the speech genre (news reading) and even the studio setting are constant across the two contexts. The implication is that the difference between the two audiences, national and more local, must be occasioning stylistic variation in the newsreaders' speech. The underlying assumption is that speech style in general is occasioned by, or determined by, or constrained by, social context, which can be analysed in terms of different concurrent dimensions. Bell expects there to be at least four relevant dimensions here. The first is 'speaker', which is held constant, because the same broadcasters are being recorded speaking on YA and ZB. Secondly, there is setting, again held constant, because they are broadcasting from the same studio. Thirdly, there is topic or perhaps genre, once again held constant, because the broadcasters are reading very similar if not the same news material. By a process of elimination, audience, the fourth factor which is not held constant, must account for the observed variation. Bell makes the point that a fifth possible factor, Labov's attention to speech, is also *not* able to account for the variation he finds. In the original paper Bell calls this explanation a 'non-starter' (Bell 1984: 147). As he says, there is no reason to suppose that the newsreaders were attending more closely to their speech in the ZB context than in the YA context.

This sort of multi-dimensional model of context is very familiar in sociolinguistics, usually associated with Dell Hymes's ethnography of speaking. We will look at a more elaborate version of it below. But we will also have to come back to the idea of speech style being contextually 'constrained', which is an idea ingrained in variationism. But Bell is very clear that he prioritises recipiency and relationality in the analysis of style. He sets out a series of programmatic claims or principles for style analysis, as follows (italicised text is direct quotation from Bell 2001: 141–48, as is quote-marked text):

(1) *Style is what an individual speaker does with a language in relation to other people.* Bell says that 'style focuses on the person. It is essentially a social thing. It marks inter-personal and intergroup relations. It is interactive – and active.'

(2) *Style derives its meaning from the association of linguistic features with particular social groups.* Bell therefore considers that socially meaningful linguistic variation between social groups is primary, and that stylistic variation is the secondary use or deployment of such variation.

(3) *Speakers design their style primarily for and in response to their audience.* Bell says that style shift 'occurs primarily in response to a change in the speaker's audience. Audience design is generally manifested in a speaker shifting her style to be more like that of the person she is speaking to'. This is also the central idea within Giles's accommodation theory (see below). Bell emphasises that response is the primary mode of style-shift, but that this responsiveness is also 'active'.

(4) *Audience design applies to all codes and levels of a language repertoire, monolingual and multilingual.* Although Bell's original data were of a classical socio-phonetic variationist sort, he wants to include other levels of linguistic variation.

(5) *Variation on the style dimension within the speech of a single speaker derives from and echoes the variation which exists between speakers on the 'social' level.* Unlike the fourth principle, this principle refers to the conventional variationist conceptions of style that we examined in Chapter 2, for example accepting that style is a 'dimension' of variation separate from 'social' variation. Bell is pointing to a common fact about the *extents* of 'social' and 'stylistic' variation, when they are measured in the quantitative variationist paradigm. 'Social' variation seems to be greater than (shows bigger numerical range than) stylistic variation. But his point is more general – that, as in (2), style variation is enabled by 'social' variation.

(6) *Speakers have a fine-grained ability to design their style for a range of different addressees, as well as for other audience members.* Some research, including my own (Coupland 1988 and below), has been able to demonstrate subtle patterns of co-variation in the speech of speakers and listeners, although Bell's model conceives of several different audience roles.

(7) *Style-shifting according to topic or setting derives its meaning and direction of shift from the underlying association of topics or settings with typical audience members.* Bell is making the interesting claim that, although response to an audience is primary, whole social situations can carry the imprint of how they are, we might say, 'peopled', and that this is what makes them meaningfully different.

(8) *As well as the 'responsive' dimension of style, there is the 'initiative' dimension where the style-shift itself initiates a change in the situation rather than resulting from such a change.* Bell links the idea of initiative style to Blom and Gumperz's (1972) idea of 'metaphorical code-switching'. In their well-known discussion of alternation between different language codes in Norway they comment on how a speaker can, for example, introduce a quality of informality or intimacy into a social event by switching into a local dialect. The idea of 'initiative' style-shifting lets the audience design model break free from what would otherwise seem to be a deterministic approach – that (as in principle 3) speakers' style is essentially responsive. The balancing of response and initiation remains one of the key problems for any theory of style, including Bell's (see Bell 1999).

(9) *Initiative style-shifts are in essence 'referee design', by which the linguistic features associated with a reference group can be used to express identification with that group.* In this claim Bell tries to link initiative or metaphorical style back into considerations of audiences. Referees, he says, are third persons not usually present at an interaction but who are salient for speakers and able to influence their style of speaking, even in their absence. Style here becomes a matter of identifying with potentially non-present groups. It therefore moves into the territory of identity management (which is the main topic of Chapters 5 and 6 of this book).

(10) *Style research requires its own designs and methodologies.* This is Bell's pitch for giving style research its own theoretical and empirical spaces, outside of variationist surveys where it was always a peripheral consideration.

We need to review these generalisations in the context of empirical research. But before doing that it is useful to set out the basic elements of 'accommodation' research, whose remit is very similar to audience design.

3.3   COMMUNICATION ACCOMMODATION THEORY

Howard Giles developed the core concepts of *speech accommodation theory* in the 1970s (Giles 1973; Giles and Powesland 1975) and the approach was renamed *communication* accommodation theory as the reach of the framework grew. Rather similarly to Bell, Giles proposed an alternative explanation for the stylistic variation that Labov's research described, also in terms of relational processes. As a social psychologist, Giles foregrounded motivational factors – what speakers might be seeking to gain through modifying their speech. Accommodation came to settle on two main clusters of motives, summarised as speakers 'seeking social attractiveness' and 'seeking communication efficiency' (although effectiveness is perhaps the more relevant term). In pursuit of being judged more likeable, for example, a speaker could be expected to *converge* her or his speech towards that of a listener in certain respects. *Divergence* could, alternatively, symbolise the desire to reduce intimacy, as could *maintenance* (implying no variation or no deviation from an existing way of communicating).

Giles gave no particular prominence to accent/dialect variation. Accommodation could relate to all manner of communicative modalities and features, such as rate of speech, pausing, levels of self-disclosure, bodily posture and key (e.g. light-heartedness versus seriousness). The accommodation model did not focus on specific meanings attached to any particular communicative feature or style, but on the degree of similarity or difference between speaker and listener. This amounts to a metaphorical reading of stylistic difference in terms of interpersonal distance. A good example is Bourhis and Giles's (1977) experimental engineering of accent divergence. They audio-recorded Welsh language learners in a language laboratory and at one point asked them to take part in a survey of second-language learning techniques. The questions were asked orally through headphones, in English and by a speaker with a 'standard' RP voice. At one point the speaker challenged the learners' reasons for studying Welsh, which he called 'a dying language with a dismal future'. Giles and Bourhis then made audio recordings of the learners' responses, which they say included them 'broadening' their Welsh accents and using some Welsh words and phrases in their answers; one person reportedly started to conjugate a less than socially acceptable Welsh verb into the microphone.

Although it offers a broadly similar understanding of stylistic variation to Allan Bell's audience design approach, research within the accommodation theory framework has usually lacked the level of linguistic (phonetic, lexical, pragmatic) detail that audience design has provided. Quite often, the analysis of stylistic shifts or differences has been done *perceptually* in accommodation theory, following the important argument that people's perceptions of communicative style are more important then their objective characteristics from an explanatory point of view. In fact, Thakerar, Giles and Cheshire (1982) proposed distinguishing between 'objective' and 'subjective' accommodation, both theoretically and empirically. They provided evidence of speakers shifting their speech to include some features (such as glottal stop [ʔ] in place of word-final [t]) which they *believed* were characteristic of their speaking partners, but which were in fact not. Distinctions of this sort break away from the rather cut-and-dried theoretical and empirical worlds of variationism.

Another important development was a series of studies of how social norms and other contextual understandings can interfere with accommodative tendencies and outcomes. Genessee and Bourhis (1988) showed, for example, how a salesman converging to the communicative styles of customers doesn't in any straightforward way enhance his social attractiveness. Customers are aware of the social norms governing commercial selling, and they form attributions of the salesman's strategies as being 'what you might expect' rather than being designed interpersonally. The social psychology of accommodation is therefore complex and sensitive, built around concepts of strategy, intention, belief, perception, attribution and normativity. This amounts to a far more complex account of relational processes than has generally been provided by variationists, even though variationists have stayed closer to the data of language variation itself. Accommodation research has been mainly experimental. Researchers have tried to set up or control contextual factors and then to measure outcomes, either linguistic or attitudinal, and this has been something of a barrier to better integration with sociolinguistics, which has favoured direct observation of one sort or another.

Accommodation has, however, sometimes been interpreted in discourse-analytic terms (Coupland, Coupland, Giles and Henwood 1988). In spoken interaction there are many ways of 'being accommodating' that need not involve linguistic convergence and divergence. We will assess the advantages of taking the analysis of style into the discursive arena in later chapters. In the rest of this chapter we should consider some of the studies that followed in a broadly variationist tradition, based on quantitative accounts of variation in sociolinguistic variables. Apart from Allan Bell's original New Zealand study, several others have been able to show audience design at work. Some use audience design concepts and others accommodation theory concepts, but it is useful to review them together. (For more detailed reviews of research in accommodation see the introduction chapter and papers in Giles, Coupland and Coupland 1991; Coupland and Giles 1988; Shepard, Giles and Le Poire 2001.)

3.4 SOME STUDIES OF AUDIENCE DESIGN AND SPEECH ACCOMMODATION

Allan Bell's tenth principle for style research (see above) called for studies designed specifically to investigate stylistic shifts. In his 2001 chapter Bell reports such a study. It involved four New Zealand speakers in their twenties being interviewed in succession by four different interviewers. The informants and the interviewers were chosen to include (in each set of four) two males and two females, and two Maori and two Pakeha people. Maori are the indigenous Polynesian people of New Zealand and 'Pakeha' is a form of reference to New Zealanders of European and mainly British descent. The participants were matched as closely as possible in respects other than gender and ethnicity. Informants were interviewed in their own homes and interviews followed a standardised schedule of questions. This sort of control also stretched to making gender differences and ethnic differences salient in the interviews 'across' these social categories (male–female or Maori–Pakeha).

Bell then analyses the frequencies of a range of linguistic features, including the discourse particle *eh*. This is an utterance tag, functionally similar to high-rising intonation at the end of an utterance (which is found in an increasingly wide range of English-speaking communities – see Britain 1992) or the particles *ie* ('yeah') or *aye* ('yes') which are found, for example, in North Wales and in Glasgow respectively. In all cases the features seem to function to elicit or check a listener's attentiveness, but they are all potentially dialect features in the sense of being used by some social groups much more than by others, thus creating some potential for social meaning-making. Bell finds that *eh* is used far more frequently (in terms of the number of uses per words spoken) by Maori males than by the three other demographically defined categories of people in his study. Then, following audience design principles, he shows that the male Maori interviewee uses far more *eh* (an index score of 46) when he is interviewed by another Maori male than when he is interviewed by the Maori female (index 26). He uses fewer again (but still a significant amount, index 19) when he is interviewed the Pakeha male. Although the female Maori informant uses far fewer *eh* than the male, she uses more of it when interviewed by a socially 'alike' interviewer (index 4) than when interviewed by a Maori male interviewer (index 2).

Looking at the data from the interviewers' perspectives, Bell finds that each interviewer, but particularly the male Pakeha interviewer, tends to adjust his or her *eh* usage in relation to who s/he is interviewing. The male Pakeha interviewer uses no *eh* when speaking to the demographically 'alike' interviewee, while he uses a lot of *eh* (index 29) to the Maori male and fewer (index 14) to the Pakeha female. This last result is surprising, but may be because the interviewee was rather reticent and had to be encouraged to respond – and encouraging response is one discourse function of *eh*. The general pattern, in terms of frequencies of use of *eh*, suggests that demographic 'alikeness' in a speaking dyad, and particulartly in the circumstance of Maori-to-Maori talk, is associated with more use of the ingroup particle. As in his analysis of newsreaders' speech, Bell can argue that 'audience' is a determining factor in stylistic 'choice'. The interviews study is designed so as to keep contextual factors constant in all regards other than speaker–addressee relationships. So audience appears to be the explanatory contextual dimension. We still need to assess whether this 'explanation by elimination' is fully tenable, but we will be better placed to do that if we look at some other empirical research first.

Another key study of audience design is John Rickford and Faye McNair-Knox's extended analysis (1994) of two interviews with Foxy Boston (names in the study, other than the authors', were fictionalised). Foxy is an African American (black) teenager from Oakland, California in the USA who was aged eighteen at the time of the study. The first interview (which was actually one in a longitudinal series of interviews and is referred to as Interview III) was recorded in June 1990. Faye McNair-Knox, an African American woman in her forties and a lecturer at Stanford University, was the principal 'interviewer', although in fact the event was often chatty and involved banter. Faye and Foxy knew each other in advance of the

Table 3.1. *Foxy Boston's vernacular usage in Interviews III and IV (adapted from Rickford and McNair-Knox 1994: 247)*

Variable	Foxy: Interiew III recorded in 1990, African-American interviewer	Foxy: Interview IV recorded in 1991, European-American interviewer
(a) Possessive -s absence e.g. *the teacher clerk*	67% (6/9 instances)	50% (5/10)
(b) Plural -s absence e.g. *they just our friend*	1% (4/282)	0%
(c) 3rd singular present -s absence e.g. *at first it seem like it wasn't no drugs*	73% (83/114)*	36% (45/124)*
(d) Copula *is/are* absence e.g. *he on the phone*	70% (197/283)*	40% (70/176)*
(e) Invariant habitual *be* e.g. *he always be coming down here*	385 (= 241 per hr)*	97 (= 78 per hr)*

Note:
Differences between asterisked percentages are statistically significant ($<.001$)

tape-recorded event. Faye's sixteen year-old daughter Roberta was also present and she was 'co-interviewed' in the same session. Roberta was also known to Foxy in advance and was part of her peer-group. The other interview, referred to as Interview IV, was conducted by Beth in 1991. Beth at the time was a twenty-five-year-old graduate student at Stanford, unknown to Foxy. Beth is a European American (white) woman.

Some of the topics of the two interviews overlapped and in many ways the later interview was designed to replicate the earlier one. But there are clear differences in how Foxy and her different interviewers are networked together, not only through racial similarities/differences but in terms of shared histories and understandings between them. Rickford and McNair-Knox analyse quantitative differences in Foxy's speech across the two events, in relation to five sociolinguistics variables. These variables are listed in Table 3.1 followed by examples provided by the authors. Each variable is linked to African American ethnicity, although the study clearly shows that these are probabilistic tendencies and not categorical (all-or-nothing) patterns. Three of the five variables show statistically significant variation between the two contexts of talk, with regularly higher frequencies of the 'non-standard' or African American-associated variants occurring in the first speech event. This means that Foxy uses significantly more instances of features such as *it seem like* (rather than *it seems like*), *you pregnant* (rather than *you're pregnant*) and *he always be coming down here* (rather than *he always comes down here* or *he's always coming down here*) in Interview III than in Interview IV.

The authors look in detail at several variables, such as third singular present tense *-s* absence, to check that linguistic-internal considerations are not skewing the results. Findings for this variable show that regular differences between the two speech events continue to appear even when statistics are examined for particular sub-categories. That is, the general pattern of variation of *-s* absence shows up when they consider regular verbs (such as *walk*) as a sub-category, and even when they consider the individual irregular verbs *have* and *do*. Even individual verb-forms such as *don't* show the same pattern of quantitative variation. Rickford and McNair-Knox comment on earlier research on *-s* absence, including John Baugh's (1979) research in Pacoima, Los Angeles (see also Baugh 1983). Baugh found that his own degree of familiarity with his informants correlated with significant differences in their use of the *-s* feature, as it did with the [r]-less variant of (postvocalic r). We have quite strong evidence, then, of quantitative differences being associated with relational closeness, and, in a wider sense, evidence of the audience design effect taking place.

There is still the problem of assessing precisely what it is that Foxy is converging towards, if we assume that it is possible to partition off contextual factors such as 'the addressee' versus 'the topic of talk'. Rickford and McNair-Knox look in detail at statistical differences in Foxy's speech when speakers are dealing with different topics. To give just one example, in the Roberta and Faye interview, Foxy uses the 'zero *is*' feature (*he on the phone*) far more frequently in topics having to do with boy–girl conflicts (average 75%) or teen pregnancies (60%) than when the topic category is drugs, thefts and murders (10%). Numbers like these are suggestive, but the authors point to the difficulty of attributing stylistic tendencies to topics, let alone to topics interpreted in the way that Bell's principle (7) interprets them.

Rickford and McNair-Knox give the following four examples (1994: 261) from Foxy's speech. The first two examples fall under the topic 'college/career', one from each of the interview settings. The second two extracts fall under the topic 'wives/slammin partners', again one from each interview. The examples illustrate Foxy's variation in respect of the 'zero copula' (absence of verb 'to be') variable and the 'invariant *be*' variable. I have italicised relevant variants:

> *Extracts 3.1, 3.2, 3.3 and 3.4*
> (1) Miss R *is* the one that- [laughter] Miss R *[zero]* the one help me get into this program, and my- and this guy name Mr O at our school, he's Chinese.
> (2) M., she goes to DeAnza's nursing school. And R and T, they'*re* going to, um, CSM, and my friend A, she's going to be going with me when I go
> (3) I *be* like, 'for real?' I *be* going, 'Tramp, you'*re* stu:pid. You *[zero]* just DUMB! Uhhh! Get away from me. You *[zero]* stupid!
> (4) You *be* in your car with your friends and they *be* like, 'hey, F, ain't that that girl they- um- B slammed the other night?' You *be* like, 'Yeah, that *IS* her.'

The 'wives/slammin partners' topic, as these extracts show, tends to include a lot of direct quotes. These are often introduced by the *be + like* quotative feature (see Tagliamonte and Hudson 1999, and section 7.3, below), which of course provides a lot of scope for variation in the specific verbal 'to be' features we are focusing on. Rickford and McNair-Knox make the important point, vis-à-vis Bell's seventh principle, that 'In the sections in which Foxy's vernacular language use reaches its peak ... Foxy is not just behaving *as if* speaking to teenagers; she is, through extensive quotations, dramatically reenacting the speaking *of* teenagers' (Rickford and McNair-Knox 1994: 261).

The Foxy study is, at one level, a cautionary tale for quantitative variationists who use sociolinguistic interviews as their data collection medium. Bell's Maori/Pakeha study can be interpreted this way too, as can some other studies. Ellen Douglas-Cowie (1978), for example, set out to study the effects of her well-educated English social persona (conveyed through her accent) on sociolinguistic interviews in Articlave in Northern Ireland. Peter Trudgill (1981, 1986) has studied variation in his own speech in his sociolinguistic interviews in Norwich. Trudgill's frequencies of [t] glottalisation ranged from 30% to 98% in his speech to ten informants of different social classes. Patricia Cukor-Avila and Guy Bailey (2001) conclude from their own interview data in 'Springville', Texas that interviewers' effects on the speech style of interviewees can be enormous. But they also draw attention to how difficult it is to identify particular causal factors or dimensions, so that race in their own data may in fact not be as potent a consideration as familiarity.

The relational framing of sociolinguistic interviews, in one sense or another, undoubtedly leaves its mark on the extent and nature of variation that they reveal. But as I noted earlier, this sort of interpretation treats stylistic variation as a set of constraints, and indeed as a methodological problem for variation research. This harks back to the observer's paradox, which still dominates variationist methodology. There is a far more positive way to read the stylistic variation that Bell and others analyse. In data relating to audience design, and perhaps particularly when we test out the limits of Bell's predictive principles, we start to see 'style' coming alive as a creative force in social interaction. The relational processes that result in quantitative indications of style-shift are probably best seen as meanings worked into interaction through the resource of linguistic variation.

I believe this is also true of some of my own early studies of style variation. I audio-recorded talk at a city-centre travel agency in Cardiff (in Wales) in 1979. I was originally interested in the diverse speech of local people in the city, following the general model of urban variationist surveys but intending to avoid the traditional sociolinguistic interview as a source of data. I reasoned that a travel agency is a service setting where people of many different social classes and ages come and go, making it a useful site for studying sociolinguistic diversity. This proved to be so in the particular agency I was observing. (Travel agency talk also features in Donald Hindle's research examining style variation in the speech of Carol Meyers, a Philadephian woman – see Labov 2001a: 438.) As my research progressed, however, I became equally interested in the talk of the agency *assistants* (service providers). Their talk at work spanned many different topics and discourse functions. Assistants (all of whom happened to be females) spent their working days talking to different clients, both face-to-face and on the telephone, giving travel advice, making bookings, taking payment and so on. They also regularly talked to other tour operators and travel companies on the telephone. Of course they talked to each other too, about their social lives as well as their work tasks and problems. This diversity of communicative modes and genres, topics and participation frameworks, also made the travel agency a particularly rich site for studying stylistic processes.

In the structuralist manner of the time, I was able to show that one of the travel agency assistants, Sue, produced what appeared to be three distinct 'levels of standardness' across different speaking contexts in the course of her day-to-day work (Coupland 1980, 1988). My approach to defining 'contexts' seems rudimentary now, but it was not untypical of taxonomic approaches at the time. I drew on Dell Hymes's well-known check-list of components of speech events

(Hymes 1964, 1972) which he summed up using the mnemonic word 'SPEAKING' (Duranti 1997: 288ff.). Each letter stands for either a single concept or a group of concepts that needed to be kept in mind when undertaking ethnographic fieldwork:

S Situation (Setting and Scene)
P Participants (Speaker, Addressor, Hearer and Addressee)
E Ends (Outcomes and Goals)
A Act Sequences (Message form and Message content)
K Key
I Instrumentalities (Channel and Forms of speech)
N Norms (Norms of Interaction and Norms of Interpretation)
G Genre

I noticed associations in the travel agency data between 'Participants', 'Message content' and 'Channel', for example in that Sue spoke exclusively to non-familiar colleagues and about work-related topics when she was speaking on the telephone. So it was reasonable to think of a generalised 'telephone' context (configured out of particular topics and addressees as well as the telephone modality of talk itself). Then there was a 'client' context, defined mainly by Sue having co-present clients as her addressees, but where Sue again spoke exclusively about work topics. Two final contexts could be called 'casual' and 'informal work-related', when Sue spoke to her co-assistants in the travel agency (who were also good friends), about non-work topics versus work topics, respectively. So this produced a hierarchy of contexts based around something like 'formality', but more specifically defined in relation to how Sue's speaking was locally organised in the recorded interactions I was analysing.

In a continuous sequence of Sue's speech like Extract 3.5, then, it was possible to identify different 'contexts', even though the physical setting of course did not change.

Extract 3.5
1 *[Sue on the telephone phone] oh hello (.) it's Hourmont Travel Cardiff (.) your*
2 *flight London Barcelona? (.) twenty-three July:? (.) the a oh- can I ring back?*
3 *(4.0) yeah (1.0) shall I ring back? (2.0) er how long? (3.0) OK then fine (.) bye*
4 [Sue hangs up the telephone and addresses another assistant] computers are
5 down (.) mm everywhere you ring lately (1.0) I better ring her back and tell
6 her not to keep her client there hadn't I
7 how's er Barbara's boyfriend enjoying his new job?

In this extract, lines 1–3 obviously fall into the 'telephone' context (shown in italics). Lines 4–6 fall into the 'informal work-related context', and line 7 falls into the 'casual' context in the sense defined. (The 'client' context is not represented in this particular extract.)

Extract 3.6 is interactionally much more complex. Sue is again on the phone at the beginning of the extract but her first utterance is probably best analysed as addressed to either herself or to her fellow assistants in the travel agency – she certainly doesn't want the Rondda Travel representative she is calling to hear her. Then we see how Sue's speech on the telephone was often recorded against the background of much less formal chat in the travel agency. In this case conversation involved Liz and Marie as well as Sue herself, while she waits for the Rhondda Travel representative to pick up.

Extract 3.6
```
 1  Sue:     come on Rhondda Travel where are you?
 2                                                [
 3  ?Marie:                          hm hm hm
 4           (4.0)
 5  Liz:     o:h I got to go shopping where d'you think I can get charcoal
 6           from?
 7  Sue:     (0.5) I don't really know
 8                                      [
 9  Marie:                              is today Wednesday?
10  Sue:     yeah
11           [
12  Liz:     Marie (.) if you're going out (.) can you just see if you can see
13           any charcoal anywhere if you're just walk- walking around
14           the shops (( ))
15  Sue:     [on the telephone] hello [high pitch] can I have Rhondda Travel
16           please?
```

The contexts of Sue's talk in Extract 3.6 could be analysed as 'informal work-related' in line 1, 'casual' in lines 7 and 10 (where she joins in the conversation about where to buy charcoal), and 'telephone' in lines 15–16.

I quantified five main speech variables, (h-dropping), realisations of (r) in word-initial and intervocalic positions separately, (intervocalic t), (ou) and (consonant cluster simplification) in three different linguistic environments. (h) is a simple present or absent phonetic feature, where voiceless onset to a vowel is either audible or not. (r) refers to variation between continuant and flapped realisations of [r]. (Intervocalic t) is the same variable as used in Allan Bell's broadcasting study. The variable (consonant cluster reduction) refers to variation between consonantal strings like [ts] versus [s] in *that's right* and between [kst#d] and [ks#d] in *next* day. (ou) refers to variation between a closing diphthong with central-position onset versus a more

Table 3.2. *Percentages of less 'standard' variants of five sociolinguistic variables in four contexts of Sue's travel agency talk (from Coupland 1988: 87)*

	Sociolinguistic variables				
	(h)	(r)	(C cluster)	(intervocalic t)	(ou)
'Casual' context	85	40	88	86	88
'Informal work- related' context	60	36	63	55	66
'Client' context	14	23	39	33	61
'Telephone' context	19	15	42	38	46

retracted onset and shorter glides in words like *home* and *cold*. The four 'contexts' proved to be associated with different frequencies of use of the sociolinguistic variables, as shown in Table 3.2 (where values for the different environments of (r) and (consonant cluster) are aggregated, and where percentages are shown for the frequencies of vernacular variants).

There appears to be a stylistic hierarchy, quantitatively speaking, of contexts, with the 'casual' context being associated with Sue's most vernacular speech, through the 'informal work-related' context, to the remaining two contexts, which are not so clearly distinguished from each other overall.

The variation ingrained in Sue's routine talk at work was potentially an interactional resource for her dealings with clients. My recordings included face-to-face interactions between Sue and 51 different clients, all of whom gave written consent for me to use the data. In the conventional variationist tradition, I gave priority to social class as the principal social dimension for arranging the 51 clients' speech data. Although they made up a convenience sample (the people who just happened to be present in the travel agency and talking to Sue when I was observing there), they fell into a familiar stratification pattern according to several sociolinguistic variables. The question from audience design and accommodation theory was therefore whether variation in Sue's speech would in some ways match the variation to be found in the clients' speech. I reported findings about this in Coupland (1984).

In his own 1984 paper Allan Bell summarises some of my findings more economically than I originally presented them. Figure 3.2 presents the findings for one variable, (intervocalic t), quantified in Sue's

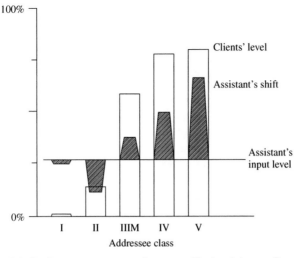

Fig. 3.2. Sue's convergence on (intervocalic t) voicing to five occupation classes of client; input level taken as Sue's speech to 'her own class' (from Bell 1984: 165)

speech and in the speech of clients she is speaking to. As in Bell's broadcasting study, this variable allows for 'standard' [t]-like variants versus voiced [d]-like or flapped variants. I calculated average frequencies of voiced/flapped variants for six separate occupational classes of client. These are referred to using the conventional sociological categories I, II, IIIN, IIIM, IV and V. Group I designates the highest occupational status category (e.g. senior managers and executives) and V designates the lowest (unskilled manual workers). IIIN refers to mid-ranking non-manual workers and IIIM refers to mid-ranking manual workers. Bell's graphic (Figure 3.2) reports five of the six comparisons, because he takes Sue's speech to group IIIN clients – and Sue's occupation places her in the IIIN class – as an 'input level', assuming this to be a sort of base-line for her style-shifting. The figure shows that variation in Sue's speech does to a large extent match the variation in her clients' speech, particularly the 'lower' socio-economic classes. In my 1984 paper I concluded that Sue's speech to clients is almost as reliable a marker of their social class as their own speech is. Frans Hinskens, Peter Auer and Paul Kerswill (2005) also reanalyse this aspect of Sue's style-shifting. They show that the ranges of variation in Sue's speech and the ranges of averaged values of her clients' speech co-vary closely in a statistical sense for four of the variables I analysed. The correlation values are: (h). 87; (ng). 90; (intervocalic t); 76 and (C cluster). 86.

3.5   LIMITS OF AUDIENCE-FOCUSED PERSPECTIVES

Audience design and accommodation are the notions that kept the
study of style alive in variationist sociolinguistics through the 1980s
and 1990s. Between them they capture a generalisation that potentially links variation research through to more general interests in the
study of language in society and in discourse analysis – the interpersonal and interactional grounding of language in social life. They
show that the study of regional and social differences in language
use – variationist research on accent/dialect – needs to connect with
long-standing sociolinguistic interests in the management of social
relationships. Yet, as a general theory (or theories) of style in spoken
interaction, audience-focused approaches have their own limitations.
In drawing these points together in this section I have no intention
of undermining the value of work done in audience design and
accommodation theory. This would be unwise, not least because
some of my own studies have been contributions to precisely these
fields! It is nevertheless important to keep some critical pressure on
established frameworks, to see what their conceptual affordances and
limits are.

Several points made in Chapter 2, reviewing the variationist
account of stylistic stratification, are equally relevant to many of the
audience-focused studies discussed in this chapter, my own included.
Analyses are once again organised around linear scales of various
sorts, and treated quantitatively. Style variation 'according to the
audience' is modelled as a speaker using more instances of, or fewer
instances of, a variable speech feature to this addressee (or group) than
to that. This maintains the category-bound assumptions about style
that we saw were characteristic of early general stylistics. For example, my own study of Sue's speech variation matching that of her
clients suggests a stratification effect. It is not the stratification of
casual-to-careful speech that William Labov posited, but it is again a
linear, quantitative stylistic ordering linked to social class variation in
the community. It is a matter of Sue 'living out' or putting into
practice a part of the Cardiff community's class-related variation in
her own speech repertoire. (When I come back to this example, in
Chapter 5, I will suggest that the social meaning of class is carried
through Sue's speech much more selectively than this.)

Audience design research makes great play of quantitative patterns.
Allan Bell's seminal 1984 paper makes a strong predictive claim about
the *extents* of 'social' versus 'stylistic' variation (see his fifth principle

in section 3.2, above). The main idea is that stylistic variation realises *less* variation, quantitatively speaking, than social variation, which Bell links to the idea that it *derives from* social variation. In commenting on my travel agency data, for example, Bell says that Sue 'goes – quite literally – more than halfway to meet her clients' (Bell 1984: 165). This argument is not fully convincing, if only for methodological reasons. It is based in a comparison of quantitative results produced from different sources, each of which has an element of arbitrariness built into it. The measured extent of 'social' variation is fundamentally related to which speakers appear in the sample and how they are surveyed. It is extremely difficult to claim that we can represent the maximal extent of sociolinguistic variation in a community. Similarly, the range of an individual's style-shifting of course depends on where and how we observe them speaking. Bell is clearly right that 'speakers cannot match the speech differences of *all* their interlocutors' (1984: 158, my emphasis) but the comparison of 'social' and 'stylistic' variation extents seems inadequately motivated.

We could think of different ways of defining the envelope of 'social variation' in this sort of account. Is it the range of variation we can measure between the typical 'casual speech' of the 'most standard-speaking' member of the 'highest social class' to the typical 'casual speech' of the 'most non-standard-speaking' member of the 'lowest social class'? Should we condense this range by adding restrictions to do with age or gender, or stretch it by including untypical outliers? The numerical values quickly come to seem rather arbitrary. Bell's original empirical case centres on the use of (intervocalic t) in New Zealand. But I wonder what it means to claim that 'social variation' in respect of (intervocalic t) contains particular speakers' stylistic variation in respect of the same feature. Janet Holmes (e.g. 1994, 1997) has produced a detailed account of the status of [t] voicing in New Zealand as a social variable. (I am grateful to her and to Allan Bell for giving me further very helpful observations on this sociolinguistic issue.) Voicing of intervocalic [t] is part of a change in progress (towards more frequent voicing) in New Zealand which originated as a working-class feature. In the 1990s it was well-established in the conversational style of working-class young people and was spreading into the middle classes. It has connotations of 'sloppiness' in speech but also of informality and Americanness, and it might even be acquiring prestige as part of changing and more positive attitudes to American influence. While there is plenty of evidence that [t] voicing is well represented as a social variable in New Zealand, it is much more difficult to explain the derivation of stylistic meaning from its complex social profile. To do this we need to see how specific meanings are made salient in contexts of use.

The more fundamental criticism (as I mentioned in Chapter 2) is that quantitative accounts assume that stylistic 'levels' in terms of frequencies of occurrence of speech variants are regularly perceived to be meaningfully different. As I suggested earlier, it has yet to be demonstrated that a 60% pattern will have a different meaning, as (supposedly) an aggregated linguistic style, from a 40% pattern, and so on. It is entirely reasonable to assume that there will be some tendency for higher frequencies of use of a sociolinguistic variant to be more robust carriers of that feature's indexical meaning than lower frequencies. But to map a linear dimension of 'social meaning intensity' precisely onto numerical arrays is extremely counter-intuitive. This procedure side-steps a theory of sociolinguistic indexicality which – in the version I develop in later chapters – gives priority to the local contextualisation of single variants in discourse.

My own travel agency study, and in fact all the studies reviewed above, are open to the charge of sociological essentialism that we also discussed in Chapter 2. Audience design and accommodation research has been tolerant of social categories such as Maori versus Pakeha, African American versus European American, male versus female, and high versus low social class. As with most variationist research, there is the risk that the sociological design of the research is over-confident in these categories, and it is possible that linguistic variation could be organised in relation to quite different social categories and perceptions if we were to look for them. They also assume that variation's relational meaning is a matter of speakers modifying their group-salient personas – being 'more like a Maori speaker' or 'more like a middle-class Cardiffian', for example, when no direct evidence in support of these interpretations is available.

There is an important counter-argument here, similar to the one I attributed to Ben Rampton in Chapter 2. While it is true that these studies do presuppose the relevance of particular social categories, they nevertheless demonstrate that social categories do *not fully* determine speech style. We can see that speakers like Foxy Boston transcend or deny the sociolinguistic patterns that we might otherwise take to be normatively associated with her being 'a young African American'. The great achievement of audience design and accommodation research is to show the malleability of sociolinguistic identity, even though the studies themselves are conceived and designed around apparently fixed categories. Giles argued that accommodation theory provided a more dynamic approach to style variation than

Labov's stratificational model (though see Labov's own claim about 'dynamism' in section 2.2). This is most obviously true in the way that accommodation theory stresses sociolinguistic contingency. Speakers' styling is, in many circumstances and perhaps even as a general rule, mutually convergent – there is a general 'set' to converge communicatively. The model invests a degree of agency in speakers, who are able to manage their relationships with others by modifying their stylistic selections. While this seems a reasonable assumption, it is difficult to locate particular instances along this (linear) scale of general tendency to local motivation.

The rubric of 'designing speech for an audience' itself repays critical examination (and cf. Clark 1993). First, we might ask whether the concept of *audience* is fully theorised here. Allan Bell (1984: 158ff.) gives us a taxonomy of audience types reminiscent of Erving Goffman's discussion of participation frameworks in talk (Goffman 1981). 'Addressees' are a known, ratified and directly addressed type of audience – the immediate and intended recipient of speech as we usually conceive it. 'Auditors' are known and ratified (the speaker knows they are there and accepts they have listening rights), although they are not directly addressed. 'Overhearers' are like auditors but they are not ratified. 'Eavesdroppers' are people who are not known to be present, and of course are not ratified or intentionally addressed. Bell's idea is that 'a speaker's style design is graded according to role distance' (1984: 160); that is, that each role exerts less of an 'effect' on a speaker's style, as the audience role becomes more 'remote'. He cites some studies that suggest a greater quantitative shift by speakers to addressees when only speaker and addressee are present in the situation, rather than when there are also auditors present. This is yet another linear principle and prediction.

But across the studies we have reviewed, addressees are socially positioned very differently. Are we dealing with 'audienceship' in the same sense? In fact we see audiences entering into very different relational configurations with speakers. In Bell's original New Zealand broadcasting study, the news announcers have 'relationships' with their listening radio audiences in only a rather abstract sense. As Bell says, they exist as an audience and as a set of addressees only in the minds of announcers and the broadcasting institutions. Foxy's addressees are physically co-present. But more than this, especially in the interview with Faye and Roberta, they build upon pre-existing social intimacy with Foxy and personally shared experience. Sue's clients in the travel agency are in almost all cases unfamiliar to her at the point where I recorded their interaction. But Sue clearly works at establishing a degree of closeness and trust in these encounters as part of her professional role, and her stylistic convergence is part of that endeavour.

Studying style through relational models is entirely appropriate in each of these cases, but the qualities of social relation being negotiated are very different across the cases. Bell (1984) offers an interesting discussion of how speech is likely to be styled to ideal rather than actual recipients, for example in brief service encounters. He gives the example of William Labov's classic study of (postvocalic r) in the speech of New York City department stores (Labov 1966). Labov surveyed store assistants' answers to his questions to them, which were designed to elicit the answer *fourth floor*, containing two opportunities for [r] pronunciation after vowels. He asked questions like 'where can I find lamps?', knowing from the store directory that these items were indeed on the fourth floor. The stratification of three stores, Saks Fifth Avenue, Macy's and S. Klein, in terms of prestige and cost seemed to lead store assistants to use different amounts of the prestige [r] feature. In the very brief encounters that Labov set up with himself as a questioning customer, the assistants were presumably targeting ideal customer types (slightly different in each store), rather than designing their speech relative to actual speech characteristics.

Following on from this, we should question what is implied in the idea of *for*, in the phrase 'style for audiences'. The idea of 'for' comes and goes in accounts of audience design, where the more common formulation is 'style is a response to an audience'. Although they are sometimes run together (see *'for and in response to their audience'* in principle 3 in section 3.2, above), these formulations are very different. 'Style for audiences' represents speaker actions as being active and agentive. 'Style in response to an audience' paints speaker actions as being more passive and automated (although Bell says not). Yet Bell's choice of the keyword *design* in 'audience design' clearly implies motivated and strategic action. In the first paragraphs of this book I argued that 'style' and 'design' have a close affiliation as concepts: design refers to the planned form of an item, and to a process of creative styling. A document, for example, is designed in the knowledge of alternative possible forms and arrangements and with particular (often aesthetic) outcomes and effects in mind. This is why, even when he talks of 'responsiveness', Bell wants to insist that a stylistic response to an audience is itself an active process. He suggests that the active–passive distinction is a false one in this context:

> If it is common that people attempt to deal amicably with each other, and if they signal that linguistically by style convergence, this should not be regarded as passivity or manipulation. It is one person's response to another. People do, after all, generally spend more time responding to others than taking the initiative (Bell 1984: 184).

Even so, the relativities of speaker responsiveness and speaker agency remain somewhat unclear in the audience design and accommodation frameworks, and probably for good reason. Some instances of stylistic convergence are undoubtedly non-strategic and fully automated. Postural and gestural convergence are good examples of this. It is very unlikely that postural 'mirroring', when one person adopts the same or a symmetrical body posture to a communicating partner, is a matter of communicative strategy or design. It may nonetheless be socially and relationally meaningful. We might say that, in these circumstances, style is passive in terms of speaker control and motivation, but active at the level of relational achievement.

Accent convergence can often happen on the fringe of speaker awareness and control. Conversation between speakers who generally have different phonetic shapes for variables creates phonetic dissonances. This is especially the case when different speakers produce different phonetic realisations of the same segment in close proximity, such as a long versus a short realisation of the words 'bath' or 'laugh' in a British context. Short [a] is a characteristically northern English pronunciation, as opposed to long [ɑː] which is characteristically southern and more 'standard' (RP). Speakers will often get a sense of unintended psychological divergence when different phonetic forms are realised in close proximity. They may then style-shift, not so much as a positive strategy to reduce social distance, but to avoid semiotic dissonance. They may or may not be aware of this shift and of its basis in relational meaning. We have to assume that speakers are entirely *un*aware and *un*able to design meaning into their styling if we model their style-shifting quantitatively. It is implausible that speakers can adequately monitor and strategically manage *frequencies* of their own use of sociolinguistic variables. On the other hand, there are cases where 'design' is a fully appropriate concept, when speakers (consciously or not, and whether or not they can account their strategies metacommunicatively) shape their speech in anticipation of particular social outcomes. At these moments, the idea of responsiveness loses its traction.

Accommodation theory has always been explicit about the role of speaker motivations. While Bell treats 'initiative style' as the marked case, relative to 'responsive style', accommodation theory has always assumed that motivated and strategic operations are the *un*marked case. Yet at one point in his 1984 paper, Bell says that 'The common factor in all these [types of public speech situation, including his own New Zealand broadcasting context] is the strong pressure to seek the addressees' approval' (1984: 172). This aligns the audience design model with one of accommodation theory's explicit motivational claims – that a speaker converges in order to boost his/her own perceived social attractiveness. This brings us back to one of the key questions for a stylistics of variation: *Who, actually, is style for?*

'Seeking approval' is rather uncontroversially a speaker-centred motive, albeit a matter of a speaker seeking to gain face through the assessment of another person. The other dominant claim in accommodation theory, converging to promote communicative effectiveness, is less specifically targeted on the speaker. It could imply mutual benefit to participants, or giving priority to an addressee's communicative needs. At the same time, being 'communicatively effective' is often taken to be a measure of speaker status and competence. Overall, it seems that imposing some general theoretical priority in favour of speakers or listeners as the targets or beneficiaries of stylistic processes is too restrictive. It risks overplaying one part of a contextual matrix and neglecting other parts. The explanatory devil is in the detail of particular social contexts and their particular relational configurations.

So it is possible to argue that audience design and accommodation theory – two remarkably cogent and productive paradigms for style research in sociolinguistics – have weighted the scales too heavily in favour of recipiency. The general concept of identity has been relatively rare in discussions of sociolinguistic style, although it is surely impossible to separate issues of social relationships from issues of self-identity. In her extremely valuable overview of sociolinguistic style research, Natalie Schilling-Estes (2004a) distinguishes 'audience design' approaches (those we have reviewed in this chapter) from 'speaker design' approaches, which she associates with my own more recent research as well as others'. The structure of the present book adheres to something like the same basic distinction, in that I will be dealing mainly with identity-related themes in the remaining chapters. But I would resist using the phrase 'speaker design' for the same reason as I gave just above. If we approach style as the deploying and making of social meaning in evolving discursive contexts, we have to remain open to reading social meanings wherever they adhere. Both self-identity and audience design are inevitably involved in this, and I have sometimes used the phrase 'the relational self'

(Coupland 2001b) to try to mark the fact that we need to treat identity and audience approaches together.

Before turning to the styling of social identities, however, we revisit the basic question of social meaning in Chapter 4. Allan Bell's work laid the ground for seeing style as the reworking of social meanings made available through sociolinguistic structure. But where do social meanings come from and what sort of resource do they constitute for styling?

4   Sociolinguistic resources for styling

4.1   SPEECH REPERTOIRES

In looking at examples of speakers' individual stylistic variability as we have done in Chapters 2 and 3 – speakers style-shifting across social situations or between recipients and recipient groups – we get a glimpse of the freedom that speakers enjoy in the domain that we are calling 'style'. In Chapter 2 we saw that William Labov tended to play down this freedom at the level of the individual. He preferred to emphasise the general, normative, uni-directional shifts that sociolinguistic interviews can trigger towards a prestige spoken norm or away from use of a 'stigmatised' speech feature. In Chapter 3 we debated Allan Bell's claim – sometimes referred to as 'Bell's principle' – that speakers' stylistic latitude derives from and is contained by the social variation visible in the community. At the same time, Bell provided the idea of initiative style shift, recognising that speakers do also have creative agency. They can use style-shifts to 'initiate' new qualities or perceptions of a local situation. So in both cases we have the idea of *constrained freedom*. For both Labov and Bell, styling is the variation that speakers can perform within certain tolerances, dictated by the boundaries of their speech communities.

The conventional sociolinguistic concept here is *speech repertoire*. Ronald Wardhaugh (2002: 127) says we can talk of a speech repertoire when (and it is always the case) 'an individual ... controls a number of varieties of a language or of two or more varieties'. So the concept of speech repertoire confirms Labov's principle that 'there are no single-style speakers' (Labov 1972b: 208) and throws the definition of an idiolect (a single person's distinctive way of speaking) into confusion. A speech repertoire seems like a closet containing a specified number of clothing items. In this conception, speakers select items from their individual clothing (or speech) repertoires. They do this either to match particular situations they find themselves in (situational conformity – dressing 'to fit in'), or to deviate to some extent from normative expectations (initiative style – dressing 'to be different'). This is very much in line with Dell Hymes's early (1974) conception of style. Hymes wanted the term 'style' to be used in a 'non-protean' sense, not significantly different from the general term 'way of speaking':

> Persons are recognized to choose among styles themselves, and the choices to have social meaning. (This is the vantage point from which a variety of phenomena treated separately under headings such as bilingualism, diglossia, standard and non-standard speech, and the like, can be integrated.) (Hymes 1974: 434–5).

Hymes's suggestion that we should not partition off the study of 'standardness' or dialect-style from other dimensions of meaningful style has proved to be important, and I try to develop this insight in later chapters.

But even if we are referring to dialect-style specifically, the idea that speakers choose styles as alternative, co-available options from defined speech repertoires is open to many objections and necessary qualifications. In this chapter I will set out different sociolinguistic arguments *against* the 'choice from pre-existing repertoire' position. One of the main objections is that the notion of speech repertoire is apolitical: it fails to engage with the political and ideological implications of sociolinguistic variation and usage. To extend the closet metaphor, we would have to recognise that some items of clothing in the closet are far more valuable than others. For example, some are perceived to be tasteless or garish, while others are dated or dull. The same is true of speech varieties. A further objection centres on the idea of 'choice' (see the Hymes quote) and the assumption that individuals 'control' the varieties in their repertoires (see the Wardhaugh quote). Do we actually *own* the items in the closet, and in what sense? What discretion have we had in the process of filling the closet? How free are we, actually, in selecting items to wear? In the linguistic domain, are ways of speaking sometimes too ingrained in us for us to be able to opt out of their identity implications and take up others? Answers to these questions lead us to think that the 'choice-from-repertoire' model is much too open. Sociolinguistic resources are less freely available to us than this.

There are also arguments, on the other hand, that the model is too restrictive. It is too restrictive if we subordinate speaker style strictly to within-community variation (as in Bell's principle). Stylistic 'wiggle-room' is in some ways more extensive than managing meanings linked to social class and formality along orderly dimensions, mirroring community variation in a slightly more curtailed form, as it has typically been depicted in sociolinguistics. This assumption is increasingly out of touch with the circumstances of contemporary life. There are potentially many more items and styles of clothing in the closet. In fact we now have to set aside the closet metaphor, with its implications of physical boundedness, and conceive of something more like *virtual repertoires* – stylistic creations of the imagination. Also, the meanings attaching to particular ways of speaking are themselves relatively unstable. What is tasteless in one era, or in one social situation, might well be fashionable in others. Styling can be initiative in a more radical sense than Bell implies, when people transcend the normative boundaries of the speech repertoires they have inherited and *cross* into sociolinguistic usage typically associated with others (Rampton 1995). But whatever sources and resources are in question, the repertoire model is too static because it pays too little attention to the *contextualisation* of speaking. Even when speakers operate 'within a predictable repertoire', they are not limited to recycling pre-existing symbolic meanings. They can frame the linguistic resources available to them in creative ways, making new meanings from old meanings.

The remainder of the chapter is structured around this debate over constraint and openness. Section 4.2 focuses on language ideology and the political weightiness of language variation. Section 4.3 introduces more deterministic arguments – that speakers are predisposed to particular ways of speaking by virtue of their socialisation, and that they therefore have quite limited control over the social meanings of their speech. Section 4.4 briefly reviews some empirical research into language attitudes, showing how prejudice against certain ways of speaking is socially structured, but also amenable to change. In 4.5 we consider the idea of metalanguage, which opens up the possibility that speakers can maintain a degree of critical distance from their own ways of speaking, introducing the theoretical importance of speech performance. This chapter cannot resolve on-going debates about constraint and openness, and it is probably naive to try to resolve them definitively. The picture that emerges is one where language variation is indeed rooted in social structure and does indeed constrain many people's senses of who they are and what they can socially achieve. But it is not inconsistent with this view to emphasise how speakers do also have potential to work free from these social constraints, and how styling plays a key part in this.

4.2 THE IDEOLOGICAL BASIS OF VARIATION

There has been a clear shift in sociolinguistic accounts of variation from the 1990s onwards, away from mainly descriptive treatments of variation to more ideologically-grounded approaches. Pierre Bourdieu's sociological research on *linguistic markets* has been influential. Bourdieu stresses the symbolic and cultural value of language varieties (e.g. Bourdieu 1984, 1991). Prestigious varieties of English, for example, have cultural *capital* which often translates into real, material advantages for speakers. They can 'cash in' their prestigious speech, for example in gaining employment in good service-sector jobs.

Bourdieu at one point theorises style directly. He says that style – linguistic style or any other form of cultural practice – is a system of social distinctiveness that is ideologically structured through socialisation:

> [Style], this particular elaboration which tends to give discourse its distinctive properties, is a being-perceived which exists only in relation to perceiving subjects, endowed with the diacritical dispositions which enable them to make distinctions between different *ways of* saying, distinctive manners of speaking. It follows that style, whether it be a matter of poetry as compared with prose or of the diction of a particular (social, sexual or generational) class compared with that of another class, exists only in relation to agents endowed with schemes of perception and appreciation that enable them to constitute it as a set of systematic differences, apprehended syncretically. What circulates on the linguistic market is not 'language' as such, but rather discourses that are stylistically marked both in their production, in so far as each speaker fashions an idiolect from the common language, and in their reception, in so far as each speaker helps to *produce* the message which he perceives and appreciates by bringing to it everything that makes up his singular and collective experience (Bourdieu 1991: 38–9, with original emphasis).

Some of the particularities of expression here are attributable to translation from French, others to the sociological rather than socio-linguistic framing of the ideas. But Bourdieu is clearly setting out an ideological programme for style research. Elsewhere he says that ideologies are 'always *doubly determined*' (1991: 169), expressing the interests of particular social classes but also serving the interests of the social actors whose voices express them. Some social styles – those associated with dominant groups – impose 'an apprehension of the established order as natural (orthodoxy) through the disguised (and thus misrecognized) imposition of systems of classification and of mental structures that are objectively adjusted to social structures' (1991: 169).

This viewpoint acknowledges variationists' traditional claim that language variation is socially structured in communities. Bourdieu regularly cites Labov. But it challenges the apparent innocence of the original variationist account. I say 'apparent' because, as noted earlier, sociolinguists of variation have never lacked the will to engage politically on behalf of linguistic minorities. Walt Wolfram (1993, 1998, see also http://www.cal.org/ebonics/wolfram.html), for example, reviews what he calls 'linguistic gratuity' or the need, established as a principle, to 'return linguistic favours to the community'. This follows in a strong tradition established by William Labov, most explicitly in his (1982) paper, 'Objectivity and commitment in linguistic science'. Apparent innocence relates to the research designs and methods of canonical variationism, which in themselves were better suited to describing variation rather than understanding or challenging its socio-cultural and ideological embedding.

Whatever, it has become increasingly obvious that the sociolinguistic structures that matter for speakers in their social lives are not simply the describable statistical patterns of speech co-varying with class and situation. They are the ideological structures that imbue language variation with social meaning, and often with social disadvantage. Lesley Milroy defines language ideologies as 'thoroughly naturalized sets of beliefs about language intersubjectively held by members of speech communities' (Milroy 2004: 162). She cites Michael Silverstein's overlapping definition, where he defines language ideologies as 'sets of beliefs about language articulated by users as a rationalization or justification of perceived language structure or use' (Silverstein 1979: 193). Ideological sociolinguistics is concerned with processes of subordination and gate-keeping, entitlement and resistance. It gives priority to ideological critique. Describing variation in 'speech communities' remains a high-volume research activity, and there are pockets of prevarication about whether, for example, 'standard English' should be accepted as a politically neutral object of description (Coupland 2000). But sociolinguistics is increasingly well positioned to engage with ideological debates in social theory (e.g. Blommaert 1999, 2005; Cameron 1990; Coupland, Sarangi and Candlin 2001; Gal and Irvine 1995).

Norman Fairclough has been a leading architect of critical language awareness (e.g. Fairclough 1992a, b; 1995b). To take one particular theme from his work, he challenges the idea of contextual 'appropriateness' in language use. The orderliness of language variation perhaps carries the implication that speakers know which ways of speaking are 'appropriate' to which social contexts, such as how to speak in formal settings. This is certainly how some British government education reports have picked up on the study of language variation. For example, the Cox Report of 1989 set out that children should be able to use 'standard' varieties of English when this is 'appropriate', and that schools should provide the means for them to learn to do this. The modality of the word 'should' in the previous sentence already hints at an appeal to social norms and prescriptions, and therefore already undermines the apparent neutrality of the concept of appropriateness.

> Appropriateness models in sociolinguistics or in educational policy documents should therefore be seen as *ideologies*, by which I mean that they are projecting imaginary representations of sociolinguistic reality which correspond to the perspective and partisan interests of one section of society – its dominant section (Fairclough 1992b: 48, with original emphasis).

Fairclough goes on to provide an important critique of normalising tendencies in language education, when programmes set out targets for young people's 'competences' in terms of specific 'communication skills' linked to perceived social needs.

Rosina Lippi-Green's (1997) book, *English with an Accent*, is a powerful critique of the ideology of linguistic standardisation in the USA. She aligns her work with Michel Foucault's writing on the disciplining of discourse (1984), and principally with the politics of 'who is allowed to speak, and thus who is heard' (Lippi-Green 1997: 64). She defines 'standard language ideology' as 'a bias toward an abstracted, idealized, homogeneous spoken language which is imposed and maintained by dominant bloc institutions and which names as its model the written language, but which is drawn primarily from the spoken language of the upper middle class' (1997: 64). Her book is a systematic cataloguing of what she calls the 'language subordination process'. 'Non-standard' varieties (and my quote-marks on this occasion reflect Lippi-Green's contention that 'standard language' is a mythical construct, as well as my own reservations) are devalued through a mixture of mystificatory politics, authority claims, misinformation about language, trivialising of vernaculars, threats and vilification (Lippi-Green 1997: 68). The empirical data in her book are wide-ranging, including surveying the accents of animated characters in Disney films. She concludes that in Disney animations, 'Characters with strongly positive actions and motivations are overwhelmingly speakers of socially mainstream varieties of English. Conversely, characters with strongly negative actions and motivations often speak varieties of English linked to specific geographical regions and marginalized social groups' (1997: 101). Lippi-Green also documents the marketing of 'accent reduction' schemes (voice training and elocution courses), and discrimination against speakers of non-mainstream English, including African American English, in education and legal settings in the USA.

These political points make it necessary to revisit a taken-for-granted assumption in variationist sociolinguistics – the idea that sociolinguistic variants are semantically equivalent, or 'different ways of saying the same thing' (see the discussion of Jack Chambers and Adonis in Chapter 1). In a famous paper, Beatriz Lavandera (1978) drew attention to the sameness requirement in variation theory. She argued that phonological and morphological variables met the sameness requirement for their variant forms because phonetic segments are, in one sense, meaningless – they do not carry referential meaning. In other words, alternation between present and absent postvocalic [r] or between single and multiple negation does not change the referential meaning of the words and utterances in which these features occur. Lavandera raised this issue in order to ask whether discourse variation, such as alternation between the phrases *and stuff like that* and *and that sort of thing* could be treated within the variationist paradigm (see Coupland 1985; Macaulay 2005). But this sort of discussion has hidden the potential for sociolinguistic variants to be *ideologically non-equivalent*. Dialect or accent variables may be alternative ways of achieving the same reference, but it certainly does not follow that they are alternative ways of saying, or meaning, 'the same thing'.

David Lee asks 'whether the differences between linguistic [dialect] varieties – specifically between standard and non-standard varieties – are simply a matter of superficial formal contrasts, or whether there are more important differences having to do with the kinds of meanings expressible in different varieties' (Lee 1992: 165). He goes on to argue that 'It is, of course, a commonplace that there are marked ideological differences associated with the use of a standard and a non-standard variety' which are 'oriented towards different meaning potentials' (1992: 165). Lee's position is that we can give a better account of the social significance of dialect-styles if we see them as 'associated with different ways of speaking, different meaning orientations, different discourses' (1992: 166). James Milroy and Lesley Milroy acknowledge the same point in saying that 'relatively low level linguistic elements [are] intertwined quite inextricably with social distinctions of various kinds important in the community' (Milroy and Milroy 1985: 96).

There is no shortage, then, of critical endorsement of the ideological loading of language variation. There are research paradigms, which we can't deal with in detail here (but see section 4.4), that empirically demonstrate structured prejudice against many 'non-standard' spoken varieties. The main implication for this chapter's concerns is that Western, anglophone countries (which is where we have most evidence available) have set particularly high stakes for language variation. We might think that they have established an ideological climate where style-shifting away from stigmatised vernaculars is highly desirable, if it allows people to escape from the punitive indexical associations of class and race. But it also seems to make style-shifting a highly charged and risky business, subject to social monitoring and threatening further sanctions when it 'goes wrong'. Another possibility, however, is that perspectives like Lippi-Green's are themselves a little one-sided and overly pessimistic. The politics of 'language subordination' are not, I would suggest, as clear-cut and repressive as her commentaries suggest. The ideological loading of ways of speaking allows speakers, on occasion, to use variation to important ends, including *subverting* dominant ideologies. But before we consider that line of argument, we need to look at theory that supports the 'language subordination' rubric.

4.3 HABITUS AND SEMANTIC STYLE

Part of Pierre Bourdieu's theorising of language and symbolic power is around the idea of *habitus*. He came to believe that acts of speaking are routinised in what Judith Butler calls 'embodied rituals of everydayness by which a culture produces and sustains belief in its own "obviousness"' (Butler 1997: 152). These embodied rituals are the habitus. As a concept it summarises Bourdieu's view that ways of speaking are intractably linked to historical and political meanings, but also ingrained in physical acts of speaking. 'Language', Bourdieu says, is a 'body technique'. He goes on:

> specifically linguistic, especially phonetic, competence is a dimension of bodily hexis in which one's whole relation to the social world, and one's whole socially informed relation to the social world, are expressed. There is every reason to think that, through the mediation of ... 'articulatory style', the bodily hexis characteristic of a social class determines the system of phonological features which characterizes a class pronunciation (Bourdieu 1991: 86).

This is a remarkable claim. It challenges the idea that we can select our speech styles 'out of the closet' freely and with agentive discretion. The concept of habitus implies that we cannot easily (if at all) shake off the ideological associations of our own ingrained ways of speaking, because they result from a slow process of being socialised into normative and acceptable ways of speaking for our social groups. Bourdieu does not give many examples, but at one point he suggests that using uvular /r/ ([ʁ], the 'standard' French pronunciation form) in place of a more vernacular trilled /r/ ([R]), 'in the presence of legitimate speakers [is] accomplished without consciousness or constraint' (1991: 51). This is the Labovian idea of predictable and presumably non-reflexive shift towards a 'standard' linguistic norm, or accommodation theory's idea of 'upward' convergence.

Habitus has some resonance with psycholinguistic theory about there being a critical period for language learning (Sankoff 2004). This refers to how primary socialisation, including language socialisation (Ochs and Schifflin 1986), takes place in a unique cognitive environment for learning. Beyond the critical period in childhood, languages and dialects cannot be acquired in the same way, even though learning and change are of course still possible. But Bourdieu is making a case about ideological and practical (practice-based) sedimentation, as well as about formal linguistic sedimentation, although we can assume that the processes overlap. Similar ideas about social class being a 'practical consciousness' are entertained by Raymond Williams, and have been brought into sociolinguistics by Ben Rampton (Rampton 2006, section 6.1; see section 5.8 of the present book). Basil Bernstein's early sociolinguistic work was controversial precisely because he interpreted the link between social class and language as a matter of learned predisposition (Bernstein 1971–1990, 1996). Bernstein argued that working-class British children were predisposed to using an *implicit* design for social interaction that he labelled 'restricted code', as opposed to the more *explicit* 'elaborated code' design through which middle-class children oriented to communicative tasks.

These approaches share two central ideas. The first is that ways of speaking and styles are not meaning-free varieties that happen to co-vary with social group membership or usage in different situations. They are fundamentally socio-semantic designs for talk. Secondly, their design qualities, their coded predispositions, are deeply embedded in our social experiences. They are therefore both socially constrained and socially constraining. There is contemporary sociolinguistic research on semantic styles. Barbara Johnstone (1996), for example, shows how grammatical and pragmatic resources used by two speakers, which could be analysed simply in terms of 'southern' versus 'northern' USA dialects, in fact constitute different meaning resources for the two speakers. To take just one particular feature, the verb *carry* for southern speakers can mean something close to what *take* means. So a southern speaker can use *carry* and *take* is ways a northern speaker can not, to distinguish willing accompaniment from forced accompaniment, as in the following examples:

> When she [Blair] wanted to go along, Sonny 'carried' her to the insurance company and to the store, but when she was unwilling, he 'taken' her to the motel. Her knowledge of southern possibilities provided Blair with a way of creating meaning that someone without her resources would have had to create another way. (Johnstone 1996: 51)

In this case, semantic variation is certainly learned and conventionalised, though Johnstone presents it as an additional communicative resources for speakers, rather than as a social constraint.

Much more in the Basil Bernstein tradition, Ruqaia Hasan develops the analysis of implicit versus explicit ways of meaning. She endorses Bernstein's view that 'the predominant semantic style for the educated middle-class English speaker is the explicit one' (Hasan 1996: 213). She contrasts the explicitness of 'standard' English syntax with Urdu, whose dominant semantic style is to use an implicit design. Urdu allows various forms of ellipsis not found in English. Subject ellipsis and complement ellipsis are conventional when these meanings are recoverable from the context, either present or known through shared history. So Urdu regularly allows expressions where complements are elided, which 'standard' English allows only in very rare instances, such as in the question *finished?* English does not allow *cooked?*, meaning 'have you finished cooking it?', or *made?* or *typed?*, whereas Urdu does (Hasan 1996: 231).

Within varieties of English also there are differences in the use of exophoric reference (referring to subjects through use of a pronoun, without linguistic specification) – expressions like *they're really taking the game to them* in the context of watching a sports event on TV. Understanding which team is referred to be *they* and which by *them* is only possible if the listener uses contextual information, following the flow of the game on TV and being able to predict the speaker's meaning. These pronouns refer exophorically – out to the social environment – rather than referring to nouns mentioned just previously (anaphoric reference). Dense social networks, where shared assumptions can be drawn on inferentially, are a breeding place for exophoric reference. So exophora is a linguistic manifestation of small social distance: 'The [exophoric] style of speaking is, then, index-ical of a qualitatively different social relation' (Hasan 1996: 215). In a personal note, Adam Jaworski explains that Polish allows similar ellipsis with past perfective participles. One possible function is to avoid the use of (commitment to) either 'tu' or 'vous' type address forms (cf. section 3.1).

Neither of these approaches (Johnstone's and Hasan's) assumes the social determinism of Bourdieu's habitus. As I suggested earlier in this chapter, the problem in assessing ideological readings of style is where, precisely, to draw the line between constraint and freedom. The attraction of Bourdieu's theory is that it articulates the potentially deep socio-political significance of language variation as a dimension of social practice. It warns us against reading stylistic choice as some-thing opportunistic or simply elective. The ways of speaking we acquire developmentally are, at least to some extent, structured into us, and for some speakers, their communicative dispositions lock them into social disadvantage. Bourdieu does not generally do a stylistic analysis of linguistic practice, but his concepts are richly suggestive for how we should analyse it. At one point he develops an account of an interactional moment captured in a newspaper story published in Béarn, a former province in south-west France. The news-paper feature describes how the mayor of Pau, at a ceremony in honour of a Béarnais poet, addressed the assembled company in the local dialect, Béarnais. The newspaper reported that 'The audience was greatly moved by this thoughtful gesture' (Bourdieu 1991: 68). Bourdieu asks how it comes to be that the audience, who spoke Béarnais, could construe the mayor's code-switch as 'a thoughtful gesture'. He says that this is only possible in an ideological climate where people assume that 'standard' French is the normatively acceptable variety for speech in public. Also, the mayor is using a 'strategy of condescen-sion' by which he earns 'profit' from this presumed sociolinguistic relationship, by constructing himself as having 'the common touch'. The hierarchical relationship between 'standard' French and Béarnais remains undiminished, and might even be consolidated by the mayor's stylistic choice.

But the general sociological model Bourdieu constructs is unremit-tingly modernist. Although his theoretical point of departure is social practice, for the most part he shows practice consolidating a fixed social order structured around class. His key idea of symbolic domination reflects a hierarchical social structure which imposes its values 'downwards'. To this he adds habitus, which is a conspiracy theory around freedom and constraint. Bourdieu says that symbolic domination manages to circumvent normal considerations of freedom and constraint, because 'the "choices" of the habitus ... are accomplished without consciousness or constraint' (1991: 51, original quotemarks). Habitus is a pre-conditioning of practice that precludes choice. In his words, 'symbolic violence' and 'intimidation' are perpetrated without awareness that any such acts are taking place (1991: 51). 'Intimidation ... can only be exerted on a person predisposed (in his habitus) to feel it' (1991: 51). The whole social structure reaches into the individual speaker. Socialisation creates a 'linguistic "sense of place"' (1991: 82) and habitus ensures that people, for the most part at least, both know and keep to their social place.

We will consider some objections to this line of argument in a short while. But let's first look briefly at some theoretical and empirical research on language attitudes and values, where much less totalising and more specific claims are made about variation as a meaningful sociolinguistic resource.

4.4 LANGUAGE ATTITUDES AND MEANINGS FOR VARIATION

The convention in variationist sociolinguistics is to attribute meanings to varieties based on patterns of variation itself. That is, if a speech feature is used more frequently by one group rather than another group, or in one speaking situation than another, it is common practice to claim that the feature has group-salient or situation-salient meaning. William Labov formalises this pattern of interpretation in his use of the terms *marker*, *indicator* and *stereotype* (Labov 1972b: 237ff.). Markers are sociolinguistic variables that show variation in both 'social' and 'stylistic' dimensions (as we discussed them in Chapter 2). Indicators show stable 'social' variation. They distinguish social classes but show no variation across speaking situations. Stereotypes are variables that are highly salient to speakers and are subject to overt comment and control. Variationists therefore talk of speech variants 'marking' the social and stylistic circumstances of their distribution. If men use a lot of alveolar [n] as opposed to velar [ŋ] of the (ing) variable, it seems reasonable, according to this convention, to say that [n] marks maleness, or (even more contentiously) 'male identity' (though see Kiesling's research, briefly discussed in section 1.4).

I have made the point, several times already, that quantitative methods give a very indirect account of linguistic practice – an account that does not match social actors' own perceptions of meaningful speech differences. But even if we set that issue aside, there are still reasons to doubt the validity of the device of inferring social meaning from speech-form distributions. First, the device has been limited to 'within community' variation, because most sociolinguistic surveys have been limited to single 'speech communities'. This generally negates meanings relating to locality because of the lack of contrastive significance, although in other circumstances we very commonly associate ways of speaking with a speaker's regional provenance. Nancy Niedzielski and Dennis Preston (2003) provide useful information on what definitions and attributes people attach to speech when they are given licence to identify whatever meanings they like. Speaking 'differently', Niedzielski and Preston find, is often characterised in regional terms. In the USA, 'the south' or 'southern speech' has a particularly high salience, for example, but there is a rich vocabulary for describing speech-styles according to other regions and their prototypical speakers: 'midwesterners', 'hicks', 'hillbillies' and so on. People also very commonly make distinctions in terms of 'everyday' versus 'high-falutin' speech, 'very distinguished' or 'snobby' speech, or 'normal' versus 'down-home' speech (Niedzielski and Preston 2003: 57). 'Correctness' and 'pleasantness' have proved to be very productive dimensions for the social evaluation of speech. These terms closely match the socio-psychological dimensions of power (or status or competence) and solidarity (or social attractiveness) in the evaluation of people and social relationships (see section 3.1).

Social meanings like (USA) 'high-falutin' or (UK) 'posh' of course relate to social class structures, although these meanings complicate the link between 'prestige' and 'standardness'. As Wolfram and Fasold found, speech can regularly be seen as 'too snooty' or 'too high-falutin' (1974: 19) – what Niedzielski and Preston call 'superstandard' or 'hyperstandard' speech. Nevertheless, the fact that 'correctness' is a common attribution goes some way to support Bourdieu's arguments about symbolic domination. But it is evident that social meanings for linguistic varieties are *not* restricted to, and in fact not normally defined in relation to, social class membership. Group stereotypes certainly feature in meaning attribution, for example in the regional attributions we have just considered – 'southern' (in a USA context) or 'Welsh' or 'Welshy' (in a British context). But these meanings are just part of a diffuse set of possibilities. The more important point is that social meanings for speech have always proved to be *multi-dimensional*. The social meanings attaching to any one speech variety, or to any single speaker, will typically be a mixture of simultaneous traits and attributions. This is one of the key findings from language attitudes research (Garrett, Coupland and Williams 1999; Garrett forthcoming).

Let's consider the two most productive dimensions along which linguistic varieties and speakers tend to be judged: prestige/status and social attractiveness/likability. Studies have generally found that evaluations within one of these systems are accompanied by (simultaneous but not necessary similar) evaluations within the other system, and this opens up important possibilities. Individual speech varieties and speakers often attract more positive meanings that compensate for more negative ones, e.g. posh speakers being judged to be prestigious but less socially attractive. The same point is summed up by the distinction that we have already noted between so-called 'overt prestige' and 'covert prestige', which Peter Trudgill interprets as a distinction between what speakers say they think and what they actually think (Trudgill 1974). Social meanings are not evaluatively absolute. Rosina Lippi-Green's critique of standard language ideology and Bourdieu's symbolic domination might therefore be too *uni*dimensional. They might also be insufficiently responsive to the effects of social change. Variationists are centrally engaged in the study of *language* change, but they do not commonly comment on changes in social meaning as they affect language variation. Shifts in social meaning – value shifts – can be rapid and decisive, once again challenging Bourdieu's sociolinguistic determinism. We have already seen how establishment values for language ideologise 'correctness' and prescribe 'standards'. Yet the ideological/attitudinal associations of Received Pronunciation in Britain have been subject to considerable shifts over time.

Lynda Mugglestone describes the movement in nineteenth-century England, on the one hand, towards 'colourless', regionally unmarked ways of pronouncing English, although she explains that this was always more of an ideal than a sociolinguistic reality. Non-regionality was an idea that partially obscured the social class alignment of 'standard' pronunciation. Daniel Jones described the focus of his *English Pronouncing Dictionary* of 1917 in these terms:

> the pronunciation used in this book is that most generally heard in the families of Southern English persons whose men-folk have been educated at the great public boarding schools. This pronunciation is also used by a considerable proportion of those who do not come from the South of England but who have been educated at those schools (Jones 1917: viii; Mugglestone 2003: 265).

The BBC in Britain took up the 'images of social unity founded on the ideal of a linguistically homogeneous nation' as a mission (where 'nation', we should add, is highly controversial as a way of referring to the British Isles). The idea of 'correctness', and 'proper' standards of speaking, were infused into this idea of uniformity. 'Standardisation' was an effort to de-localise 'educated speech'. But Mugglestone explains that, post 1960 in Britain, '"talking proper" gradually came to be seen as "talking posh"' (2003: 274). The normative BBC broad-casting voice came to be heard as 'plummy' and began to be coded negatively. RP took on a more complex identity:

> it has increasingly been seen not as neutral and 'accentless' – the images implicitly traded on by the early BBC – but instead as being heavily marked in accent terms, signalling elitism and exclusiveness rather than that 'passport to wider circles of acquaintance' which has so often been proclaimed in the past (Mugglestone 2003: 274).

Mugglestone (2003: 273) talks of the 'rise of the regional' in and after the 1960s in Britain, perhaps linked to a general upsurge in the vitality of popular culture, including British pop music, the Beatles, the Swinging Sixties, and so on.

There is a growing view that accent discrimination in Britain is on the wane. Ben Rampton (2006: 271) quotes Deborah Cameron's view of over a decade ago (Cameron 1995: 27–8) that standard language ideology is being resisted by a 'variation ideology', where variation is positively valued, possibly as a general feature of late-modernity. We hear speculations that 'Estuary English' is a new, classless, non-elite, accessible voice in Britain, with traces of it to be found in the speech of Prime Minister Tony Blair and, earlier, Princess Diana for example in their use of intervocalic glottal stops in expressions like *there's a lot of it about* (Mugglestone 2003: 280). But the Estuary English debate confu-ses two sorts of change which are always concurrent and inter-related – language change and value shifting. The speech of elite groups (sometimes referred to as 'The Queen's English') changes over time (Mugglestone: 283, 287). But value shifts, which are a clear factor in promoting linguistic change, also rework social meanings for varie-ties, new and old. The social group in Britain that came to be known as 'Thatcher's children' (benefiting from the right-wing mone-tarist policies of Margaret Thatcher's government) were also called 'yuppies' (young, upwardly-mobile professionals, especially those working in money markets and the Stock Exchange). They often originated in the south-east of England and their profit motives were legitimised by government policy in favour of free market economics.

It became far more 'respectable' to be rich and to have become rich at others' expense, through what might otherwise have been seen as economic opportunism and sheer greed. So south-eastern English, non-RP speech, loosely called Estuary English, had a new source of social validation. Then, the growth of regional broadcasting in Britain and increasing interest in political devolution validated regionalism.

The result has been a new and evolving language-ideological climate in which it is less necessary and less feasible to respect a British 'standard' variety of English, which has started to be seen as 'old school'. Mugglestone (2003: 284) suggests that Greg Dyke, a recent Director of the BBC, was in favour of greater regionalisation of voice on the BBC. It is certainly not safe to talk of a general British democratisation of ways of speaking, although the onward march of popular culture brings vernacular speech to prominence more and more (e.g. in the voices of footballers, TV presenters and soap opera performers). Some regional voices attract more positive values than others. For example, there is a marked 'Celticisation' of the UK TV networks, with (particularly) Scottish but also some Irish and Welsh voices newly considered to have desirable social resonance in prominent and 'serious' media roles, such as news reading. Other voices, like the urban vernaculars of most large English cities, are still considered thoroughly 'unsuitable' for these roles, although they are finding new media niches where they have definite positive appeal (see section 6.6).

It is difficult to assess the current standing and meaningful associations of different spoken varieties through language attitudes research, partly because of methodological limitations (Garrett forthcoming). Language attitudes research has been conducted in different ways, and some of its most direct methods seem to access conservative judgements, leading informants into recycling familiar, taken-for-granted beliefs about language variation (that is, language ideologies). A study that colleagues and I designed with the BBC in 2004–5 was of this sort (Bishop, Coupland and Garrett 2005; Coupland and Bishop 2007). We designed a simple but broad online survey of more than 5,000 British adults' responses to 34 accent varieties, presented simply to them in the form of speech variety labels. We asked respondents to judge the 'prestige' and 'attractiveness' of each voice-type, and to provide social information about themselves. The survey was in some ways rudimentary, but it provided more extensive comparative information than has been available previously about the social meanings of British accents of English.

The main results, in terms of descriptive statistics, are summarised in Table 4.1. The table shows average values of people's ratings

Table 4.1. *Mean ratings (whole sample, 5,010 informants) of 34 accents of English according to social attractiveness and prestige*

	Social attractiveness	Prestige
— 1. Accent identical to own	4.87 **(2)**	4.14 **(3)**
2. Afro-Caribbean	3.72 **(21)**	2.90 **(30)**
3. Asian	3.21 **(31)**	2.74 **(33)**
4. Australian	4.04 **(13)**	3.51 **(11)**
5. Belfast	3.67 **(23)**	3.11 **(27)**
6. Birmingham	2.92 **(34)**	2.70 **(34)**
7. Black Country	3.16 **(33)**	2.81 **(32)**
8. Bristol	3.64 **(25)**	3.22 **(21)**
9. Cardiff	3.67 **(24)**	3.16 **(25)**
10. Cornish	4.22 **(8)**	3.38 **(13)**
11. Edinburgh	4.49 **(5)**	4.04 **(4)**
12. French	4.09 **(11)**	3.74 **(9)**
13. German	3.20 **(32)**	3.21 **(23)**
14. Glasgow	3.45 **(29)**	2.93 **(29)**
15. Lancashire	3.90 **(15)**	3.24 **(20)**
16. Leeds	3.73 **(20)**	3.15 **(26)**
17. Liverpool	3.40 **(30)**	2.82 **(31)**
18. London	3.70 **(22)**	3.89 **(6)**
19. Manchester	3.61 **(27)**	3.22 **(21)**
20. Newcastle	4.13 **(10)**	3.21 **(23)**
21. New Zealand	4.37 **(6)**	3.84 **(7)**
22. North American	3.90 **(15)**	3.80 **(8)**
23. Northern Irish	4.05 **(12)**	3.30 **(17)**
24. Norwich	3.81 **(18)**	3.38 **(13)**
25. Nottingham	3.78 **(19)**	3.39 **(12)**
26. Queen's English	4.28 **(7)**	5.59 **(1)**
27. Scottish	4.52 **(4)**	3.98 **(5)**
28. South African	3.51 **(28)**	3.34 **(16)**
29. Southern Irish	4.68 **(3)**	3.63 **(10)**
30. Spanish	3.88 **(17)**	3.29 **(18)**
— 31. Standard English	4.96 **(1)**	5.44 **(2)**
32. Swansea	3.64 **(25)**	3.11 **(27)**
33. Welsh	3.95 **(14)**	3.29 **(18)**
34. West Country	4.16 **(9)**	3.36 **(15)**

of each accent on a seven-point scale, where 1.0 represents the lowest possible rating and 7.0 represents the highest possible rating. The original published sources give formal statistics which allowed us to check for significant differences between judgements for social attractiveness and for prestige, also for significant differences across the different demographic groups of people who evaluated the 34 accent types.

The study found mixed evidence of stability and change in social evaluations of English accents over the 30-year period since an earlier, comparable survey was conducted. There is evidence in Table 4.1 that speech varieties approximating to 'standard English' (the variety labelled that way and so-called 'Queen's English') are not uniformly judged most favourably. For example, several 'non-standard' accents are judged to be more socially attractive than 'Queen's English' – Southen Irish English, Scottish English, Edinburgh English and New Zealand English. There is certainly evidence of regular downgrading of some vernaculars associated with urban areas, especially Birmingham, and some ethnic minorities. The survey, though wide, referred to these minorities only very briefly and elliptically. There was statistical evidence (not summarised in the table) of women informants regularly being more generous in their judgements than men, and of younger informants being less well disposed to the 'standard' accent types than older people. Several regional groups were especially 'loyal' to their own varieties (giving them higher ratings than other groups did), especially in Scotland, Wales and Ireland. The main points to emerge were that social meanings for variation are clearly multidimensional, inherently variable and potentially unstable.

4.5 METALANGUAGE, CRITICAL DISTANCE AND PERFORMATIVITY

One of the premises of a critical approach to language and society is that it is possible to launch some sort of resistance to ideological constraint. Sociolinguists are interested in language ideologies because exposing taken-for-granted, social-structuring assumptions about language might provide the means to challenge and to loosen their effects. This is why Norman Fairclough (1992a), for example, writes about critical language *awareness* and its importance, and particularly about the responsibility of education systems to increase levels of awareness. Awareness is a precondition for change, and the term 'critical' is often taken to imply a commitment to bringing about social change. But we shouldn't assume that it is only academic 'critics' who have the potential for awareness, for achieving critical distance from the social power of language and for achieving social change. The general case against sociolinguistic determinism is that speakers – all of us – are indeed invested with language awareness and a potential to engage critically. People's potential for bringing about social change is part of their/our potential as speakers. The social action of speaking is, we might say, social change at a micro-sociological level, and we need to consider how 'style' has a particular role to play in effecting change.

The theoretical starting point here is the idea of *metalanguage* (Jaworski, Coupland and Galasiński 2004). In Chapter 1 we considered Roman Jakobson's outline of linguistic functions, which included a *metalingual function* – language referring to itself. Metalinguistic capacity underlies many different linguistic designs and genres, such as linguistic jokes, artful and playful language use, poetry and other literary and quasi-literary genres, quoting or 'voicing' of other people's speech, irony and so on. What all these designs, spoken or written, share is the 'designer' having a degree of awareness of the consequences of his or her own linguistic/stylistic operations and attending creatively to the form of a linguistic product. Indeed, this is the classical arena for stylistics. In these cases it is quite apt to talk of motivated choices between alternative linguistic or other semiotic forms, even though people may not be fully conscious of alternatives or able to explicitly rationalise the choices they make. Metapragmatic awareness (awareness of the functional and indexical implications of our utterances) is a core quality of all communicative interaction (Silverstein 1993; Verschueren 2004). Nevertheless, it is useful to maintain a distinction between designs for talk that are based in specific sorts of metapragmatic awareness, linked to genres and outcomes (like those listed above), and others where metapragmatic awareness has no specific implications.

Several of the approaches to style that we have already considered have appealed to metalinguistic processes. Labov's 'attention to speech' principle suggested that being more aware of our own acts of speaking triggers speech convergence towards a prestige norm. Bell's use of the term 'design', as noted in section 3.2, perhaps implies speakers construing alternative forms of talk. Giles's accommodation theory makes explicit claims about communicative strategies (e.g. boosting social attractiveness), as does Brown and Levinson's politeness theory. Language attitudes research often takes a direct approach which imposes a metalinguistic frame on respondents, asked to evaluate accents or speakers. But 'doing style', styling, has not typically been seen as a fundamentally reflexive activity. We have found arguments *against* this position, such as Bourdieu's claims that the habitus is beyond speakers' reflexive awareness and control. But there are powerful arguments in favour of reflexivity too.

Judith Butler (1997) takes issue with Bourdieu's determinism. She shares Bourdieu's assumption that speaking is a bodily act – she is thinking of the physical or near-physical impact of racist language and other forms of *symbolic violence*. She accepts Bourdieu's idea that social norms impose a sort of 'foreclosure' on what speakers can say and how they can speak. But she argues that this bodility, and especially what she calls the *performativity* of speaking, resists and challenges social norms:

> I would insist that the speech act, as a rite of institution, is one whose contexts are never fully determined in advance, and that the possibility for the speech act to take on a non-ordinary meaning, to function in contexts where it has not belonged, is precisely the political promise of the performative (Butler 1997: 161).

Performativity implies that utterances break with the social contexts in which they occur. Making 'non-ordinary' meaning is a potential of speech performance, and speakers can perform 'insurrectionary acts' (1997: 145). Bourdieu stresses *doxa*, the inculcated ideological meanings that prevail in society and that speech recycles. People, he thinks, tacitly let the social structure speak through them. Butler thinks that speakers can 'resignify' or reshape meanings in their speech performances. Their meanings can be 'incongruous'. This is a political reading of J. L. Austin's (1962) speech act theory. Performative utterances in Austin's sense are utterances that change social arrangements. The performative utterance *I declare the meeting closed* 'performs' the closure of the meeting; it changes the socially agreed structure and status of the meeting event. For Butler, all acts of speaking have this potential to undermine established, conventional meanings (doxa): 'the efforts of performative discourse exceed and confound the authorizing contexts from which they emerge' (1997: 159).

Bourdieu was not consistently such a social determinist, however. He too writes about subversion, about the role of critical discourse, and about possibilities of 'counterposing a *paradoxical pre-vision* ... to the ordinary vision' of the social order (Bourdieu 1991: 128, with original emphasis). He even writes about the political dimension of performative speech and possibilities for heretical discourse, for example through 'the labour of dramatization' (1991: 128). He is certainly aware of Mikhail Bakhtin's ideas about the subversive potential of carnivalesque language and events (Bakhtin 1968; Rampton 1995: 314). Bourdieu provocatively mentions (in translation) 'outspokenness whose daring is less innocent than it seems since, in reducing humanity to its common nature – belly, bum, bollocks, grub, guts

and shit – it tends to turn the social world upside down, arse over head'
(1991: 88). This is presumably Bourdieu's personal performance of
insurrection.

Bakhtin himself wrote about the tension between inherited normative 'speech genres' and speakers' reworking of them:

> All the diverse areas of human activity involve the use of language . . .
> the nature and forms of this use are just as diverse as are the areas of
> human activity . . . Language is realized in the form of individual
> concrete utterances (oral and written) by participants in the various
> areas of human activity. These utterances reflect the specific
> conditions and goals of each such area not only through their content
> (thematic) and linguistic style, that is the selection of lexical,
> phraseological, and grammatical resources of the language, but above
> all through their compositional structure. All three of these aspects –
> thematic content, style and compositional structure – are equally
> determined by the specific nature of the particular sphere of
> communication. Each separate utterance is individual, of course, but
> each sphere in which language is used develops its own *relatively stable*
> *types* of these utterances. These we may call *speech genres*. (Bakhtin
> 1986: 60)

In his paper on 'The problem of speech genres' (written in 1952–3 and
reproduced in Bakhtin 1986) Bakhtin writes about how any speaker
presupposes not only 'the existence of the language system he is
using, but also the existence of preceding utterances – his own and
others' (Bakhtin, 1986: 69). Current speech enters into one kind of
relation or another with these preceding utterances, It might 'build on
them' or 'polemicize with them'. This is the idea of *multiple voicing* and
Bakhtin's famous view that 'Our speech . . . is filled with others' words,
varying degrees of otherness and varying degrees of "our-own-ness",
[which] carry with them their own evaluative tone, which we assim-
ilate, rework and re-accentuate' (Bakhtin 1986: 89). In double or multiple voicing, speakers can adopt different stances towards preceding
utterances (1986: 189). *Uni-directional* double voicing is when speakers
use forms of language 'belonging to others' and, as Rampton says, 'go
along with the momentum of the second voice, though it retains an
element of otherness' (Rampton 1995: 223; cf. Bakhtin 1981). *Vari-
directional* double voicing is when there is a clash between the speaker's stance and that of the voice s/he is appropriating. This is where we
can talk of sarcasm, irony, subversion and so on. I discuss Bakhtin's
ideas further, and Rampton's development of them, in later chapters,
where the concepts of performance and performativity will also feature strongly.

4.6 SOCIOLINGUISTIC RESOURCES?

In this chapter's wide-ranging but still very selective review, I have gone well beyond the normal boundaries of sociolinguistic style research. This is necessary if the field is to connect with wider currents of discourse analysis, language ideology and general social theory. Where does it leave the concept of sociolinguistic 'resources'? All speakers have a linguistic competence available to them as a resource for speaking. They have access to lexico-grammatical and phonological systems through which they can create meaningful utterances. Their *sociolinguistic resources* are usually discussed under the heading of *communicative competence*, which originally invoked the difficult idea of speaking 'appropriately', but which generally attended to speakers' awareness of social rules and norms for speaking (Hymes 1972; see Duranti 1997: 20ff. for a discussion). An obvious part of speakers' engagement with social norms is their knowledge of the variable forms of speech that they have some representation of and familiarity with, based on their social experience. Dennis Preston makes the point that variable speech features are differentially *available* to speakers, in the sense of their ability to perceive them and their propensity to evaluate and discuss them metalinguistically. Speakers also have varying amounts of *control* over these features, in terms of their ability to speak them and analyse them (Preston 1996; Niedzielski and Preston 2003: 22ff.). Availability and control are two considerations in determining the 'repertoire' of linguistic forms that speakers can apparently 'select' from for stylistic purposes, although we have noted the limitations of these concepts too.

However, sociolinguistic resources are not just linguistic forms or varieties themselves, allied to competence in using them. They are forms or varieties imbued with potential for social meaning. This chapter's review has suggested that social meanings are more than just the statistical correlates of variation distributions. 'Birmingham English', for example, doesn't just bear the meaning of its geographical location or its generalised association with the working-class people who speak that variety most distinctively. It continues to have an ideological profile among British ways of speaking that includes the meanings 'least attractive variety' and 'least prestigious variety'. Even so, these meanings might simply be conventional tropes about British language variation. Other meanings might well be forged around Birmingham speech in actual social practices. 'Received Pronunciation' doesn't simply bear the meaning 'prestigious' or 'supra-local'. Social meanings are multi-dimensional evaluative constructs built up around language varieties that speakers can bring to bear in discourse. This multi-dimensionality is clearly visible, even in the sterile methodological circumstances of the *Voices* survey that I referred to above. Received Pronunciation (if we can have enough confidence in what this term or others like 'standard English' designate) apparently has less social attractiveness for some people than some other British ways of speaking. Younger people showed rather less deference towards it than older people. For Bourdieu, varieties like RP are the focus of a mechanism of symbolic domination, so it can only be a 'resource' for some segments of the social system. But, looked at evaluatively, this does seem too negative and too static a conclusion.

We have to think of social meaning as being a set of dialectical relationships between people, practices and language varieties or features. These meaning-form-practice resources are also historical. This is obviously true in the sense that a linguistic variety's social profile changes over time, as we saw in Mugglestone's history of Received Pronunciation in Britain (and the same sort of shift might be suggested in the age differences just referred to). But arguments from Bourdieu and Bakhtin, although they reach radically different conclusions, suggest a more fundamental historicity. We inherit linguistic varieties and their meanings from social arrangements that were in place during earlier time periods. Language change occurs incrementally over the generations, meaning that children do not speak entirely like their parents. But the critical period for language learning generates a tendency for adults to largely maintain their learned speech patterns through their lives, at least in terms of accent and dialect, and if we are thinking of general tendencies rather than specific contextualisations or performances. There is therefore a sense in which social meanings for language variation are always out of date and needing to be reworked into contemporary relevance.

The basic ideological contrasts between 'standard' and vernacular speech and between high and low social class, which sociolinguistics still readily accepts, are more consistent with the modernist social arrangements of the industrial period (which only began to 'run out of steam' around 1960) than with today. Meanings for linguistic variation in terms of privilege and oppression of course still have social relevance today, and people still know and can account for language variation in these terms. But the hierarchical social world evoked by social class dialects is anachronistic. It would not be surprising if speakers of vernacular varieties, in the twenty-first century, had a sense that their speech was 'all dressed up with nowhere to go', or at least that where these varieties 'go' is far from obvious. No wonder that vernaculars start to occupy new social spaces in late-modernity. In new spaces, their earlier 'stigmatised' associations (although some vernaculars were not obviously that) may still be relevant, or they may be *much less* relevant, or put to service in *new* interpretive frames.

As a communicative resource, meaning-imbued language variation does not simply present itself to speakers to fill out social identities and social positions as they choose. Speaking *is* often routinised and, within limits, socially predictable. It is not surprising that variationists can continue to match abstract patterns of social and linguistic structure. If we go some way to believing in Bourdieu's habitus, the predictability of ingrained speaking dispositions may be more of a penance than a resource. But speakers have the additional resources of reflexivity and performativity. They can be active critics of the social meanings of their own and other people's speech and can (in fact, they *must*) contextualise their speech for local purposes. In Chapter 1 the verbal sense of 'styling' was introduced to refer to precisely this creative design potential for speaking. Being aware of social meaning and actively constructing social contexts are themselves socio-cognitive resources for using variation. Socio-historical 'data' (forms and meanings) are available for reworking and recontextualising – in Bakhtin's term they are available for 'reaccentuating'.

This is the basic *resource and contextualisation framework* I would like to carry forward into the next two chapters, where we examine the identity-making potential of style. We will continue to focus most directly on the constructive potential of styling through accent/dialect, although it becomes more and more difficult to separate dialect from discourse as we get deeper into the detail of local contextualisation. We move away from universalist claims about style – away from claims like 'there are no single-style speakers' or 'people shift upwards when their attention to speech is greater' or 'there is a general set to converge towards the audience's speech characteristics'. We can see styling as an interactional practice where some people have more facility than others, and where the interactional accomplishments can be either quite mundane or quite spectacular. Chapter 6 deals with more spectacular instances than Chapter 5.

5 Styling social identities

5.1 SOCIAL IDENTITY, CULTURE AND DISCOURSE

The last three decades have seen a general shift in social scientific theorising of identity, away from relatively static models towards dynamic models. A significant voice arguing for this realignment was that of George Herbert Mead in the early days of social psychology (Mead 1932, 1934). Mead argued that social interaction was where people's appreciation of social forces could be seen at work. He stressed people's understandings of the social implications of their actions in specific situations. He said that agentive social action was a necessary focus for psychology. Much later, in anthropology, Frederick Barth argued a similar line, challenging a static, structural-functional understanding of the social world (Barth 1969, 1981). In his historical review of anthropological research on ethnicity, Richard Jenkins says that Barth's perspective has become the dominant one in that discipline (Jenkins 1997: 12). Barth suggested that we should not treat identities as fixed social categories associated with different cultural traits. Rather, we should focus on relationships of cultural differentiation and the sorts of 'boundary work' that people do in practice.

Many contemporary perspectives on social identity in different disciplines take this general line, stressing the need for a dynamic approach to identity as an active discursive process. Anthony Giddens says we need to see identity as a personal 'project' pursued reflexively by people as they go through the events and stages of their lives (Giddens 1991). Theorists in cultural studies have argued vociferously against the assumption that people inhabit unitary identities. A key source is Edward Said's treatise on the repressive politics of 'Orientalism' (Said 1978) – the 'Western' presumption that people and cultures 'of the Orient' have simple determining traits and characteristics. Contemporary theory is often more comfortable with the idea of plural identities and with the idea of cultural and social *hybridity*, implying a form of mixing and non-discreteness. Politically, these ways of referring to identity are felt to resist unwarranted and dangerous assumptions of ethnic purity or social exclusiveness. They stand in ideological opposition to essentialist representations (see section 2.5) and to the tendency to 'other' socio-cultural groups perceived to be different, perhaps by homogenising them or devaluing them (Coupland 2000; Riggins 1997).

In anthropological linguistics Richard Bauman and Charles Briggs give us a discursive model of culture (Bauman and Briggs 1990). A culture, for them, in fact *is* 'a discourse', and we reproduce culture through discursive performance. Members of cultural groups perform their culture by creating 'texts' of various sorts – the process of *entextualisation*. Members of cultural groups are aware of, and engage in, distinctive ways of speaking and interacting, and some of these are ritualised into familiar speech genres. Culture therefore lays down or 'sediments' texts, which in turn realise the culture (Bauman 1996; Hanks 1996; Irvine 1996; Urban 1996). So cultural belonging is itself an active, iterative, reconstructive process. It is not simply the perpetuation of an identity state, indexed by symbols such as the use of distinctive languages or dialects. A sense of culture resides in local processes of enacting or reconstituting culture. When we replay or reconstruct cultural forms, we inevitably work them into new contexts – the process of *recontextualisation*.

Cultural identification is therefore a tension between given and new, which is very much where we left the discussion of normativity and performativity in Chapter 4. Richard Bauman writes that:

> one of the key issues on which understanding of the process must rest is the dynamic tension between the ready-made, socially given element, that is, the persistent cultural entity that is available for recontextualization in performance, and the emergent element, the transformation of this entity in the performance process (Bauman 1996: 302).

Anthony Giddens, from a sociological perspective, makes similar points about the notion of 'tradition'. He says that tradition is a form of 'formulaic truth' recreated in the present:

> I shall understand 'tradition' in the following way. Tradition, I shall say, is bound up with memory, specifically . . . 'collective memory'; involves ritual; is connected with what I shall call *a formulaic notion of truth*; has 'guardians'; and, unlike custom, has binding force which has a combined moral and emotional content . . . [T]he past is not

preserved but continuously reconstructed on the basis of the present . . .
Tradition, therefore, we may say, is *an organizing medium of collective
memory*. The 'integrity' of tradition derives not from the simple fact of
persistence over time but from the continuous 'work' of
interpretation that is carried out to identify the strands which bind
present to past. (Giddens 1996: 63–4, with original emphasis)

This is another account of the importance of history in a resources
model of social identity. But it also forces us to attend to what is *not*
replicated from convention and social norms. Creative rendering of
socio-cultural content and forms (entextualisation) does not necessarily mean faithful cultural reproduction. Whether cultural reproduction happens, and what new glosses are added to social meanings
when they are performed, depends crucially on the local formatting
or framing of meanings.

This is where *discourse analysis* comes into focus. Approaching social
identity through discourse is not simply a methodological alternative
to, for example, quantitative indexical approaches. According to the
theoretical arguments reviewed here, discursive social action is where
culture and social identities 'live' and where we can see them taking
shape. The styling of social identities against a backdrop of social
norms and 'collective social memories' is the heart of the process.

5.2 ACTS OF IDENTITY

In sociolinguistics, Robert Le Page and Andrée Tabouret-Keller's *acts of
identity* framework is an important appeal to a constructivist, process-
centred perspective on language and social identity (Le Page and
Tabouret-Keller 1985). The phrase 'acts of identity' itself evokes an
anti-essentialist stance – identity construction being seen as a consequence, perhaps a target, of social action. Le Page and Tabouret-Keller
say they see 'linguistic behaviour as a series of *acts of identity* in which
people reveal both their personal identity and their search for social
roles' (1985: 14). They studied conversations and story-telling in
Belize, St Vincent and in London, tracing the evolution of Caribbean
and Creole linguistic varieties, referring back to Le Page's linguistic
survey of the British Caribbean in the mid 1950s. Their data were not
only people's speech itself, but also people's accounts of language use
and of ethnic and social differences. The 1985 book is a repository of
historical, sociological and linguistic details of ethnic movement and
fusion in the Caribbean and of 'West Indian' immigration into Britain.
('West Indian' is a term that has no relevance to the demographic and

linguistic donor Caribbean communities; it is a British label, representing a reinterpretation and coalescing of diverse ethnic and linguistic groups.)

The theoretical centrepiece of Le Page and Tabouret-Keller's analysis is well summarised in a famous dictum:

> [T]he individual creates for himself the patterns of his linguistic behaviour so as to resemble those of the group or groups with which from time to time he wishes to be identified, or so as to be unlike those from whom he wishes to be distinguished. (Le Page and Tabouret-Keller 1985: 181)

This generalisation relates primarily to how, in social situations involving complex mixtures of language and dialects (such as the Caribbean, but also Malaysia and Singapore, sociolinguistic settings that Le Page and Tabouret-Keller also consider), people have a degree of autonomous control over how they project themselves in terms of ethnic and national identity. Acts of *projection* involve 'the speaker . . . projecting his inner universe, implicitly with the invitation to others to share it, at least insofar as they recognize his language as an accurate symbolization of the world, and to share his attitudes towards it' (1985: 181). A speaker reaches out to others who may or may not endorse the cultural validity of what is being socially projected. If there is acceptance and 'reinforcement' of a particular projection, a speaker's 'behaviour in that particular context may become more regular, more focused'. Speech may also be relatively 'diffuse', for example through linguistic accommodation to others, but will settle over time into a focused pattern as a newly evolved linguistic system.

Le Page and Tabouret-Keller acknowledge the overlap between their own theoretical approach and Howard Giles's accommodation theory (section 3.3). In fact they list constraints on acts of identity in rather similar terms to those we find in the accommodation model. For example, speakers can only engage in identifying with other groups to the extent that they 'identify' (recognise) them, have access to them and to their ways of speaking (compare Preston's idea of 'availability'), have ability to modify their own ways of speaking (compare Preston's idea of 'control') and have adequate motivation to 'join' the relevant groups. (A more detailed comparison could be made between Le Page and Tabouret-Keller 1985: 182ff. and Giles, Coupland and Coupland 1991: 1–68.) The main difference is that Le Page and Tabouret-Keller are principally interested in mid-term to long-term shifts in community speech norms (similarly to Peter Trudgill's use of accommodation theory concepts to explain contact effects between dialects – see Trudgill 1986), while Giles has been mainly interested in the more local contexts and consequences of interpersonal and intergroup accommodation.

In their own empirical work, Le Page and Tabouret-Keller do not validate their acts of identity dictum by analysing local instances – local discursive acts – of identity projection, although this is clearly entailed in the general claims they make. They do present some fascinating sample texts, but no stylistic analysis of them. Viewing language variation as accomplishing acts of identity sits comfortably in the dynamic, constructivist tradition described above. In fact Le Page and Tabouret-Keller (1985: 207) quote Barth (1969) when he says that 'we can assume no simple one-to-one relationship between ethnic units and cultural similarities and differences'. The idea of 'from time to time' in the quoted dictum opens a window on the local occasioning of social identities in discourse and takes us away from a linear stylistics of variation. One of Le Page and Tabouret-Keller's main observations is that there is no clear continuum between 'standard' English and 'broad' Creole vernacular. Linguistically mediated identities are not restricted to their national or group-original incumbents.

All the same, Le Page and Tabouret-Keller's framework leaves many issues unresolved. First, it makes too little play of cultural and socio-linguistic inheritance, no doubt because it is tailored to social settings with relatively new and very complex admixtures of people and varieties. In the country newly named Belize at the time of their fieldwork, for example, identities such as 'Spanish' (or 'Guatemalan' or 'Mexican'), 'Bay-born' (or 'Creole'), 'Carib', 'Maya' (or 'Kekchi'), 'Waika', 'English', 'Irish' and 'American' were all available. But in the more focused Western communities (where, as noted earlier, most dialect-style research has been done), the idea of a 'variety of origin', or indeed a variety ingrained in a speaker's habitus, can not be entertained quite so open-endedly.

Second, the phrase 'wishing to identify with' in the Le Page and Tabouret-Keller dictum is rather ambiguous as to ownership and commitment. Allan Bell makes the point that what he calls referee design covers a wide range of different types of relationship between a speaker and the referred-to group (see section 3.2). At one extreme this might be simple reference to or 'evocation of' the other's voice. At the other extreme it could be 'whole-hearted identification with the group to which the code belongs' (Bell 1999: 525). Projecting a social identity is not the same as feeling or living a social identity with personal investment in it and felt ownership of it – if identities can in fact be 'owned'. The subjective/affective/affiliative dimension easily gets lost in practice-oriented theories of social identity, just as practice and achievement, and process as a whole, tend to get lost in both descriptivist and cognitivist approaches.

This is not at all to say that sociolinguistic acts of identity are always expressions of positive affiliation to a social category. We are coming to several examples, in this chapter and in Chapter 6, where this is very far from the case. But the rubric of creating styles 'to resemble those of the group or groups with which from time to time [a person] wishes to be identified' doesn't shed sufficient light on how styling acts are subjectively designed or affectively motivated. 'Resembling' can imply different sorts of indexical relationship and different stances, such as projections made playfully or with some degree of identity fictionalising or qualification, versus projections designed to allow a speaker to 'pass as' a member of a particular social group.

The overriding limitation is therefore that we get little sense of the contextual factors involved in projecting identities. The key concepts in Le Page and Tabouret-Keller's framework are speakers, varieties and communities, with little attention paid to contexts or contextualisation. Like all discursive acts, acts of identity need to be woven into particular social contexts. Their meanings will reflect their contextual placement and shaping.

5.3 IDENTITY CONTEXTUALISATION PROCESSES

The social constructionist perspective on identity – people constructing identities in social interaction – is fairly well captured by Le Page and Tabouret-Keller's term 'projecting'. Other general terms could be 'launching' or 'deploying' identities. Each of these words suggests a partly controlled process of outward-directed self-representation through some mode of styling. Erving Goffman (1959) makes the distinction between expressions 'given' and 'given off', reminding us that identities are not fully controllable and subject to strategy or management. When we 'give' expressions or self-identities, we have reasonably strong strategic control. When we 'give off' expressions or self-identities, we have low control and they 'leak' from our behaviour and our verbal and non-verbal displays. But where there *is* an element of control, we need to introduce more precision into the account of how a projective act of identity engages with personhood. Although, by definition, social contextualisation is contingent and subtle, I suggest it will be useful to recognise the following processes: *targeting, framing*, *voicing*, *keying* and *loading*. I introduce each concept briefly in this section, then draw on them in reviewing empirical studies in the rest of this chapter and the next.

Targeting is involved in making acts of identity because discursive action is often directed at shaping the *persona* of one particular participant, most typically either a speaker or a listener. (This assumption lies at the heart of Brown and Levinson's politeness model, which we considered in section 3.1.) Le Page and Tabouret-Keller discuss only self-targeted acts of projection, although a great deal of social identity work in talk targets recipients. It is *ascriptional* – it ascribes identities to others. But third parties (Bell's category of 'referees', see section 3.2) can be the target of identity work. So can particular relationships or groups – constructing meanings for 'us' together, 'how we are'. Language variation can index all of these targets and add particular nuances of social meaning to them. Identity projections can be targeted at people's identities as individuals, or at their identities as members of social groups. (This picks up on social psychology's conventional distinction between 'personal identity' and 'social identity'.) At the same time, our personal identities are in many respects collages of different social category characteristics, complete or fragmentary.

Framing is a core term in Erving Goffman's analysis of social interaction (Goffman 1974). It is crucially involved in determining how particular identities are made relevant or *salient* in discourse. Social interaction often leaves many or most potential social identities latent, and the linguistic features and styles that might index them are just unactivated meaning potential. Linguistic and other semiotic features and styles need to be contextually *primed* before sociolinguistic indexing happens. The potential metaphorical transfer through which a linguistic feature comes to stand for or to mean something social (iconisation, cf. Irvine 2001) has to be occasioned in a discourse. The identificational value and impact of linguistic features depends on which discursive frame is in place. That is, when we approach linguistic variation as a meaningful resource, we can expect that particular discursive frames will present specific affordances and constraints for interactants at specific moments of their talk. Certain types of identity work that can potentially be done at those moments, in those frames, will be foregrounded. They will give relevance and salience to certain sorts of indexical features and meanings, or they will deny them relevance and salience. At least three types of discourse framing need to be recognised. I discuss them as theoretical options here; we will use these concepts in later analyses.

First, *socio-cultural framing (macro-level social frames)*. We have already seen that social class is the socio-cultural frame most regularly appealed to in variationist sociolinguistics. It is an important part of the socio-linguistic ecology of urban 'speech communities', or at least it has been treated as such. So we have to ask what linguistic resources (forms and associated potentials for meaning) are validated by the sociolinguistic structure of a particular community to the extent that they might become active in a discourse frame. Reciprocally, what socio-cultural values to do with social class do these resources indexically mark, and what stakes are there to play for in relation to them? In socio-cultural frames, acts of identity are undertaken by speakers positioning them-selves, or others, in relation to a pre-understood social ecology. Identities to do with gender and sexuality, age or ethnicity also operate at this level of framing. How, for example, is age constructed in a particular culture and what ideological associations are available for meaning-making in relation to age when it is made salient?

Second, *genre framing (meso-level social frames)*. Genre or 'generic' frames set meaning parameters around talk in relation to what con-textual type or genre of talk (e.g. conversation versus set-piece perfor-mance, business talk or informal chat) is understood by participants to be currently on-going and relevant. Acts of identity can be made in relation to a specific genre, for example in terms of participant roles (what social role a speaker has in carrying forward a particular speech genre). A particular generic frame might consolidate identities that are foregrounded in the wider socio-cultural frame, or it might con-tradict them or make them much less relevant at a given moment. Participants might find their identity options prefigured or constrained by the speech genre at hand, or the genre frame might edit away identity options that would otherwise apply. The same linguistic feature that would mark a social identity in the socio-cultural frame might carry different resonance in the generic frame. As we saw in Chapter 2, genres are typically sustained by particular communities of practice. But in any one community, specific norma-tive expectations about social identities will be held for specific com-municative genres.

Third, *interpersonal framing (micro-level social frames)*. The issue here is how participants dynamically structure the very local business of their talk and position themselves relative to each other in their rela-tional histories, short- and long-term. Personal and relational identi-ties can be forged and refined linguistically in subtle ways within a consolidated genre and community of practice. A sociolinguistic feature that might otherwise bear, for example, a social class or a participant role significance might do personal identity work in the interpersonal frame. By using a particular feature, a speaker might style himself or herself as, for example, more or less powerful within a particular relationship, or style the relationship as being a more intimate or less intimate one.

Voicing refers to how a speaker represents or implies *ownership* of an utterance or a way of speaking. In the domain of style, it is rash to assume that people speak exclusively in and through their own voices. In section 4.5 we looked at Mikhail Bakhtin's ideas about multiple voicing and how speakers can align differently with other voices – unidirectionally and vari-directionally. But in a simpler sense, speakers often quote or reconstruct the words of other people, and in so doing they can inflect those source voices in various ways, giving them particular identity traits and qualities. This takes us towards processes of imitation and parody (see section 6.3), but subtleties of voicing are involved in most acts of identity. If we all have a degree of meta-linguistic awareness of our own speech, then 'ordinary speech' might be better described as people 'voicing themselves'. People can style the normative speech of their own 'speech communities' and sometimes imply less than full ownership of it.

Keying is a term borrowed from Dell Hymes's taxonomy of the components of communicative events (see section 3.4). William Downes says key relates to the 'tone, manner or spirit of the act, mock or serious' (Downes 1998: 303). The identificational consequences of an act or projection depend crucially on its keying, because key allows us to infer – sometimes more guesswork than inference – a speaker's communicative motivation. Talk in the genre of 'banter' or verbal play commonly involves the playful projection of identities targeted at recipients. Voicings can be playful or malicious, acts of teasing or put-downs. Irony is a quagmire for reading acts of identity, because 'as if' identities can wholly subvert the apparent meaning of a projection. Particularly in the area of stylised identities (see section 5.8 and chapter 6), identity 'effects' can be designed and achieved that are entirely at odds with their first-level signification.

Loading is an extension of keying, referring to the level of a speaker's *investment* in an identity being negotiated. 'Straight' or seriously keyed identity projections or ascriptions can be light or even routine in their effect. In other contexts the same acts can be weighty or telling, because the loading of an act of identity has to be read relative to the contextual assumptions that are in play. Bell suggests that an extreme case of referee design is the 'appropriation' of another group's code, which a speaker 'takes possession of' (Bell 1999: 525).

Armed with these concepts, we now turn to a series of worked analyses of identity styling.

5.4 FRAMING SOCIAL CLASS IN THE TRAVEL AGENCY

To assess the importance of an active contextualisation approach to social identity, we can take another look at the Cardiff travel agency context introduced in Chapter 3. In fact we can look again at a particular sequence of talk and reinterpret it with more contextual sensitivity than I managed in the original analysis.

Extract 5.1: Travel agency assistants

```
 1  Sue:     come on Rhondda Travel where are you?
 2                                            [
 3  ?Marie:                           hm hm hm
 4           (4.0)
 5  Liz:     o:h I got to go shopping where d'you think I can get charcoal from?
 6  Sue:     (0.5) I don't really know
 7                                       [
 8  Marie:                             is today Wednesday?
 9  Sue:     yeah
10           [
11  Liz:     Marie (.) if you're going out (.) can you just see if you can see any
12           charcoal anywhere if you're just walk- walking around the shops
             (( ))
13  Sue:     (on the telephone) hello (high pitch) can I have Rhondda Travel
14           please?
15  Marie:   ((      I'm only going        laughs))
16  Liz:     oh (laughs) (high pitch) where you going then?
17  Marie:   I'm going to the solicitors
18  Liz:     oh (laughs) my dad's been up there ((he ought to ))
19                                               [
20  Sue:                                 hello it's Hourmont Travel here (.)
21           um was I talking to you about Evans (.)
22           [                            ·
23  Marie:   ((            ))
24                                [
25  Liz:                        barbecue
26  Sue:     to Dallas? well the problem i:s I've held an option on them for you (.)
27                                   [
28  Marie:                          ((            ))
29  Liz:     will they?
30  Sue:     but I can't book them in full cos you have to take full payment (1.0)
31           [
32  Marie:   ((                                   ))
33  Liz:     do they? I've never seen it
```

```
34                      [
35  Sue:                        you see so they'll hold them for me now until Friday
36                                      [
37  Marie:                              ((
38              (laughs)    ))
39          [
40  Liz:                    (laughs) they don't sell things like that
41  Marie:  (1.0) course they do
42  Sue:    well I've booked them and they're all alright (.)
43              [
44  Liz:                 where would I get it from?
45  Sue:    but I can't give them ticket numbers until they pay
46                  [
47  Marie:              ((                    ))
48                                      [
49  Liz:                                charcoal
50  Sue:    (closing) (breathy voice) OK?
51  Marie:  ((        Blacks        ))
52  Liz:    yeah camping stuff innit yeah
53  Marie:  ((and Woolies))
54  Sue:    mm (.) alright
55              [
56  Liz:            (( )) reckoned Woolies as well but I don't think so
57          (1.0) I'll just go down to Blacks
58                  [
59  Sue:                    that'll be great (1.0) we'll let you know if you can-
60          o:h Friday morning (.) yeah that's OK the option's till Friday anyway
61          (.)
62  (other client conversations in the background)
63  Sue:    OK then fine (1.0) OK then (.) bye (.) Sue (1.0) (breathy) OK? bye
64  Marie:  (faint) is anyone else (( )) starving?
65  Sue:    well I was going to have one but I'm not going to now
66  Marie:  well have one don't pay any attention to what I say
67      [ ]
68  Sue:                        no
69  Marie:  I talk a load of rubbish
70                  [
71  Sue:                    I'd rather you know no you know about them
72          don't you
73  Marie:  no I don't I don't know anything
74  Sue:    that's all I've had to eat then though
```

Extract 5.1 is a longer version of one of the extracts I used to illustrate Sue's talk at work in the travel agency (Extract 3.6 in section 3.4). As the extract opens, Sue, the travel agency assistant, is trying to connect on the telephone to a coach tour operator, *Rhondda Travel*. The extract then allows us to follow two concurrent conversations. One is Sue's telephone conversation, where we don't have access to the other party's voice. The other conversation is among the three travel agency assistants in the office, Sue, Marie and Liz, about buying charcoal, then about eating lunchtime sandwiches. We hear this chatty conversation with some gaps, partly because of overlapping speech and partly because the recording microphone is positioned closest to Sue's service position in the office. Once again, Sue's talk on the telephone is represented in italics, to help distinguish the two separate conversational flows. All three women have similar Cardiff vernacular voices in what Labov would call their 'less careful' speech.

Sue is minimally involved in the charcoal conversation early on, at line 9. She comes back into the three-way conversation after hanging up the phone at the end of line 63. Let's focus on the transition achieved between lines 64 and 66, as Sue rejoins the triadic conversation to talk about sandwiches. Some detail on the phonological variation in the extract is needed first, extending the list of variable features we considered in the earlier account of this extract. In general, the three women do not use centralised-onset forms for variable (ou) in *go*, or the wedge vowel [ʌ] in *come*, or the close RP-type variant [æ] in *can*, all of which would be marked as posh ('standard' or hyperstandard) in Cardiff. They tend to use [ɔu], [ə] and [a], respectively. On the other hand, (iw) is never RP-like [juː] in *you*, being [jɪw] throughout. There is audible variation within the extract, however. Sue has markedly more open onset to (ai) in *Friday* (line 35) than in all the first-person pronouns (*I*) at the end of the extract (lines 65–74) where the first element of the glide is in the area of [ə]. There is a powerful clustering of vernacular variants of the consonantal variables too in Sue's speech starting at line 65. (h) is [Ø] in *have* (65) and *had* (74). *going to* is ['gɔnə] (65); *about them* is [ə'barəm] (71). *don't you* is ['doːnɪw] (72). In line 1, Sue has fronted long [aː], [æː], as a realisation of *are*, which is a strongly stereotyped feature of English in Cardiff, before she speaks to the Rhondda Travel representative. Similarly, Liz's *camping stuff innit* at line 52 contrasts starkly with Sue's 'careful' speech in the same time slot, but in a different conversation.

What acts of identity can we say Sue is performing in this extract? We need to focus on how the evolving context brings different social frames in to relevance, and how variation in Sue's speech, and her identity projections through them, become meaningful in those different frames. There is no doubt that social class meanings are, in a general sense, in the air in this extract, as they generally were in the travel agency talk that I observed and recorded. We saw in Chapter 3 how Sue's speech, quantitatively analysed, tracks the speech of her clients, who can be grouped into different occupational classes. The variation just described is variation that can easily enough be associated with social class arrangements in the city of Cardiff. Cardiff is Wales's biggest conurbation, and it is one of rather few environments in Wales where something like the classical Labovian class-stratification model applies (see Mees and Collins 1999). But the travel agency is an interesting sociolinguistic setting because talk there spans public and private domains.

When Sue's speech has schwa-like first elements in the diphthong in *my* and *I*, [h]-less *have* and *had*, and flapped [t] in *about them*, we might say she 'sounds working class'. Alternatively, when her speech has open onset to (ai) in *Friday* on the telephone, she 'sounds more middle class'. But is this actually the most contextually satisfactory reading of her stylistic variation? We should take the perspective of the participants, as best we can, and ask how this variation is likely to impact on them. What identity work is being done through the meaning potential of socio-phonetic variation, and how does that mesh with identity work being done at other levels of the discourse? Specifically, how do the three types of framing I introduced in the previous section apply to Sue's acts of identity in Extract 5.1?

Public discourse is where we expect socio-cultural frames to be generally relevant, as in Sue's face-to-face talk to clients and in her talk to non-familiar tour agents on the telephone. We have already seen that sociolinguistic variation in her speech is active in each of these domains of talk. Public discourse 'loads up' the sociolinguistic variables that are most sensitive to social class in Cardiff. The relevant phonological features include (h), (ng) and the high/low articulation variables such as (consonant cluster simplification) and (intervocalic t), where more elided forms are sometimes judged to be 'common' or 'slovenly' ways of speaking. Conservative language ideologies are brought to bear on these features in public discourse, and a social judgement like 'common' is of course a social class related attribution. Talk to non-familiars in Cardiff, when a speaker might be held to be publicly accountable for her social persona, is amenable to social class inferencing. So Sue's identity work on the phone is very plausibly class-work, and she may be seeking a more middle-class persona of the sort that still tends to gain status in public and especially workplace discourse in Cardiff and many other mainly English-speaking cities. On the other hand, several other factors impinge, which I come to below.

In contrast, it would be very unconvincing to try to read 'working-class' meanings into Sue's speech and social identity when she is talking about her sandwiches and her dieting, later in Extract 5.1. Being of a social class is neutralised once the frame shifts from public to private discourse, where class is not salient because it is non-contrastive among the group of colleagues and friends. On the other hand, Sue's being in some ways 'powerful' or 'powerless' at personal and relational levels *is* relevant there. But also, back in the socio-cultural frame of public discourse, we can't be sure that the class-work being done in Sue's acts of identity is in fact being achieved through phonological indexicality, or solely by this means. Notice how Sue's telephone conversation, at the level of ideational or referential meaning, invokes commercial power practices. In her own words, Sue has *held an option on* a booking for the tour operator who has to *take full payment* before the deal can proceed. Compare this with the 'walking round the shops to try and buy charcoal' theme of the competing conversation, or Sue's own personal powerlessness in the face of a depressing diet at the end of the extract (see below). Class as control *is* relevant in the public projection on the telephone, and class semiosis through dialect constitutes part of Sue's identity in her professional mode of discourse.

In terms of genre, however, there are clear transitions between professional talk and everyday-lifeworld talk in the extract. Overlaid on the social class reading of Sue's talk, the genre structure of the episode positions her as abruptly moving out of the role of professional representative at the end of line 63. She does give her personal name while operating in the professional frame – *Sue*, at line 63 – but she does this in that minimalistic form of person reference that is conventional in telephone service encounters. She is the voice of this specific travel agency, Hourmont Travel, and she and other participants may feel that there should be some resonance between her vocal style and a smoothly, competently functioning travel agency. Notice the build-up of professional jargon through Sue's telephone talk. Also the vivid disjunction between Sue's rhetorically abrasive and Cardiff vernacular *come on Rhondda Travel where are you?* (with semi-close fronted long (a), [æ:], in *are* and flapped [r]) at line 1 and her concerned, solicitous demeanour as the telephone conversation closes. The genre frame facilitates identity readings in terms of professional versus personal roles as relevant social meanings for Sue's talk.

Sue's talk between lines 64 and 74 is not only non-public discourse and non-professional discourse; it is personally intimate discourse. It deals with a topic that was very active in the travel agency over the many weeks of my recording there – eating and dieting. This is a topic in which the three travel agency assistants, and Sue in particular, invest heavily in emotional terms. There is regular relational politics around dieting among the three assistants. Moves to eat lunch at all, and certainly decisions about the timing of *when* sandwiches are eaten, are interpersonally very significant. Sue's utterance *I was going to have one but I'm not going to now* at line 65 raises delicate issues. 'Having one' here means eating a sandwich before the due lunchtime hour, when it would have become more legitimate to eat the sandwich, according to the assistants' mutual dieting pact. At line 64 Marie has transgressed by asking if anyone is *starving*, when it's taken for granted that the others, and especially Sue, are self-consciously holding back from eating their sandwiches. Talking about hunger is taboo. Disclosing her eating regime to her co-assistants, so that they know what she eats and when (*I'd rather you know . . . about them*, line 71), is a strategy Sue uses to help her to resist 'eating too early'.

The exchanges about sandwiches invoke issues of entitlement, trust, blame and potential praise – a moral agenda – in an intimate relationship between the assistants. What part could dialect style have in this relational work? One semiotic principle at work at this point in the talk is implicitness. Contrasting sharply with the on-the-surface explicitness about professional procedures in the telephone talk, Sue falls into a way of speaking, triggered by Marie's question about being *starving*, where the dieting agenda, its components, its participant roles and its pressures are all thoroughly known to the group. Lexico-grammatically and semantically, 'having one' is sparse. So, discursively, is the coherence link between Sue's saying she isn't going to 'have one' and Marie's response that Sue shouldn't pay attention to what she says. The offence and Marie's recognition of it are only understandable if we (and of course they themselves) are aware of the relational history around eating and the dieting pact.

In heavily implicit talk, it is perhaps unsurprising that phonological processes also shift towards elision and economy, and this is what we see in the phonetic description of Sue's final utterances in the extract. But there is also a personal standing or status meaning in play. Sue is very audibly depressed at having been forced to confront her dieting regime. Perhaps she thinks she is a failure, or at least that she needs Marie and Liz to keep policing her diet. Her act of identity in the interpersonal frame is to mark this 'incompetence', and the dialect semiosis does contribute to achieving this. What is made relevant in the interactional frame is neither 'lower-class' nor 'non-professional status'; it is low personal competence and control. We might gloss Sue's dialect style in this sequence as 'under-performance', which is also marked in reduced amplitude and a flatter pitch range.

This example suggests that the variation resources available to speakers are multi-valenced. They are 'called into meaning' by discursive frames and have their effects in diverse social dimensions. Sue's personal identity is at stake in the relational politics of dieting, and when the travel agency assistants settle on this theme as the business in hand, variation can style identities in that frame. In professional work-mode, and in the genres of talk that constitute work at the travel agency, an entirely different frame is in place and the meaning potential of variation also shifts. 'Competence' means something quite different for Sue in this frame, and the same variation resources can style different identities there. As suggested ealier, there is always a cache of potential identities that are deactivated or made non-relevant by discursive frames. For example, the 'Cardiffness' of Sue's speech – and the speech of her agent-friends and most of her clients – is not relevant because this is a taken-for-granted and shared attribute. Variation of the sort we have seen can on occasion be read in social class terms, only because the discourse context frames place or region out of relevance (everyone involved is part of the Cardiff sociolinguistic ecosystem). In other contexts of talk, the same sort of variation can style place.

5.5   STYLING PLACE

The conventional assumption from dialectology, carried over into mainstream sociolinguistics, is that regional provenance is imprinted onto vernacular speech, and that vernaculars therefore index regions or places. This remains an entirely plausible general assumption, even under contemporary circumstances where people are geographically very mobile and where we can't avoid experiencing place – multiply and repeatedly – through mass media and through our personal contacts with 'moving people'. Barbara Johnstone makes the important point that sociolinguistics has tended to conceive of place 'in objective, physical terms' (Johnstone 2004: 65). It has designed survey research on the presumption of regional coherence in language within particular communities or networks. An alternative approach is to conceive of place as a culturally defined category, and indeed as a social meaning amenable to being styled.

Johnstone cites Anthony Giddens's (1984) idea that place is another aspect of context which may or may not be symbolically relevant, and Benedict Anderson's influential writing about 'imagined communities' (Anderson 1983). We can easily fit Nancy Niedzielski and Dennis Preston's perspective on folk understandings of regional speech varieties, and indeed surveys of attitudes to linguistic varieties generally (see Chapter 4), into a subjectivist and social constructionist conception of place. When we investigate cultural diasporas – groups maintaining a sense of cultural belonging, physically distant from their 'homelands' – we get a strong sense of the potential power of imagined community. For example, the North American Welsh diaspora, although it is small and thin relative to other ethnically-aligned groups there, sustains strong affiliation to Wales and to the Welsh language (Coupland, Bishop, Evans and Garrett 2006). A sense of local belonging can therefore transcend physical distance, which supports Giddens's theorising of the compression of time and space under globalisation (Giddens 1996). Fast modern telecommunication shrinks both time and distance in our experiencing of these dimensions. It breaks the conventional link between locality and 'local language'. Technologised social interaction is associated with new genre conventions, in both speech and writing, and offers new potential for stylistic creativity (Androutsopoulos 2006).

But even within local spaces, a *sense* of the local needs to be achieved – to be made socially meaningful. Language variation therefore isn't only something that happens 'naturally' within 'speech communities'. It is a resource for styling a meaningful sense of place, or indeed place*s* (plural) in meaningful contrast to each other. Barbara Johnstone has analysed the discursive construction of (American) 'southernness' and what it means to be a Texan (Johnstone 1995, 1996, 1999; Johnstone and Bean 1997). She quotes a particular woman, Terri King, as saying, 'My southern drawl makes me $70,000 a year ... it's hilarious how those businessmen turn to gravy when they hear it' (1999: 305). Johnstone explains the wider context for this sort of reflexivity about Texan speech. Anglo-Texans, particularly from the eastern part of the state, have to deal with their complex relation to southernness and to the stigmatised speech variety associated with the south. Hispanics, on the other hand, can invoke south-western identities for themselves, unconnected with the south. This uncertainty and reflexivity about regional identity through speech can lead to careful contextualisation of southern-sounding speech and *metalinguistic displays* of various sorts (cf. Eastman and Stein 1993).

The phrase 'southern drawl' is an interpretive reading of the diph-thongization or 'multiphthongization' of vowels. But Johnstone resists the idea that this is a 'feature of southern speech', because the effect of southernness is the result of contextualisation processes which need to be understood ethnographically, just like careful make-up and hair-styling (Johnstone 1999: 509). In her interviews with southern women Johnstone gets accounts of the 'gentility' of southern ways of speaking, but also 'closeness and friendship' as well as the more manipulative economic function that Terri King reported. The social meaning of southernness is a consequence of its contextualisation, and quite specific local meanings can be negotiated.

It is interesting that this general argument, like my argument about Sue in the previous section, *inverts* the general assumption about identity *hybridity*. It is not that people in complex and fluid social environments come to have necessarily more complex or less singular or less pure identities. Rather, it is the case that, given a level of reflexivity about language meaning potential and social identity options, people work at achieving a sense of local singularity by discursive means. As Johnstone (2004: 78) says in relation to another context of her research, Pittsburghers might suggest that theirs is the only USA community that uses the word [jɪnz] – a variant form of 'you'uns' as a second-person plural pronoun, when the form is probably more widespread. Pittsburghers therefore treat 'yinzers' as people who have strong local identity with Pittsburgh, iconising the part-real, part-imagined local dialect feature as an ingroup marker.

Like Pittsburgh, most places that have strong sociolinguistic distinctiveness within a principal language zone – major cities, national territories like Wales, Ireland and Scotland in Britain, or regions like the American south or the English south-west – have familiar metalinguistic discourses of accent and dialect variation focused on sociolinguistic stereotypes. These stereotypes are not only matters of metalinguistic reference, however. They can be incorporated in *performances* of accent and dialect, in particular discursive contexts and frames.

In 1985 I analysed a Cardiff local radio DJ's dialect styling, which took in his self-styling as a Cardiff speaker (see also Coupland in press c). Frank Hennessy is well known in Cardiff and Wales not only as a radio presenter but also as an entertainer, folksinger/songwriter and humorist. His popular image is built around his affiliation to, and promotion of, local Cardiff culture and folklore, in large measure through his speech. For some, he typifies the vernacular Cardiff voice, perhaps even the Cardiff worldview – a nostalgia for dockland streets and pubs, a systematic ambivalence to 'Welshness' (even though Cardiff is the capital city of Wales), a sharp, wry humour and a reverence for the local beers, in particular 'Brain's Dark Ale'. In general, his show is a celebration of Cardiff cultural forms.

The resources Frank draws on are partly referential. In their letters to Frank some listeners mention local places and practices of interest in the city, such as *Wimbourne Street in lovely old Splott*, a long-established working-class Cardiff city district, and the names of six paddle-steamers which operated in the Bristol Channel after the Second World War. Other resources are stylistic, for example when listeners' letters open with forms of address that have intimate but also regional resonance, such as *[h]ello Franky Boy, [h]i [h]i Frank,* or *[h]ow's things our kid* (where the bracketed aitches point to just one of several phonetic features that evoke a Cardiff accent). But the show's sense of place is constituted dialectally in many other respects too. Cardiff-associated speech characteristics permeate much of Frank's performance on-air. In particular, fronting and raising of long (a:) to [æ:] in *dark* and *park* (as we saw occasionally in Sue's speech), but also [æ] in short [a] environments, as in *cat* or *pal.* Frank's radio show at the time I recorded it had the informal title *Hark hark the lark,* being introduced and punctuated by a distinctive jingle – a whimsical, sung fanfare of the words *Hark, hark the lark in Cardiff Arms Park* with [æ:] predominating throughout. ('Hark, hark the lark' is a traditional song, without any connection to Cardiff; 'Cardiff Arms Park' is the celebrated rugby ground in the middle of the city.) Frank would perpetuate this phonological theme in his own catch phrases, such as *it's remarkable, well there we are* and *that's half tidy.* These phrases all provide phono-opportunities for [æ:], sometimes in sequences where Frank does self-deprecating humour around his own incompetence. In one sequence he complains that *the pints* [of dark ale] *are gettin' heavier, or is it me gettin' weaker?* His suggested remedy is to drink *six halfs* (pronounced with 'non-standard' [fs] not 'standard' [vz]) instead of his *three usual darkies* [pints of dark ale].

The mediated context, particularly when the show first launched, constructed a frame in which place – even though this was a Cardiff-based radio station broadcasting mainly to the Cardiff and south-east Wales area – was highly relevant and where voicing the ingroup was highly distinctive. In Frank's early career, Cardiff voice was otherwise *never* heard in broadcasting contexts. Frank was a lone pioneer of Cardiff speech in the public sphere. His fundamental act of identity was to target Cardiffness dialectally, and to build a Cardiff-rich dialect persona for himself as its prototype. The authenticity of this projection was challenged by some vernacular speakers in the city who felt Frank's performances were self-consciously exuberant and stylised, and this was undeniably the case. Frank generated meanings of community nostalgia and personal niceness and ordinariness. This styled the city and Frank himself into types that were not necessarily 'ideal imagery' for a developing capital city. Contemporary slogans about Cardiff being 'Europe's youngest waterfront capital' certainly project different meanings for the city. But the importance and 'weight' of

Frank's identity work was in its historical timing, breaking a taboo about the 'acceptable' voice of Welshness through English.

The *marketing* of places often draws on linguistic symbolism. As tourism becomes increasingly important as a revenue stream, especially in small countries and low-employment zones, places are sold and bought, most obviously as tourist destinations (Jaworski and Pritchard 2005). To be sold, destinations have to be packaged and styled; they need to be distinctive but accessible. This is the commercial context for Allan Bell's (1999) stylistic analysis of an Air New Zealand video commercial that displayed successive versions of a well known Maori song. Although the song is familiar, most New Zealanders, Maori as well as Pakeha, would not understand it, because levels of linguistic competence in Maori are low. The first in a sequence of renditions of the Maori song in the commercial is sung by the opera singer Dame Kiri Te Kanawa. Then there is an Irish-styled version, using familiar visual stereotypes of Ireland and the song sung in Irish jig style. Then an American 'cool' rendition, with visual references to New Orleans and African American performers, and phonetic traces of 'American' pronunciation (although the song is still sung through Maori). In fact the 'American' pronunciation is indexically African American, when the Maori word *mai* is pronounced with a long monophthong [a:].

This is clearly a projection of a globalised New Zealand – a globally accessible New Zealand, culturally focused on the Maori language but accessible from different cultural points of view and styles. Bell says the advertisement implicitly stakes the claim that 'they're singing our song here' (1999: 534). The final rendition of the song is socio-phonetically 'local' in the sense of overlaying features of Pakeha English onto Maori lexico-grammar. Visually it foregrounds young New Zealanders travelling in London, which of course thematises global travel – the business of Air New Zealand, whose product is being promoted through the commercial. In the commercial there are intriguing intimations of how language variation and languages are linked to places, in this archetypally late-modern domain. The Maori language is iconised as a symbol of a distinctive and perhaps exotic New Zealand place and culture, even though it is not widely understood at anything other than an expressive level of associative social meaning. But there is also the strong implication that English is *the* world language whose phonetic varieties, including New Zealand's own, play a part in connoting regional distinctiveness. Accents of global English, even 'in translation', are positioned as having the remarkable affordance (remarkably efficient, commercially) of connoting difference while allowing global communicative access.

5.6 VOICING ETHNICITIES

In 1972 William Labov made a case for inherent variation in spoken language using an extract from the speech of a 12-year-old black boy named Boot. Labov called him the 'verbal leader' of a pre-adolescent street gang in south-central Harlem, New York City. In Extract 5.2 Boot is explaining the rules of the game of Skelly.

> *Extract 5.2*
> 1 An 'den like IF YOU MISS ONESIES, de OTHuh person shoot to skelly;
> 2 ef he miss, den you go again. An' IF YOU GET IN, YOU SHOOT TO
> 3 TWOSIES. An' IF YOU GET IN TWOSIES, YOU GO TO tthreesies.
> 4 An' IF YOU MISS tthreesies, THEN THE PERSON THa' miss skelly
> 5 shoot THE SKELLIES an' shoot in THE ONESIES: an' IF HE MISS,
> 6 YOU GO f'om tthreesies to foursies.
>
> (Labov 1972b: 189)

Labov's argument is that, on the one hand, we shouldn't treat this sort of variation in speech as 'free variation' within a linguistic grammatical system. The variation, he implies, has social meaning and needs to be accounted for. Labov transcribes the 'standard English' forms in Boot's speech in upper case, and the African American Vernacular English (AAVE) forms (which at the time he called Black English Vernacular forms) in lower case, as above. But on the other hand too, he argues that we shouldn't treat this sort of variation as code-switching – Boot switching repeatedly between two independent linguistic codes or systems. He says that his transcription, using the upper-case and lower-case convention, is 'an unconvincing effort' (1972b: 189). This is because most features in Boot's speech are shared between 'standard' English and AAVE, and the transcription assigns forms to one code rather than the other 'by the accidents of sequencing'. As he says, in line 2 *you go again* is assigned to AAVE only because it happens to follow *den*, where the [d] for [ð] in the first consonant is a common AAVE feature. Similarly in line 1, the transcribed word *OTHuh* is an attempt to indicate that the final syllable has no postvocalic [r] – hence the transcription 'uh' – and 'r-less-ness' is a common feature of AAVE, and so on.

Since the variation in Boot's speech is not adequately analysed as free variation or as code-switching, Labov feels he confronts an analytic problem. Implicitly, his solution is to treat variation of this sort as being inherent in the system. He explicitly resists treating the variation as stylistic:

> Without any clear way of categorizing this behavior, we are forced to speak of 'stylistic variants', and we are then left with no fixed relation at all to our notion of linguistic structure. What is a style if not a separate sub-code, and when do we have two of them? We normally think of language as a means of translating meaning into linear form. Where and how do stylistic meanings enter into this process? (1972b: 189)

This quotation is quite revealing. It shows that Labov's general orientation to style is a structural, system-bound one (see Chapter 2) rather than being based in social meaning. The acts of identity and resources and deployment perspective we have been adopting in this chapter makes quite different assumptions, and particularly that the meanings of social categories, identities and relationships are constructed discursively. In fact many studies have shown how specifically *ethnic* meanings are woven into talk, subtly, progressively and interactionally.

Cecilia Cutler (1999) gives a clear example of ethnic styling through speech, where a young white boy, Mike, over time moved into (but eventually back out of) a black and hip-hop personal identity, partly through incorporating AAVE features into his speech. The phenomenon of white speakers adopting speech features associated with black speech is described in several other studies too, many of them inspired by Ben Rampton's theorising of linguistic *crossing* (see section 5.6). Using AAVE features allows white young people to share symbolically in a generalised urban youth identity. The instance that Cutler deals with is interesting, particularly for the cultural range of Mike's persona shift and for its time-scale. Mike lived in a wealthy New York City suburb, referred to as Yorkville, and attended an exclusive private high school where most of his friends were white. He first began using AAVE features in his speech and hip-hop style clothing (baggy jeans, reverse baseball cap, designer sneakers) at age 13, and held that style through his mid-teens, but was tending to revert to more 'standard' speech by age 19, when Cutler's article was written.

The AAVE features that Mike adopted were phonological more than grammatical, although he did occasionally say things like *what up?* (copula deletion – absence of the verb 'to be', as opposed to *what's up?* – Cutler 1999: 431). But he regularly used [d] for [ð] and schwa [ə] rather than [i] in *the* before vowels. So we have utterances like *dass de other side that fucks it up* realised phonetically as [dæs dɔ ˈəðɔ saːd dæt fʌks ɪɾ ˈʌp] (1999: 431). Mike also produced a high frequency of [r]-less forms, which also patterns with the statistical norms for working-class black speakers from survey research. Prosodically, he lengthened many second syllables in polysyllabic words, as in [spoːz] for 'suppose'

and [fɪfti::n] for 'fifteen'. Lexically, he used words like *shit* for 'stuff',
phat for 'great' and *bitches* in reference to girls.

Cutler says that Mike had little direct contact with gang culture so
'had to seek it out, inspired no doubt by the proliferation of "gangsta
rap" in the early 1990s' (1999: 435). This leads her to say that Mike's
orientation to AAVE and hip-hop was a commodified life-style choice.
Cutler quotes an episode where Mike and two friends are rubbishing
the 'wannabe' inadequacy of other Yorkville white boys styling themselves as black street-gang members:

> *Extract 5.3*
> 1 Funny: they [white Yorkville crew kids] wouldn't step a foot over like
> 2   (.) you know they wouldn't (.) they're like (.) you know they
> 3   wouldn't they're like (.) set foot in Harlem but they try to act
> 4   like they're from Harlem you know (.) I (.) I mean last year (.)
> 5   he gotta go round and like "yo (.) dis is Yohkville (.) dis is
> 6   Yohkville"=
> 7 Joey: =yeah they're like (.) "get outta Yohkville (.) muthafucka!"
> 8 Funny: [continuing the imitation] "wes side (.) eas side we at woh
> 9   [war] (.) we at woh"
>   (The sequence is re-transcribed from Cutler 1999: 438, with
>   orthographic representation of pronunciation as in the source.)

Funny and Joey were not regular users of AAVE features, so Mike's
participation in the ridiculing positioned him awkwardly, raising
potentially complex issues of personal and social authenticity.
Funny and Joey's parodic mimicry of the (white) Yorkville crew kids'
ways of speaking targets the inauthenicity of white kids' crossing into
black-associated speech styles – a crossing process that Mike himself
had at that time undertaken quite 'successfully'. To call this process
'ethnic styling' is appropriate only up to a point. The Yorkville crew,
and Mike, are certainly adopting black-associated styles and enjoying
the indexical associations of coolness and hardness that flow from this
way of identifying (cf. Bucholtz 1999b). But the 'African Americanness'
of the act of identity is arguably almost incidental, reflecting the
historical origins of hip-hop culture rather than its current values
for young people. The social difference that is being negotiated
seems to have as much to do with Harlem versus Yorkville, and social
class as part of that, and a feeling of personal 'cool' versus 'uncool', as
it has to do with black versus white. However we categorise it, Mike's
styling was a metalinguistically rich and culturally meaningful – in
fact a culturally intense – discursive process. Mike and his friends were
drawing on specific historical and linguistic relationships as resources

against which they could design their own personal identity projects and their relationships with their peers.

In Britain, ethnic styling is sometimes focused around variation between local urban vernaculars and laguage forms historically linked to Caribbean Creole speech (Alladina and Edwards 1990-1991; Sutcliffe 1982). Mark Sebba (1993) analysed variation in 'London Jamaican' in the discourse of young black people from the London suburbs of Leyton, Catford and Southwark. Sebba uses the general term 'Creole', which can also be referred to as 'Patois', 'black talk', 'bad talk' or even 'Jamaica'. But in fact Creole is 'a collection of stereotypical features which are associated with Jamaican Creole as spoken in Jamaica' (Sebba 1993: 18). The young people in Sebba's data learned these features in early adolescence, so once again we are dealing with adoptive and somewhat reflexively based style resources.

London English and Creole speech forms can't be clearly distinguished as fully separate codes. The label Creole designates a range of grammatical forms, such as *did go* for 'went', *them* or *dem* or *mi* as subject pronouns and expressing question function by intonation alone, as in *Leonie have party?* It has some distinctive lexis, such as *seh* as a relative clause marker after verbs like 'think', and *stay* for 'be' when it refers to a prolonged state of being. The set expression *you know what I mean?* can be used as an expression of agreement with a preceding utterance, similar to 'yes I know', rather than as a request for confirmation. The variety also includes lexical tags such as *man*, *guy*, *star*, *spar*, *y'know* or *cho*, and swear-words like *raas*, *turaatid* and *bomboklaat*. Phonetically, 'girl' can be [gyæl], 'the' can be [di], 'long' can be [laŋ], and so on (Sebba 1993: 21-3, 62-4, 70-1).

Sebba gives an analysis of the subtle interactional effects of introducing Creole forms in young people's conversation, as in Extract 5.4, where the most clearly Creole-styled utterances are set in italics.

Extract 5.4

```
 1  Brenda:  then I just laughed (.) and then 'e (.) 'e just pulled me for
 2           a dance (.) I didn't mind dancing wiv 'im 'cause me know say
 3                                      [    ]
 4  Joan:                              yeah
 5  Brenda:  me no 'ave nothin inna my mind but to dance (.) and then
 6                                      [   ]
 7  Joan:                              yeah
 8  Brenda:  we started to talk and all the rest of it and that's it full stop!
 9                                      [  ]  [  ]
10  Joan:                              yeah   yeah
                              (Re-transcribed from Sebba 1993: 111.)
```

Brenda has been talking with her friends about an incident at a party when a boy had been tricked into thinking that Brenda fancied him, and he had approached her. She says she agreed to dance with him, but had nothing more in mind. Sebba says that the crucial utterance in Brenda's account is the one at lines 2 and 5, where she is trying to explain to Joan why she danced with a man whose approach had shocked her. This particular account of Brenda's state of mind is given in Creole, even though Brenda begins and ends her turn in non-Creole London English. Joan's supportive back-chanelling with *yeah* picks out the key rhetorical segments of Brenda's account and coincides with the 'shifts' (if this is the best way to describe them) 'in' and 'out' of Creole speech. Sebba's overall reading of the effect of Creole in this instance is that it helps to focus the main point in an utterance, which is 'worked up to' and 'worked down from' in non-Creole speech. Similar rhetorical functions are the use of Creole for one-liner jokes and for delivering punch lines.

As John Rickford and Faye McNair-Knox showed (see section 3.4), sociolinguistic interviews can be sites for styling social/ethnic identities, even though studies orienting to audience design/accommodation don't generally read variation in terms of acts of identity. Acts of affiliation and disaffiliation – reducing or increasing social and linguistic distance between speakers – might of course entail ethnic (re)alignment – achieving greater or less intimacy in group membership. In fact accommodation theory makes precisely this claim as the basic motivational account of convergence and divergence. Natalie Schilling-Estes (2004b) takes both quantitative and qualitative approaches in analysing ethnically salient variation in sociolinguistic interviews involving two people from Robeson County in south-eastern North Carolina. Robeson County is in the heart of the American south, where a bi-racial (black/white) classification system has been historically in place. Lumbee Indians/Native Americans in the county have resisted being forced into this system, asserting their own independent ethnic identity.

Some linguistic features distinguish Lumbee speech from both black and white local vernaculars. These include *I'm forgot* ('I have forgotten') and an inflected form of the more widely heard AAVE habitual *be* form *he be talking all the time, he be's talking*. Phonologically, the Lumbee share in the southern pattern of monophthongal [a:] in [ra:d] for 'ride' and [ra:t] for 'right', but use the feature less than both white and black people locally. Postvocalic [r]-lessness is more strongly associated with African American speakers than with Lumbee speakers (Schilling-Estes 2004b: 168–171). Schilling-Estes relates variation in the speech of an African American male postgraduate student, Alex, and a Lumbee male undergraduate student, Lou, to the structured content of the interview, where Alex was positioned as the interviewer and Lou as the interviewee. Pre-set topics spanned race relations, family and friends. In a quantitative variationist analysis, she finds that, predictably, Alex and Lou use different frequencies of [r]-lessness and monophthongisation of [ai], matching the general tendencies for their respective ethnic groups.

But in some parts of the interview dealing with race relations, the speakers diverge more from each other – more than when they discuss family and friends. It might seem that the topic of the interview is 'determining' Alex and Lou's stylistic variation relative to each other. But Schilling-Estes shows that topic is far too gross a concept, and that in some segments of the race relations topic, the speakers gradually find more interpersonal consensus. This is partly symbolised through Alex increasing his linguistic alignment with Lou with respect to third-person singular -s absence and copula deletion, also in terms of [r]-lessness. The speakers seem to detach themselves from their personal connections to ethnic groups, for example starting to refer to African American and Lumbee groups through the pronoun *they* rather than *we* (Schilling-Estes 2004b: 181). In the family and friends segments there are instances of direct echoing of vernacular forms, as in the close repetition of habitual *be* forms, italicised in the following extract. Lou and Alex are discussing a mutual friend who has joined a cult.

Extract 5.5
```
 1  Lou:   Jack [term of address] (.) they be telling them some crazy
 2         stuff Alex
 3  Alex:  how you know that's the one [name] is in?
 4  Lou:   'cause 'cause (.) uh [name] told me to watch it [a TV special on cults]
 5  Alex:  you joking (.) what's the name of it? you don't know what the
 6         name of it is? what- what they- what- what they be telling
 7         them?
 8  Lou:   they be telling them stuff like (.) uh (.) you got to twenty
 9         members by the time you get in here (.) you get settled in (.)
10         then you get twenty members or you can't stay in this church
```
(Re-transcribed from Schilling-Estes 2004b: 185)

Lou and Alex have resources to style themselves as Lumbee and African American, respectively, although the sociolinguistic ecology in which they operate is complex and there are few clear-cut indexical relationships for them to draw on. Schilling-Estes suggests that Alex and Lou's high levels of [r]-lessness, for example, probably index southernness rather than African American group identity, particularly when the topic of their talk has opened up a space for shared south-ernness to be meaningful. On other occasions, for example in occa-sional moments of interpersonal tension between the two speakers, the simple fact of linguistic similarity probably has meaning at an interpersonal level. This contextual account of social meaning there-fore re-emphasises the role of discursive frames for meaning construc-tion, even though Schilling-Estes does not use this concept directly.

In an active contextualisation approach to ethnicity it is the rela-tionality of ethnic meaning that tends to come to the fore. As Penelope Eckert says (2004: 113, using Gal and Irvine's 1995 theoretical con-cepts), we make certain ethnic categories salient by downplaying or erasing others. Through recursivity (re-applying distinctions) we give ideological categories more apparent coherence, working up new oppositions and distinctions around primary criteria. Eckert gives the example of 'black' versus 'white' ethnicity being reinforced by using relative darkness of skin as a basis for ever-finer racial catego-risations. Iconization makes arbitrary differences, for example in speech style, seem to be 'natural' bonds between practices and social categories.

5.7 INDEXING GENDER AND SEXUALITY

The limitations of assuming that a direct indexical link exists between language use and social group membership are just as apparent with gender and sexuality as they are with categories such as race and class. Much has been made of probabilistic positive correlations between sex of speaker and dialect 'standardness' in variationist sociolinguis-tics (see section 2.2). Women tend to use 'standard' forms more fre-quently than men do in otherwise similar speaking situations. But speaking 'standardly' does not directly or reliably index 'femininity', if only because 'standard' varieties have other indexical associations – most obviously, as we have seen, in the meaning-frames of high social class, professional public role and personal competence. It is much more plausible to argue that some regional vernaculars are historic-ally associated with manual work and predominantly male work-forces – for example in Britain in the coal mines of South Wales or the ship-building yards of Liverpool or Belfast. Those sociolinguistic networks (Milroy 1987) have mainly lapsed nowadays, and the con-temporary distribution of work-roles is less clearly gendered. Sociolinguistic variation by gender, where one could argue that gen-der meaning-associations were in some cases sedimented into speech over decades past, therefore seems to be another of those cultural legacies that are anachronistic – somewhat out of synch with late-modern social arrangements. So, if 'non-standard' did once directly index 'masculinity' (or if it did this in some frames for some social groups), it is less likely to do so directly now.

Of course, ideological values *are* mapped onto ways of speaking that are held to be gender-linked – stereotypes of women's tentativeness, powerlessness and co-operativity, for example, and of men's direct-ness, aggressiveness, silence and power. At the level of individual speech features or vocal prosody, there are instances where voice comes close to directly indexing gender. One British example might be young middle-class female speakers' realisation of the vowel in words like 'shoe' and 'goose', for which /u/ is the usual phonemic symbol in RP. It is commonly now realised as [ʊu] or ɨ (Foulkes and Docherty 1999: 13), for example in the word *thank you*. Ann Williams and Paul Kerswill say that this feature is heard pronounced as [y:] 'particularly in young female speech' in both Milton Keynes and Reading (Williams and Kerswill 1999: 144–5). Anecdotally, these real-isations are judged to be particularly 'girly'. The physiognomy of [u] fronting, involving more lip-pursing, might play some part in this perception, although there may also be a general sound-symbolic process at work – high front vowels have a stereotypical association with smallness and, in the ideology, 'femininity'. It might also be relevant that *thank you* utterances are positively polite and often defer-ential. Another example is vocal pitch itself, where there is a general biological correlation between pitch and sex by virtue of the different average sizes of men and women's larynxes, although of course this is only a probabilistic correlation.

But, back in the field of accent and dialect 'standardness', it really is difficult to accept that quantitative gender tendencies in the use of sociolinguistic variables are necessarily socially meaningful at the level of gender. Jennifer Coates takes a strong stance on the import-ance of 'difference' in the 2004 edition of her book, *Women, Men and Language*. Her final sentence in the book is:

> We understand that women and men are similar in many ways, but it is difference which fascinates us, and so we will continue to be in thrall to research which we can read as telling us about women's ways of talking, men's ways of talking, and differences between them. (Coates 2004: 221)

Let's consider just one example. Coates summarises Jenny Cheshire's (1998) analysis of gender differentiation from her study of working-class, adolescent peer groups in Reading in England (Coates 2004: 75–82). Cheshire reports gender variation in relation to eleven morphological/syntactic forms in terms of mean percentages for boys and girls' usage of each variable feature. The quantitative differences range from around 1% (e.g. for 'non-standard' -s, as in *we goes*) to around 30% (for 'non-standard' *what*, as in *the bastards what hit my son* and 'non-standard' past-tense *come*, as in *I come down here yesterday*). Even so, Cheshire also reports quantitative differences between the speech patterns of 'good girls' and 'bad girls', reflecting how strongly the girls adhered to 'vernacular culture norms', like not attending school regularly. The quantitative differences between 'good' girls and 'bad' girls are generally larger than those between boys and girls overall. But the girls did decrease the amount of 'non-standard' verb-form usage in school as opposed to outside school.

Can we imagine a scenario where a person's repeated contact with boys and girls, whose speech shows these sorts of quantitative differences, does lead over time to a gendered perception of verb grammar in Reading – where verb grammar might begin to take on the social meanings of 'girl-like' and 'boy-like' usage in Reading? The first difficulty is that, as mentioned earlier, there has been no demonstration that people are sensitive to subtle frequency differences in the use of linguistic variables. In the Reading case, girls provide counter-evidence on a case by case basis to any proto-theory that 'non-standard' verb grammar is 'boyish' or 'not girly'. Also, it seems there is too much interference from other salient meaning-potentials for a gender inference to be clearly supported. The strongest correlations in Cheshire's data are between 'standardness' and the vernacular culture index that she sets up. This distinguishes kids' levels of embeddedness in vernacular practices like carrying knives more clearly than gender, although this sort of claim is itself a risky extrapolation from numerical patterns. Should we say that the social meaning 'gender' depends on a more basic 'vernacular culture' meaning, or is vernacular culture more of a 'boys' thing' in itself? As Duranti implies, it is safer to bring cultural inferences into the interpretation (Duranti 1997: 209ff.). In the Reading case we can't say that 'non-standard' verb grammar connotes gender. But it might be true that in context it connotes an anti-establishment, anti-school stance, which in turn is open to being interpreted as gender-relevant.

This argument is put incisively by Elinor Ochs (1992). Ochs says that patterns of linguistic/discursive usage, for which she uses the general terms *stances*, can come to carry indexical meanings at the level of social identity. The sense of 'identity' here is ascriptional – identity being ascribed to a speaker by others. Ochs means that people or cultural groups can come to attribute the meanings 'female' or 'male' to ways of speaking that have no necessary association with those categories. And this brings us back to a generalisation that has already emerged several times in relation to styling. It is entirely possible for a particular linguistic form or style to be attributed social meaning in relation to *different* social or situational categories – it can mean different things.

This point applies to so-called 'queerspeak' (Livia and Hall 1997), where the analytic quest for directly-indexed gay and lesbian 'languages' or 'lects' is unlikely to succeed. We can say that the quest is itself part of an ideological assumption about social difference. Deborah Cameron and Don Kulick (2003) are strongly hostile to this approach and it leads them to suggest that an 'identity' perspective on language and sexuality is not worth pursuing. Bucholtz and Hall (2004) reject this argument, although the contest between these two analytic positions seems to be based on false premises. I think Cameron and Kulick are arguing against reductive and essentialist approaches to language and sexual 'identity', approaches that try to establish ways of speaking as being uniquely 'lesbian' or 'gay'. Bucholtz and Hall want to maintain a focus on identity, but not, of course, in these terms. As they say:

> regardless of how we want to classify any given set of socially
> meaningful linguistic practices ... indexicality works the same way:
> In every case, language users both draw on and create
> conventionalized associations between linguistic form and social
> meaning to construct their own and others' identities (2004: 478).

Conventionalized associations often link social categories together, for example masculinity and ethnicity. There are many ways of being and talking 'like a man' or 'like a black person', but in some sociocultural contexts the formation 'masculine' or 'manly' can come to be defined in terms of 'blackness'. This is one dimension of the social construction we saw around the would-be hard and street-wise Yorkville crew. Mary Bucholtz explores a similar linkage in her analysis of a white Californian boy's fight narrative (Bucholtz 1999b). The boy, Brand One, gives this account (an extract from the original transcript) of another kid approaching him trying to steal from his backpack.

Extract 5.6

1 two months ago this dude um (1.5) [tongue click] I was walking up to
2 uh (.) to the bus stop and he- and he was in my backpack right? (.)
3 this black dude was like six (.) maybe like fi:ve ten he was big (.)
4 he was a lot bigger than me (.) he was in my backpack and I felt him
5 and I turned around and I was looking at him and I was like
6 "what are you doing?" (.) and he was like [slow rate, low pitch] "nothing
7 pu:nk" (.) and I was like [tongue click] "ma:n (.) get <u>out</u> of my backpack
8 du:de" (.) and then he walked up beside me right? (.) and there was like
9 a wall [high pitch] right there kinda you know (.) and then ((I pushed
10 him up against it)) and he's like [slower rate, lower pitch] "what you
11 gonna do you little <u>punk</u> ass <u>whi:te</u> <u>bi:tch</u> and I was like "just get out of
12 my backpack"

(Re-transcribed from Bucholtz 1999b: 458-9)

The narrative is Brand One's (re)construction, and he voices both his own utterances as well as the attacker's (lines 6–8, 10–12). He refers to the attacker as *this dude* (line 1) and then as *this black dude* (line 3). Although Brand One therefore makes a racial attribution in identifying the attacker as a *black dude*, he also quotes the attacker addressing him using labels associated with both race and sexuality. The attacker is reported to have called Brand One *punk*, which Bucholtz says is a term originating in African American slang as a derogatory term for gay men, and *punk ass white bitch*, which mixes in racialising and gendering with sexuality attributions. In contrast, Brand One (re)constructs his own forms of address to the attacker as *man* (line 7). There is also the interesting contrast between *what are you doing?* (line 6), attributed to Brand One himself, and *what you gonna do?* (lines 10–11), attributed to the attacker. The first of these uses 'standard' English grammar while the second, with absent 'are', conforms to AAVE. Bucholtz says that 'Together with the lexical choices in each utterance, these dialectally contrasting syntactic structures now construct Brand One as nonconfrontational, reasonable and *white*, and his antagonist as confrontational, threatening and *black*' (1999b: 451, with original emphasis).

As the story develops, Brand One tells how he was helped out by a friend who is inferably black – he refers to him as a *big ass fool* (where 'fool' has no negative connotations) and describes him as *hella scary*. So Brand One's own speech (that is, as narrator rather than as a voiced protagonist in the story) incorporates some AAVE features. He even voices Stephen, the helper, as referring to him (Brand One) with the phrase *my nigger*. The utterance voiced for Stephen, challenging the attacker, is: *you punk motherfucking <u>bitch</u> (.) going in my nigger's backpack* (1999b: 460). So, outside of the contrast, as narrated, between Brand One and the attacker, which is styled partly as a black/white antagonism and partly as one person asserting his aggressive masculinity over another male he calls a 'bitch', Brand One styles himself as *sharing in* black identity, when the story moves on to show Stephen acting supportively to him, and styles Stephen as incorporating him into African Americanness. The social meanings for black and white speech remain relatively stable through the narrative. But the identity work that they are made to do is subtle, context-specific and contrastive. Racial categorisation is appropriated into a story about male aggression and male resistance to aggression.

Norma Mendoza-Denton's study of Mexican American girls in northern California rather similarly shows how being Mexican American, or Chicana, is deeply associated with other identities such as class, gender and toughness. As Penelope Eckert says in summary, 'being Chicana [in Mendoza-Denton's analysis] is tied up with a variety of local and nonlocal issues ... Class and gender ... may be associated with stances such as toughness or intellectual superiority. A single linguistic feature, therefore, may be deployed in multiple styles, and combined with others to create a style rich in social meaning' (Eckert 2005: 101–2). Mary Bucholtz's analysis of the social identities of 'nerd girls', also in northern California, again shows how different semiotic features are combined into a projection of a powerful, pro-intellectual, competent femininity (Bucholtz 1999a). Part of this projection is avoidance of 'non-standard' syntax and current slang words. Another element is the use of word-final voiceless stops with audible release, which sounds 'British' in this context and hypercorrect. In Britain itself, Emma Moore analyses how morpho-syntactic variation (for example *was/were* levelling and negative concord) quantitatively differentiates 'Townie' from 'Popular' girl groups at a school in Bolton in north-west England (Moore 2003). See also Scott Kiesling's (1998) research on college fraternity men's complex social identities (referred to in section 1.4).

5.8 CROSSING

Published in 1995, Ben Rampton's book *Crossing* put the sociolinguistic study of style, and of interethnic styling in particular, on a new footing. His work shares many assumptions and priorities with the studies I have been reviewing in this chapter and it has been an important stimulus to many of them. Rampton wants to understand the social construction of identities through qualitative, ethnographic analysis of language practice. He explores the local meanings and politics of styling. The term 'crossing', in its most basic definition, refers to a speaker's use of a linguistic feature or variety that is usually associated with a social group that the speaker doesn't obviously or 'naturally' belong to. So the crossing perspective resists the community-bound assumptions of variationism. Rampton endorses Mary Louise Pratt's criticism of the form of sociolinguistics that has an instinct to find orderliness and uniformity in speech communities, imagined to be self-contained and closely structured (Pratt 1987: 56; Rampton 1999: 421–2). Crossing, as Rampton formulates it, sits in the centre of constructionist approaches to sociolinguistic style.

The distinctiveness of Rampton's work lies in its ethnographic depth, theoretical openness and empirical specificity. Many 'post-variationist' sociolinguistic studies, even when they focus on trans-category styling, work with fairly straightforward understandings of the social categories they deal with – African Americanness in the USA, social class in Cardiff and so on. Analysing social construction through style has generally meant exploring the new meanings that speakers can fashion from 'old' social categories in discourse. My discussion of 'resources' in Chapter 4 took that line. But Rampton works from theoretical and empirical first principles in trying to understand what ethnicity and social class might mean for his inform-ants – British-born school kids in multi-ethnic schools in the south Midlands of England (Rampton 1995) and in London (Rampton 2006). This first-principles stance (which is my interpretation not Rampton's own) is, I think, dictated by his research context, partly because of the ethnic fluidity of the groups he studies and the developmental aspect of identity for school-age kids. The wider socio-cultural context is also complex – the historical complexity and indeterminacy of race and class arrangements in contemporary Britain. The sociolinguistic data for the 1995 study are 'the use of Panjabi by young people of Anglo and Afro-Caribbean descent, the use of Creole by Anglos and Panjabis, and the use of stylised Indian English by all three' (Rampton 1995: 4).

Roger Hewitt (1986) had analysed the sensitive politics of Creole use by white adolescents in south London and the potential for new cross-racial alignments to emerge from these cross-over strategies. Rampton's work shares these priorities, but avoids an 'inter-cultural' framework. He is interested in non-discrete 'styles', where fragments and vestiges of speech varieties associated with ethnicity are worked into kids' speech, often in very complex and fleeting interactional contexts at school. His primary data are audio-recordings of kids' talk, captured via radio-microphones, as they live out the everyday routines of school life. Rampton develops micro-analyses of sequences of interaction, richly contextualised, interpreted in relation to dense theoretical frameworks. Although the research is certainly politically sensitive, and although the wider social environment of the kids' lives certainly involves racial discrimination and disadvantage along race lines, Rampton seems committed to avoiding mapping a conventional politics of race onto his data. The ethnographic imperative is to try to establish what social meanings are created at the intersection of linguistic styling, contextualisation and ethnicity. We can consider only a few short examples here.

Rampton identifies a mode of talk that he labels Stylised Asian English (SAE). (A reasonable approximation to SAE from global popular culture might be the speech style of the Apu character from the TV show *The Simpsons*.) Its linguistic features include 'deviant verb forms and ... the omission of auxiliaries, copulas and articles ... verbal auxiliaries were rarely contracted ... stressing of every syllable ... retroflexion [of consonants] ... voiced and voiceless plosives were either heavily aspirated, or unaspirated completely ... /w/ could be changed to [v] or [b] ... diphthongs were usually changed to monophthongs ... a short central open vowel [being] very common as a replacement for [a range of] vernacular English [vowels]' (selective quotation from Rampton 1995: 68). Informants found this assemblage of features to constitute a distinctive social style that they were familiar with and could often produce. Extract 5.7 is a detail from a scene where two students – Asif, wearing a radio-microphone, and his friend Alan – are in detention (being kept in a classroom during the lunch break as a punishment for defacing desks during lessons). A teacher, Miss Jameson, arrives outside the detention room at about the same time as two other of Asif's friends, Salim and Kazim. Miss Jameson has arrived to take over supervision from another teacher, Mr Chambers.

Extract 5.7
1 [Kazim and Salim arrive at the door.]
2 Asif: Kaz (.) [in Panjabi] stay here stay here
3 Mr Chambers: ((see you messing around))
4 Alan: ((   ))
5 Asif: [chants, in Panjabi] "your [obscenity] nonsense"
6 Miss Jameson: after you
7 Asif: [in SAE] *after you::*
8 Salim: [higher pitch, in SAE] *after you::*
                 (Re-transcribed from Rampton 1995: 72.)

Rampton says that SAE (the utterances set in italics) occurs at moments when boundaries are at issue. In this extract Miss James was negotiating access through the door with the two arriving students, going into the detention room. SAE signals a stereotyped politeness that could not be taken at face value, not least in Asif's case because he is already inside the room and not in a position (spatially) to let the teacher go first. The *after you::* utterances in lines 7–8 are voicings, but with indeterminate targets. The utterances, in their literal semantics, are addressed to a teacher, Miss Jameson. But Asif at least is fictionalising a role for himself in letting Miss Jameson go first. The utterances seem to refer to and undermine the authority of the teachers, although Rampton points out that this exchange did not lead to hostility between Miss Jameson and the students, and that Mr Chambers was said by the kids to indulge in multiracial Panjabi speech himself on occasions. In fact Rampton says that Miss Jameson's first use of *after you* (line 6) was itself 'falsely polite', equivalent to saying 'please, do come and join us in detention', and so was 'the first move away from straight, untransformed talk' (1995: 72). He therefore suggests SAE here was part of a form of 'sport' or 'verbal duelling', more than political resistance.

The more recurrent theme in Rampton's analysis of SAE among multiracial school kids is its destabilising potential. When students approached adults, including approaching Rampton himself as the ethnographic participant-observer, for example to make a request for a lift in a car, they might do this in SAE, in utterances like *we want lifting* or *you could take me in your car?* The kids, Rampton says, were registering

> an identity contrary to the kind of cognitive recognition that the recipient might be expected to make in the circumstances. It foregrounded a *social* category membership ('Asian who doesn't speak vernacular English') at a moment when the adult would normally be setting him/herself up for interaction in a primarily *personal/ biographical* capacity. And in so doing, it promised to *destabilise* the transition to comfortable interaction and the working consensus that phatic activity normally facilitates (1995: 79, with original emphasis).

Some adults said they felt that kids' SAE established social distance and made them feel embarrassed, as Rampton says he himself felt. This suggests that SAE played a part in unsettling established socio-cultural frames and other, more local discursive arrangements that operated at school. It is impossible to say whether these micro-moments of destabilisation function as acts of resistance to wider ethnic, white–black dominance arrangements. Perhaps they are acts of resistance to institutional arrangements in the school, unless we see that institutional framework as a localised instantiation of British authority structures. Rampton stresses their ambiguity, but also speculates that social movements necessarily have a local interactional dimension.

SAE fits the definition of crossing because kids like Asif, although of Asian extraction, generally use London vernacular. They cross into SAE occasionally as a marked social style. But Creole (or Creole-associated styling) was also part of their 'repertoire' and its use was sometimes to symbolise rather more antagonistic stances than SAE achieved. Rampton says that Asian-associated sociolinguistic issues had some overt recognition in the school at the level of policy. They fitted into the school's conception of 'multiculturalism'. Creole, on the other hand, was less dignified in this regard, and in any case it sometimes blended seamlessly into local vernacular speech (cf. Hewitt 1986). Even so, in Rampton's data there are suggestions of more focused Creole usage marking annoyance or aggression.

A little later on in the event from which Extract 5.7 is taken, Asif challenges Miss Jameson about her reasons for arriving late at the detention room. She says she had had to see the headmaster but Asif abruptly asked her *why?*, implying he doesn't accept her account. Miss Jameson then tells the boys she is going to get her own lunch.

Extract 5.8
```
 1  Miss Jameson:  I'll be back in a second with my lunch (( ))
 2                                                       [
 3  Asif:                                           NO [click]
 4                 dat's sad man (.) ((I'll b      ))
 5                 I had to miss my play right I've gotta go
 6                 [
 7  Alan:          ((          with mine            ))
 8                 (2.5) [Miss Jameson has left the room]
 9  Asif:          l:unch (.) you don't need no lunch
10                 not'n grow anyway ((laughs))
11                 [
12  Alan:          ((laughs))
13  Asif:          have you eat your lunch Alan
                   (Re-transcribed from Rampton 1995: 120–1.)
```

Asif of course has no power to determine his own leaving of the detention room and he resorts to insulting Miss Jameson, presumably out of her hearing after she has left. Saying she doesn't need lunch (line 9) is a comment on her physical size, which the boys laugh about.

Rampton uses Erving Goffman's idea of 'afterburn' – verbally attacking a conversational opponent after their face-to-face encounter has
ended (Goffman 1971: 152; Rampton 1995: 121). There are Creole
influences in parts of Asif's speech (italicised in the transcript), but
they can't be very clearly categorised. His click at line 3 is not quite the
dental click associated with some Creole speech. Line 4's *dat's sad man*
has a Creole feel, and the 'pitiful' sense of the word *sad* is apparently of
Creole origin. The lengthened [l] in *l:unch* and first syllable vowel in
Asif's *not'n* pronounced with [a] (lines 9 and 10) are more clearly
Caribbean variants. Rampton's interpretation is that Creole helps
Asif to articulate his seriously felt sense of injury at being defeated
by Miss Jameson's abrupt leaving and at her dismissing of his questions to her. If this is correct, it would be an interesting case of an
outgroup style being used to voice an interior emotion in serious key –
Asif targeting Miss Jameson's authority over him and insulting her for
her fatness, but reflecting his damaged personal standing and identity. At another point Rampton suggests that a 'basic disparity
between speaker and voice ... is fundamental to language crossing'
(Rampton 1995: 278), and that this makes crossing a fundamentally
metaphorical process. It generates a complex chain of inferencing that
leaves symbolic resonance around an utterance.

   Rampton's research in London schools (reported in the 2006 book) is
primarily concerned with education practices and foreign language
learning. However, it also consolidates and develops his earlier work
on identity styling and stylisation, specifically in relation to social
class identification and the categories of 'posh' (privileged, 'standard'-
type sociolinguistic styling) and 'Cockney' (local London vernacular
styling). I refer to Rampton's theorising of stylisation in more detail in
Chapter 6, where is it centrally relevant. The analysis of social class
meaning in Rampton (2006) is once again highly abstract at the level of
theory and highly specific in its sensitivity to local contextualisation.
It is not a matter of kids styling themselves in a direct way as being
'of a social class'. Instead, Rampton suggests that social class is part of
the meaning structure of their lives, an ingrained sense of social
hierarchy, which they evoke obliquely:

> In their everyday negotiations of the mundane, my informants did not
> actually say 'this is a class issue', but in putting on posh and Cockney
> voices, they did the next best thing. In these acts of stylisation, they
> momentarily stepped back from the flux of activity and suggested that
> more general qualities and/or categories associated with posh and
> Cockney were relevant to the proceedings on hand. (Rampton 2006:
> 369–70)

In Extract 5.9 from a playground recording, again made via a radio-microphone, Joanne and Ninette notice a boy that Ninette fancies; his name is Ricky.

Extract 5.9
1 Ninette: oh oh oh my boyfriend's here (2.0)
2 Joanne: ((([?short kissing noise])) mwa (3.0)
3 Ninette: [audibly moving away from Joanna] my little
4   scooby doo thing (2.0)
5 Joanne: [higher pitch] *oh you are: here Ricky (.) Ricky*
6   [quietly with slight laugh] *Ninette's here*
                  (Re-transcribed from Rampton 2006: 334.)

Joanne's italicised utterances are marked for posh. In line 5, for example, *oh* is [əʊ] and *here* is [hɛə]. In line 6 the same word *here* is [hɪɑ] which is a very conservative RP form. Rampton feels that Joanne's stylisation of posh creates a meaning of politeness and restraint in a context where Joanne, probably speaking out of the hearing of the other two, knows that Ninette has amatory and perhaps sexual designs on Ricky. The stylistic analysis is a form of psychoanalysis, reaching for rather profound dimensions of selfhood and cultural meaning. Here is Rampton's summary of the main meanings of posh and Cockney:

> it looks as though a relatively *standard accent* is used to articulate an incompetent or uneasy relationship with the body and with feelings and emotions ... that the words selected express an apparent regard for social decorum ... and that there is an association with literate cultivation rather than oral spontaneity ... A *Cockney* accent, in contrast, is associated with bodily activity, with the expression of feeling unconstrained by social manners ... with profane language that emphasises sexual activity ... A pattern emerges, then, in which vigour, passion and bodily laxity appear to be associated with Cockney, while physical weakness, distance, constraint and sexual inhibition are linked to posh. In fact, at an abstract level, this can easily be accommodated within a more general set of contrasts between mind and body, reason and emotion, high and low (2006: 342, with original emphasis).

Rampton's ethnographic analysis of particular sequences in which these meanings surfaced is painstakingly detailed. It is necessary to work through his many analysed instances to get a cumulative sense of his interpretations being authoritative, but the analytic detail gives us (as readers) similar access to these stylistic constructions as Rampton's own. The approach is both liberating and constraining as a sociolinguistic analysis of style. We have to ask how wide is the range of sequences and situations where (some of) these meanings are likely to be triggered, outside the London school context as well as inside it. There is the familiar problem of ethnographic analyses being unreplicable. But a general cultural semantic of class does emerge strongly from the London school data and the central argument – that social class and ethnic meanings are a resource available to be invoked and inflected in many different ways in relation to local interactional concerns – is entirely convincing.

One point where Rampton's analysis diverges from the more general approach we have been considering in this chapter is when he distances social structure seen as a form of 'practical consciousness', from social structure seen as ideology. As mentioned earlier, Rampton gives credence to Raymond Williams's analysis of class as a 'structure of feeling', rather than as an ideology or as a more definitive assemblage of beliefs or stereotypes. Here is Rampton overviewing the structures of feeling concept, intercut with quotations from Raymond Williams (1977):

> 'Structures of feeling' are socially and historically shaped, and they are trans-situational, drawing on experiences prior to the communicative present, to the extent that one can speak of the structures of feeling characteristic of a person, a set of people, a collection of texts, or indeed a period. The 'structure' part of 'structures of feeling' involves 'a set [of affective elements of consciousness and relationships] with specific internal relations, at once interlocking and in tension'([Williams] 1977:132), and ... the historically grounded, high-low/mind-body/reason-emotion binary might be identified as one such structure. In terms of their relationship with interaction, structures of feeling 'exert pressures and set effective limits on experience and action' ([Williams] 1977: 132), but they are much more indeterminate than 'ideology' and 'cannot without loss be reduced to belief-systems, institutions, or explicit general relationships' ([Williams] 1977:133). Instead, structures of feeling are 'practical consciousness of a present kind, in a living and interrelating continuity', and 'can be defined as social experience *in solution*, as distinct from other social semantic formations which have been *precipitated* and are more evidently and more immediately available' ([Williams] 1977:133). (Rampton 2006: 344–5)

It may not be necessary to force this division between ideology and practical consciousness. In analysing stylistic operations in discourse, social meanings can be more or less determinate and explicit. When we are dealing with more overtly socio-political contexts (and perhaps more typically in adult than in adolescent interaction), it is more likely that consolidated social meanings will be brought into play in more 'precipitated' forms. All the same, social meanings 'in solution' are a new concern for sociolinguistics and pull us further away from the over-confident, over-consolidated theorising that has held back the sociolinguistics of style.

5.9 OMISSIONS

The examples I have discussed in this long chapter are a small subset of the research in which sociolinguistics has dealt with the styling of identities. I have included no studies of age-identity processes (Coupland, Coupland and Giles 1991), although age has come in under the wire in some of the extracts we have examined, where 'youth' seemed to be part of speakers' targeted identities. The variationist paradigm has generated a lot of quantitative data on age differences, although the same problems arise in turning the account to stylistic meaning-making. On the whole, age has been of interest to variationists because it gives some insight into generational stages of linguistic change, not because age is a key identity category that we have to manage and rework throughout our lives (Coupland 2001d).

The themes of ethnicity, gender and sexuality return in Chapter 6, although it should be clear by now that it is unwise to approach social identity on a category-by-category basis. The main division – again an uncertain one – between this chapter and the next is to do with *performance*. Performance has been a hidden theoretical concept in this chapter's arguments and I start Chapter 6 with a review of it. In stressing creativity and active contextualisation, we have already been dealing with styling as a performed discursive practice. Judith Butler's concept of performativity, introduced in section 4.5, has similarly been a highly relevant but latent notion. But we also need to consider 'strong' performances, where the gap between a speaker's social incumbency (his or her 'natural' social position) and targeted identities is larger than in most of the instances we have discussed so far. Those are cases where the term *stylisation* becomes indispensable, and where cross-category social identification is more radical and more spectacular.

6 High performance and identity stylisation

6.1 THEORISING HIGH PERFORMANCE

It would be apt to invoke the idea of performance as a quality of most and probably all of the styling practice we have considered in the book so far. There has been a tendency in linguistics to strip away any specific meaning for the term 'performance', by virtue of Noam Chomsky's long-standing but sometimes-disputed distinction between linguistic competence and linguistic performance. One of the founding ideas in sociolinguistics was to challenge the idea that language in use could be dismissed as 'mere performance', if that notion implied everyday language use or actual behaviour. As we saw in Chapter 1, a concept of 'everyday language' has been important to sociolinguistics since its inception, even though that concept has raised interpretive difficulties of its own. Chomsky's corresponding emphasis on linguistic competence, speakers' knowledge of the linguistic system, ignored the social dimension of language that is at the heart of sociolinguistics. I have already referred to communicative competence as Dell Hymes's alternative formulation (see section 4.6). Alessandro Duranti (1997: 14ff.) discusses this complex of issues in detail. But once we recognise speakers' agentive role in constructing meanings in how they contextualise variation, and when we also recognise that speaking involves a degree of metalinguistic awareness (see section 4.5), it seems right to talk of speakers *performing* speech. What we are generally implying is that speakers design their talk in the awareness – at some level of consciousness and with some level of autonomous control – of alternative possibilities and of likely outcomes. Speakers perform identities, targeted at themselves or others, when they have some awareness of how the relevant *personas* constructed are likely to be perceived through their designs.

But there is also a distinction to be drawn between what we might call *mundane performance* and *high performance*, or at least we should recognise a scale that runs between these two performance types or formats. In exactly that spirit, linguistic anthropology, particularly through Richard Bauman's work, has developed useful accounts of contextual factors that distinguish what I am calling high performance events from others (Bauman simply uses the term performance). Bauman (1992: 46ff.) allows us to infer a list of particular characteristics that all high performance events share. He says they are scheduled events, typically pre-announced and planned, and therefore programmed. They are temporally and spatially bounded events, marked off from the routine flow of communicative practice. They are co-ordinated, in the sense that they rely on specific sorts of collaborative activity, not least in that performers and audience members will establish themselves in these participant roles for the enactment of the performance. High performances are typically also public events, in that the membership of the audience will not be especially exclusive. Even if it *is* exclusive, audience members are positioned as parts of a more general social collectivity. These characteristics are material aspects of how high performance events are contextualised, but Bauman also identifies the heightened *intensity* of performance events as a key characteristic. (See also Bauman 1977, 1996; Bauman and Briggs 1990.)

We can reorganise this list of characteristics and extend it a little if we say that high performance involves, in several related senses, communicative *focusing*. This is not the linguistic focusing that Le Page and Tabouret-Keller invoked. It is the focusing of a communicative event. Seven dimensions seem relevant:

- *form focusing* The poetic and metalinguistic functions of language comes to the fore and considerations of 'style' in its most commonplace sense become particularly salient.
- *meaning focusing* There is an intensity, a density and a depth to utterances or actions, or at least this is assumed to be the case by audiences.
- *situation focusing* Performers and audiences are not merely co-present but are 'gathered', according to particular dispositional norms. People know their roles.
- *performer focusing* Performers hold a 'floor' or a 'stage', literally or at least in participants' normative understandings of speaker rights and sequencing options.
- *relational focusing* Performances are *for* audiences not just *to* audiences (cf. our discussion of this distinction in relation to audience design in section 3.5). Although audiences are often public,

performers will often have designed their performances for specific groups.

- *achievement focusing* Performances are enacted in relation to more or less specific demands. 'Stakes' (gains, losses and risks) are involved, with potential for praise or censure for good or bad performance.
- *repertoire focusing* Performers and audiences are generally sensitive to what is given and what is new in a performance. Performances may be versions of known pieces, or at least known genres. Innovative interpretation can be commended. Rehearsal is relevant.

To say that an event is framed as a high performance event carries all of these implications to some degree, although it is of course possible for reframings to be achieved within communicative events, for example when a speaker in a conversation (to use Dell Hymes's 1975 expression) 'breaks through into performance'. Bauman is mainly concerned with institutionalised performance events, although some 'ordinary conversations' can take on the relevant situational aspects, for example when a speaker tells a set-piece narrative to a gathered group of listeners who afford him or her the floor (Coupland, Garrett and Williams 2005).

Bauman also develops the idea of *cultural performances*. He emphasises the role of reflexivity in (high) performance, and how such events have the particular facility of opening up cultural norms to reflexive scrutiny:

> Perhaps the principal attraction of cultural performances for the study of society lies in their nature as reflexive instruments of cultural expression ... First of all, performance is formally reflexive – signification about signification – insofar as it calls attention to and involves self-conscious manipulation of the formal features of the communicative system ... making one at least conscious of its devices. At its most encompassing, performance may be seen as broadly *metacultural*, a cultural means of objectifying and laying open to scrutiny culture itself, for culture is a system of systems of signification ... In addition to formal reflexivity, performance is reflexive in a socio-psychological sense. Insofar as the display mode of performance constitutes the performing self as an object for itself as well as for others, performance is an especially potent and heightened means of taking the role of the other and of looking back at oneself from that perspective. (Bauman 1996: 47–8, my emphasis)

This is a particularly useful perspective for the analysis of identity, especially if we extend Bauman's notion of culture to what sociolinguistics generally calls social groups. Bauman says that the distinction between performer and audience is one of two significant distinctions in the participation structure of (high) performance events. The other is between the performer–audience pair (together), and people who constitute the membership of the cultural/social group itself. The (high) performance frame establishes a relationship between the meanings co-articulated in the performed event and the meanings that define the wider cultural or social formation. This relationship, and this duality of meaning, are laid open to scrutiny when social styles are performed.

In this chapter we look at some different high performance events and see their metasocial/metacultural potential to construct social identities, again paying attention primarily to indexically loaded variables such as accent/ dialect features. As Rusty Barrett says, 'In identity [high] performance, out-group stereotypes concerning the behavioral patterns of the group associated with the performed identity are likely to be more important than actual behavior or the group's own behavioral norms' (Barrett 1999: 318). Performers' projected identities are constructed and read relative to prevailing meanings for the social categories invoked. I think we can therefore say that acts of identity in high performance events encourage a critical dialogue about the real versus the projected content of identity categories, such as maleness and femaleness, Welshness or other forms of localness or ethnicity, and so on. As we saw in the previous chapter, form-focusing is also a quality of stylisation. Again, metasocial/metacultural acts of identity involve lifting a particular identity out of its immediate context. We therefore need to consider some further theory around the concept of stylisation and around the idea of decontextualisation. These ideas complement the above definition of high performance.

6.2 STYLISATION

Stylisation is a concept originally associated with the literary and cultural criticism of Mikhail Bakhtin (1981, 1986; see also Wales 1989; Rampton 2006, section 6.3). For Bakhtin, stylisation has both specific and general meanings. It is 'an artistic image of another's language' (1981: 362). But it is also a general quality of language use. He wrote that 'Modern man does not proclaim'; rather, he 'speaks with reservations'; 'he stylizes ... the proclamatory genres of priests, prophets, preachers, judges, patriarchal fathers, and so forth' (1986: 132). Bakhtinian stylisation is therefore not only 'artistic'. It is a

subversive form of multi-voiced utterance, one that discredits hegemonic, monologic discourses by appropriating the voices of the powerful, and reworking them for new purposes. For Bakhtin, stylisation
is a core instance of the dictum that we met earlier – 'our speech ... is
filled with others' words, varying degrees of otherness or varying
degrees of "our-own-ness", varying degrees of awareness and detach-
ment' (Bakhtin 1986: 89).

In his analysis of Stylised Asian English (see section 5.8), Rampton
was drawing attention to form-focused ways of speaking that incorporate selective elements of recognisable socio-cultural styles. School
kids were performing Asian-linked ways of speaking and throwing
them into contrastive relief against the backdrop of their more habitual speech styles. The subversive effect of some stylisations was a
result of the complexities of ownership that they raised. It was pretty
clear that the kids were not speaking in their own 'true' voices or
personas, yet not altogether clear that they were speaking in other
groups' voices or personas either. In high performance events, which
are often staged institutionally, reading ownership of voice is just as
complex and interesting.

Radio presenters, for example, may be expected to project preferred
and designed personas rather than in any simple sense their real
selves. Many dimensions of authenticity relating to personhood and
talk itself – for example the factual accuracy of what is said, consistency of self-representation or cultural coherence – are subordinated
to the priority to entertain or just to fill out the performance role. The
demand of projecting identities consistent with particular media genres or media institutions might also be an important consideration.
This was certainly true of Frank Hennessy, the radio DJ described in
section 5.5, although Frank's performance generally involved him
keeping within the bounds of language variation as we hear it in the
city of Cardiff. Apart from a few brief and playful forays into Ameri-
canised speech and a few other regionally marked varieties, Frank did
not indulge in complex or multi-layered identity play. But radio talk
can sometimes involve layers or laminations of stylistic meaning of
this sort.

I analysed a series of extracts from a morning light-entertainment
show on BBC Radio Wales, broadcasting to the whole of Wales and
adjacent regions of England in English (Coupland 2001c). I chose one
particular show, *The Roy Noble Show*, because it carries a daily short
feature involving banter between the show host, Roy Noble, and a
guest astrologer, John Dee. John does a horoscope feature around the
mid-point of Roy's show followed by a segment I called 'today in

history', done interactively with Roy. The show as a whole, and the 'today in history' sequence in particular, repeatedly touch on traditional rich points of cultural Welshness (Agar 1991; Coupland 1995). For about five minutes John and Roy chat in a part-scripted, part-extemporised way about historical events with some relevance to Wales. As I know from their published writing and other broadcasts, each of them is particularly knowledgeable about history and Welsh cultural life. But in the 'today in history' sequence, they style themselves as *gossiping* about history – a curious mixed genre. John self-presents as a quite camp male and 'camps up' the gossip-value of historical moments, while Roy generally plays the interested dupe who feigns to have limited knowledge of the historical facts but makes witty side-comments to John's accounts.

The event is accent-stylised in that John produces what would usually be thought to be extravagant and chaotic variation between more 'standard' and more vernacular South Wales English values for a wide range of many phonetic variables. In Extract 6.1 John is in the middle of listing and commenting on some historical events linked to the day and month of the current broadcast.

Extract 6.1

```
 1  John:  battle of the pyramids as well (.) Napoleon had a very good day
 2         (.) he
 3           [
 4  Roy:   was that in the sand then?
 5  John:  oh: ye:::s in the sand (.) he defeated the Mamelukes (.)
 6  Roy:   did he?
 7  John:  and there's nothing worse than a case of Mamelukes in
 8         in seventeen ninety eight
 9           [
10  Roy:   where were they from then the Mamelukes?
11  John:  oh the Mamelukes ruled Egypt (.)
12  Roy:   oh did they?
13  John:  they did
14  Roy:   so they were from all over Egypt
15  John:  yeah y you could say that they were (.) u:m (.) they were um (.)
16         they were um (.) they were slaves technically (.) they were very
17         posh slaves
18  Roy:   wa like your Spartacus?
19  John:  oh I oh posher than Spartacus oh all silk tents and curved swords
20  Roy:   did they?
21  John:  yes a un unfortunately some of the Mamelukes (.) er lacked
22         certain attributes (.) that the rest of us take for granted
23  Roy:   never
24  John:  they di::d
```

25	Roy:	didn't they?
26	John:	oh: yeah
27	Roy:	never had their pudding did they?
28	John:	no weren't allowed to breed see
29	Roy:	oh I see [sniggers]
30		[
31	John:	(breathy sniggers) and the Tate gallery opened
32	Roy:	did it?
33	John:	yes of course this was Tate (.) as in Tate and Lyle
34	Roy:	as in sugar
35		[
36	John:	the sugar magnate
37	Roy:	yeah
38	John:	he opened the Tate gallery and this opened in eight eighteen
39		ninety seven

John and Roy build a cartoon-like representation of Napoleon's defeat of the Mamelukes (or Mamluks), incorporating the stereotypical cultural themes of sand, silk tents and curved swords. These semantic images are bright and tightly specified, but economically drawn, which is what cartoon drawings are like. There is a recurrent dissonance between the required factual accuracy of history and John and Roy's generic reframing of it as gossip. See Roy's mock-surprised recipiency tokens *did he?* and *never* (lines 6 and 23). The historical event is knowingly trivialised as Napoleon 'having a very good day'. John's phrase *a case of Mamelukes* (line 7) plays with the idea that the name sounds like a disease. John says that the Mamelukes were *technically ... posh slaves* (lines 16–17), which is a knowingly non-technical account, in the same way that Roy suggests they *never had their pudding*, referring to their being castrated. The collocation *posh slaves* is semantically incongruous, again drawing attention to semantic form. Roy's phrase *like your Spartacus* (line 18) feigns no knowledge of the cultural category Mamelukes, only of the more widely popularised Spartacus character, known to many people mainly through the film epic. The phrase with *your* is a working-class implicative way of connoting familiarity with a class of items or people.

John's post-posed *see* (line 28) has a similar 'unsophisticated speaker' value. Dialect semiosis adds to the non-technical, mildly subversive and cartooning representation, for example when John produces long monophthongal [e:] in *slaves* (lines 16, 17). The word *slaves*, and especially its second mention in the phrase *posh slaves*, is very prominent. John works up to it progressively during his turn beginning at line 15 and anticipates that a keyword is coming by saying *you could say that they were* followed by several pauses. This draws attention to phonetic form, also because John's more habitual pronunciation of this segment is a more RP-like [ei]. In fact John stylises the same vernacular monophthong feature in the three realisations of *Tate* (lines 33 and 38), even though he produces a very clear and dissonant RP-like [ei] in the stressed word *magnate* (line 36, placed between the occurrences of the word *Tate*).

Roy, and even more so John, give us enough stylistic data to infer that their identity constructions are 'put on', somewhat fictionalised and in different respects hyperbolic – extravagant phonetic styling, exaggerated surprise at historical facts, vivid stereotyping of historical characters. Even so there are clear socio-cultural referents for the performed personas that they fitfully construct for themselves during 'today in history'. The 'unsophisticated speaker' is a social class persona, and on accent/dialect criteria it is clearly a Welsh working-class persona. The 'over the garden fence gossiper' persona is again a projection of working-class communicative practice, but also stereo-typically a female practice. Audience members acculturated to the show can read these targets *as being* stylised rather than 'straight', and to that extent they/we collude with and participate in these identity games. But it is important that their collusion is with the semiotic association of Welsh ways of speaking with low sophistica-tion, even if at the same time there is an assumption that, like John and Roy, we (Welsh people) are not necessarily 'like that'.

This is far from a pure image of the Welsh (female) working class, however, and several other resonances come in. John's camp self-presentation sometimes echoes the voices of well-known gay male characters and impersonated 'housewife' figures in a range of British comedy shows. The first incarnation was in the comic gay characters of Jules and Sandy from the 1960s BBC radio programme *Round the Horn*, carried forward through the Charles Hawtry and especially Kenneth Williams figures in the long series of studiedly down-market British *Carry On* films. A similar stylistic configuration occurs in Monty Python's gossiping housewife characters (played by men), and in the similar but north of England comic female characters performed by Les Dawson and Roy Barraclough on British TV. John's *oh: ye:::s* (line 5) and *oh: yeah* (line 26) have long glides to [u] on *oh* from onsets in the region of [ɔ], heavily nasalised and rising to very high pitch which is then sustained on the *yes* (or similar) syllable. To British listeners these utterances sound 'very Kenneth Williams'. Ben Rampton does not find the stylised identities in his own data to be 'characterolo-gical' (Rampton 2006: 360), but John's (and to a lesser extent Roy's) projections are precisely this. They are stylistic echoes of very familiar media characters who have quite regularly been targets of vocal impersonation by others.

What are the defining criteria of stylisation, based on this instance and analysis? Here is a schematic summary (adapted from Coupland 2001c), building on important insights in Ben Rampton's work:

- Stylised utterances project personas, identities and genres other than those that are presumedly current in the speech event; projected personas and genres derive from well-known identity repertoires, even though they may not be represented in full.
- Stylisation is therefore fundamentally metaphorical. It brings into play stereotyped semiotic and ideological values associated with other groups, situations or times. It dislocates a speaker and utterances from the immediate speaking context.
- It is reflexive, mannered and knowing. It is a metacommunicative mode that attends and invites attention to its own modality, and radically mediates understanding of the ideational, identificational and relational meanings of its own utterances.
- It requires an acculturated audience able to read and predisposed to judge the semiotic value of a projected persona or genre. It is therefore especially tightly linked to the normative interpretations of speech and non-verbal styles entertained by specific discourse communities.
- It instigates, in and with listeners, processes of social comparison and re-evaluation (aesthetic and moral), focused on the real and metaphorical identities of speakers, their strategies and goals, but spilling over into re-evaluation of listeners' identities, orientations and values.
- It interrupts a current situational frame, embedding another layer of social context within it, introducing new and dissonant identities and values. In doing this, its ambiguity invites re-evaluation of pertaining situational norms.
- It is creative and performed, and therefore requires aptitude and learning. Some speakers and groups will be more adept at stylisation than others and will find particular values in stylisation.
- Since the performer needs to cue frame-shift and emphasise dissonant social meanings, stylised utterances will often be emphatic and hyperbolic realisations of their targeted styles and genres.
- Stylisation can be analysed as strategic inauthenticity, with complex implications for personal and cultural authenticity in general.

6.3 DECONTEXTUALISATION

It is useful to link up these ideas about stylised performance with ideas about cultural entextualisation. In section 5.1 I mentioned Bauman and Briggs's explanation of how cultures lay down or sediment texts which are then performed and shaped into texts (entextualised) in new contexts. Cultural continuity can be understood as an iterative process of performed entextualisation. If we add in the idea of metasocial or metacultural function, we have an argument that cultural continuity is achieved through creatively performed reiterations at the level of practice, alongside a process of critical reassessment of what these practices are like and how they define 'us', and us relative to others.

To elaborate on this, drawing on Bauman and Briggs (1990), we can say that high performance events build socio-cultural meaning not only in how they are entextualised, but also in how they are *de*contextualised. A high performance in many ways abstracts away from the current situational context of telling. Performances are therefore both within and outside the culture that they characterise: 'poetic patterning extracts discourse from particular speech events and explores its relationship to a diversity of social settings' (Bauman and Briggs 1990: 61). High performances and the identities they create are not only for the moment. They are detachable or transportable. This is another way to think about their metasocial or metacultural function. High performances focus cultural forms and practices and invite audiences and performers themselves to reflect on them and apply them to other contexts:

> A text, then, from this vantage point, is discourse rendered decontextualizable. Entextualization may well incorporate aspects of context, such that the resultant text carries elements of its history of use within it. (Bauman and Briggs 1990: 73)

This very abstract theoretical argument is significant because it challenges the assumption that high performance events are 'unreal' or 'merely fictive'. High performance is important *because of* the gap it establishes between what we think of as real social practice and performed social practice, and because of the critical reflexivity it encourages. This qualifies Bakhtin's position on the ubiquity of historically inherited ways of speaking. It suggests that high performance is a specific discursive format which packages up stylistic and socio-semantic complexes and makes them transportable.

We can now turn to a range of performance genres and contexts to see how at least some of these ideas can underpin a stylistic analysis. The first example, in section 6.4, is of historical interest in the UK,

showing how a famous left-wing politician of the 1950s, Aneurin
Bevan, used fleeting vocal stylisations to construct his own political
stances and to undermine those of his adversaries. I will need to
explain the historical context of Bevan's political contribution in
some detail. In section 6.5 we turn to the world of drag queens and
transgendered identities. Finally in this chapter, I draw together wide-
ranging examples of accent/dialect performances where linguistic
varieties and features are 'exposed' through one form of media representation or another.

6.4   VOICING POLITICAL ANTAGONISM – NYE

Aneurin Bevan, affectionately known as 'Nye', is an iconic figure
in the history of British politics. He is *the* icon of British socialism in
the twentieth century. His reputation centres on his role in founding
the British National Health Service, which was the most radically
transformative institution introduced by any administration on the
British political left. Bevan's career symbolises successful working-
class resistance, through mainstream political processes, to large-
scale and destructive capitalist exploitation of working communities.
Aneurin Bevan was a class warrior. The roots of his life and politics
were in South Wales. Coal mining and steel fabrication defined the
South Wales Valleys' position as the hotbed of nineteenth- and twentieth-
century industrialisation. Rapid deindustrialisation, mass unemploy-
ment and waves of extreme social deprivation from the 1920s
through to the 1980s, whose legacy is far from eradicated today,
decimated the Valleys communities. But they also further galvanised
working-class consciousness and radical political action in South
Wales (Williams 1985; Smith 1999). Born in 1897 in Tredegar, on the
eastern extremity of the South Wales coalfield, a colliery worker from
age thirteen, Bevan quickly engaged with and moved up through local
political groups, becoming a member of parliament for Ebbw Vale in
1929. He went on to become a cabinet minister with responsibilities
for health and housing in the post-1945 Labour government, and
deputy leader of his party. (See Coupland in press for a more detailed
account.)

Bevan's personal identity was complex. He was a socialist ideologue
fervently committed to principles of social justice through public
ownership and redistributive taxation, and enraged by capitalist
exploitation. He could be ruthless and aggressive, although his bio-
graphers say he was also highly sociable, and even tender and shy in

dealings with friends and non-political acquaintances. He was fiercely proud of his Welsh social origins in Tredegar and appealed passionately to his childhood experiences as a basis for his political philosophy. All the same, he developed a wide social circle of friends, including the newspaper proprietor Lord Beaverbrook and other members of the English cultural elite. He had a reputation for sharp dressing and enjoying good food and drink. Kenneth O. Morgan calls him 'an aristocrat in outlook and taste' (1989: 13). On this count, as Morgan explains, he was criticised as 'a Bollinger Bolshevik, a ritzy Robespierre, a lounge-lizard Lenin' (1989: 13). The phrase 'champagne socialist' was also used by his political opponents.

Bevan had, and still has, an unparalleled reputation as a political speaker. His oratory at public political rallies and in the House of Commons was legendary. He made vicious attacks on the Conservative Party (the 'Tories', a term Bevan used almost as an insult). His speeches were spontaneous but based on extensive rehearsal. He often made capital from aggressive rejoinders to hecklers and attacks on opponents who were present in the debating chamber. He often segmented utterances into short, matched strings, punctuated by even-length pauses, in the grandiose manner of public political oratory. He would manage speech rhythm and pausing, amplitude and intonation to produce swooping rhetorical sequences that often culminated in key political points. At other times his speeches would create a surprising intimacy and audiences would be drawn into quasi-dialogic debate with him, or even actual dialogue.

His dominant voice was strongly South Wales Valleys, which is a major sub-variety of Welsh English (Garrett, Coupland and Williams 1999, 2003). But he sometimes used RP-like variants of some variables, and it is this aspect of his speech-making and what meanings it allowed him to construct that deserve to be analysed as stylisation. A small set of fragments of audio- and video-recordings of Bevan's speeches has been in circulation since his death. Contextual information about the sources of these recordings is limited, although it is possible to reconstruct some general characteristics of the settings from the recordings and sometimes to identify a precise time and place. For reasons to do with the availability of audio-recording technologies, the extracts available are from the later years of Bevan's life. I know that one recording in the set I analyse in Coupland (in press) was made in 1959, one year before Bevan's death from cancer.

In the 1950s the dominant accent of the London House of Commons was what we would now call conservative RP, even among senior Labour Party politicians on the political left (including Clement Attlee

Table 6.1. *Phonetic variables generally distinguishing South Wales Valleys English and Received Pronounciation*

	Valleys	RP	Conservative RP	
(ou)	oː	ɔʊ	əʊ	oː – ɔʊ contrast is available in one lexical set, e.g. *coal, although, so, over*; ɔʊ is normative in a second set, e.g. *told, knows, ownership*; əʊ is the conservative RP realisation for both sets
(ei)	eː	eɪ		This contrast is available in one lexical set, e.g. *educating, Ebbw Vale, misbehaving, nation*; eɪ is normative in a second set, e.g. *train, day, neighbour*
(au)	əʊ	aʊ		e.g. *pounds, out, now*
(ai)	əɪ	aɪ		e.g. *might, private, why*
(a)	a	æ		This contrast is available in stressed 'short a' contexts, e.g. *fact, national, established*, including in words that have a short vowel in South Wales but a long vowel in RP, e.g. *circumstance*, where lengthening is another option
(aː)	aː	ɑː		This contrast is available in 'long a' contexts, e.g. *argue, laugh, tarnished*
(y)	i	ɪ/ie	ɛə	These contrasts are available in orthographic final 'y' words and in '-ly' adverbials, e.g. *finally, city, integrity*
(ɜː)	ɜː/œː	ɐː		e.g. *heard, perfectly, years*
(ə)	ə	ʌ		This contrast is available in stressed syllables, e.g. *dull, must, come*
(iw)	ɪw	ju		e.g. *opportunity, constituency, you*
(h)	Ø	h		Ø (zero) in word-initial orthographic 'h' contexts, e.g. *house, hands*, and favoured in *have, had, he, his*, etc.
(ing)	n	ŋ		n in verbal '-ing' contexts and lexical compounds with '-thing', e.g. *educating, going, nothing*

who was Labour Party leader between 1935 and 1955). Bevan's Tredegar accent was starkly different. I have already mentioned some of the phonetic features usually associated with South Wales versus RP in earlier sections. Table 6.1 gives a more orderly list.

Extract 6.2 is a famous sequence. The speech is at an outdoor venue to a large crowd. Almost certainly this is Bevan's speech at the 'Law not

War' Labour Party rally in Trafalgar Square in London at the time of the Suez crisis, November 1956. Tory Prime Minister Sir Anthony Eden had called on Egypt and Israel to withdraw their forces ten miles from the Canal. When they did not comply, Britain and France attacked Egyptian airfields the very next day, in defiance of the United Nations' Charter. In the extract I have noted particular values for phonetic variables just above the syllables in which they occur. I have marked occurrences of Bevan's slight speech block with /.

Extract 6.2

```
                          ŋ
1  Sir Anthony Eden has been pretending (2.0)
       Ø  h  Ø              e: ŋ
2  that he has he is now invading Egypt (.)
                          ai     ei
3  in order (.) to strengthen the United Nations (3.0) [laughter; audience: rubbish]
4  er every every um (.)
          з:                    e:
5  every burglar of course (.) could say the same thing (2.0) [laughter]
   Ø        a:       Ø        ŋ    həʊ
6  he could argue that he was entering the house in order to ≪step up≫
       train the police (4.0) [loud laughter]
   o:                              Ø        ŋ
7  so if Mis- Sir Anthony Eden (.) is sincere in what he is saying (.)
       Ø
8  and he may be (2.0) [laughter; audience: ah:: with low-fall intonation]
   Ø
9  he ≪fall-rise≫ may be (1.0) [slight laughter; 'yeah']
       Ø              Ø      ŋ
10 then (.) if he is sincere in what he is saying (.)
                      ɪw              əi
11 then he is ≪step-up≫ too stupid to be a Prime Minister
                                                    [
                                            [wild laughter]
(There is a break in the recording here, and the extract may therefore not be continuous,
   although it appears to be.)
       a:      ae
12 we are in fact in the position today (1.0)
       ha  ŋ                  e:          ei
13 of having appealed to force in the case of a small nation (1.0)
                                  ə
14 where if it is appealed to against us (1.0)
          ə          ə          ei
15 it would result in the destruction (.) of Great Britain-
       ou        ei
16 -not only as a nation
```

                  ŋ   ŋ
17   but as an island con / taining <u>li</u>ving men and women (2.0) [audience:
      hear hear]
18   ≪quieter≫ therefore I say to Anthony Eden (1.0)
                    ə
19   I say to the British / government (2.0)
            o: əʊ
20   there is no / <u>count</u> at <u>all</u> upon which they can be de<u>fend</u>ed (2.0)
          h   ɜ: e:
21   they have be<u>smirch</u>ed the name of Britain (3.0)
     Ø   ə   e:
22   they have made us ≪high pitch≫ a<u>shamed</u> of the <u>things</u> (.) of which
                 əʊ
      formerly we were <u>proud</u> (4.0) [loud cheers]
     Ø   ou   εə
23   they have (.) <u>off</u>ended against every principle of <u>decen</u>cy (2.0)
               ou   ə
24   and there is only <u>one</u> <u>way</u> in <u>which</u> they can (.) even be<u>gin</u> to re<u>store</u> their
              a: u ei
      ≪harsh≫ <u>tarn</u>ished repu<u>ta</u>tion [audience: *get out*]
                           əʊ   əʊ   əʊ
25   and that is to ≪high pitch≫ get <u>out</u> (.) get <u>out</u> get <u>out</u>
                                      [
                                   ((loud cheers))

In the first 11 lines Bevan represents Eden's policy of military intervention in Egypt as motivated by a desire to strengthen the United Nations. This is a curious proposition, presumably reworking some specific comment by Eden that the policy of attacking Egypt would show the power of the United Nations. Bevan parallels the invasion with burglars breaking into a house, and *strengthening the United Nations* with *training the police* (lines 5 and 6). This of course imputes criminality to the attack and criminal behaviour to the Tories, as well as exposing the ludicrous nature of the supposed motivational reasoning. Then we have the mock-serious concession that Eden may be being sincere in his (ludicrous) beliefs (lines 7–9), before the abusive put-down that Eden's being sincere would leave stupidity as the only available explanation.

Bevan has invited the audience to reflect on the illogical motivation of *to strengthen the United Nations* up to line 3, and a supportive audience is already audibly rubbishing this motive in the pause between lines at that point. Bevan's apparent fumbling for a comment sets up an anticipation of a derisory remark to come. He then tantalises his audience with his as-if accepting of Eden's sincerity, presenting the opportunity for them to reach their own denial of this sincerity before he articulates it himself. Some audience members duly give him laughter and a prolonged low-fall *ah::* after line 8 (to the effect, 'ah, we don't believe that') and slight laughter and an ironic *yeah* after line 9. But then, Bevan's debunking of Eden in line 11 turns out not to be simply a refutation of sincerity, but the more damaging suggestion that Eden cannot be sincere without also being *too stupid to be a Prime Minister*. This is a true Bevanite discursive ploy – eliciting an audience evaluation then *transcending* or trumping that evaluation in his own punch-line comment.

From line 12 Bevan drops out of the mock-moral evaluation of Eden's sincerity and moves into denunciation. He loads up his censure with direct and extreme morally evaluative expressions, especially over lines 20 to 24. He asserts his own authority in the highly formal metapragmatic design *I say to Anthony Eden . . .* (lines 18, 19). Interpersonally, the frame is not participative in the way the earlier frame was. Bevan moves out of personal attack into attacking Tory policy, from sarcasm to direct evaluation, and from light-hearted play to heavy condemnation. How does accent semiosis work as a resource here?

Bevan's delivery over lines 1–5 is slow and deliberate, with a small non-fluency in line 4 possibly resulting from his wanting to 'correct' an aitchless realisation of *he*. There is variation between [e:] (the prototypically South Wales value) in *invading* (line 2) and *same* (line 5) and RP-like [ei] in *Nations* (line 3). (The word *Nations* in the phrase *the United Nations* is less amenable to phonetic vernacularisation than non-proper-noun items, although Bevan seems to favour RP-like [ei] in the word *nation* generally.) But when Bevan draws the 'burglar' parallel, the complete line (line 5) has a strong vernacular quality. This is partly because Bevan has lexically relegated the status of the grammatical subject from *Sir Anthony Eden* to *every burglar*, but the semiotic associations of vernacular [ɜː] in *burglar* add to the effect. Bevan constructs a second parallel contrast between Eden's grandiose purpose (*to strengthen the United Nations*) and his feeling that anyone *could say the same thing*, with vernacular [e:] in *same*. We begin to see that there are two voices in Bevan's account. The first is not Eden's own voice, but it is a voice which superficially endorses Eden's stances and claims. The second is a critical and sceptical voice, drawn from and evoking a vernacular culture of unreliable burglars.

These phonetic images are fleeting and not fully consistent, although features in utterance-stress position, and probably vocalic more than consonantal features, have most salience. They cannot in isolation carry the values I am attributing to them, although I am sure we can say that they are part of the ideological contrasts that Bevan is constructing. The 'sincerity-stupidity' sequence has something similar about it. The ideational/pragmatic thrust of his talk at that point is to offer respect to Eden's being *sincere in what he is saying*. But the *too stupid to be a Prime Minister* phrase (line 11) is the anticipated punchline, and is delivered on a markedly higher pitch, with increased amplitude, *and* with a resoundingly South Walian [ɪw] in *stupid*. This is the critical voice returning, speaking abrasively and personally, but from a vernacular social base, willing to drop out of polite and respectful parliamentary protocols of 'trusting the sincerity of opponents'. As a personal judgement, *too stupid to be a Prime Minister* is uncompromisingly disrespectful, direct and unhedged. Lexically, *stupid* sets up a self-consciously unsophisticated and perhaps even puerile basis for personal judgement; socio-phonetic imagery adds support, implying a specifically South Walian 'no nonsense' intolerance. But the utterance is also voiced from a position of superiority – Bevan's reputed intellectual elitism, added to the moral basis of his critique of invading Egypt. Intellectual and moral elitism with vernacular authority is very much Bevan's distinctive political persona, and indeed it is a key part of the mythology of working-class Welshness.

There are contrasting socio-phonetic nuances in the powerful, censorious sequence in the second frame, down to and including line 24. Some keywords have resonant South Wales Valleys pronunciations: *no count* at *all* in line 20, *ashamed* in line 22, *tarnished* in line 24, and of course the final *get out get out get out*. In that string, three flapped intervocalic [t] sounds lend support to a Valleys image, and Bevan voices the communal rhythmic chant that the crowd itself might adopt. Yet there are also several RP-like realisations of (h), (ng) and (ei), and the phonetically striking line, *they have offended against every principle of decency* (line 23). Within this line we have the unusual, hypercorrect, spelling-pronunciation of (ou), realised as [ou], in the first syllable of *offended*, and the highly conservative RP realisation of written 'y', [ɛə], as the final syllable of *decency*. Bevan produces this [ɛə] for final 'y' on some other occasions too. To my ears it is evidence of him fleetingly accommodating Westminster's patrician phonological style, before, on this occasion, the sequence ends with a rousing return to vernacular values and class action, in *get out get out get out*. The moral high ground he is claiming in this sequence in some ways naturalises the conservative RP variant – reversing the polarity of vernacular authority in the earlier sequence. 'Principles of decency', Bevan is implying, ought to be values shared by all people in government. At the same time, [ɛə] undoubtedly also contributes to the impression of Bevan's 'champagne socialism' that his left-wing critics disapproved of.

So Aneurin Bevan marshals semiotic resources to construct diverse social personas in and through the different interactional frames that are characteristic of his public speech-making. This is not to say that his political identity is in some way deeply compromised – it could hardly be more resolute. But his enduring commitment to what he often called 'his own people' on the working-class Welsh side of the class war of 1950s Britain required him to fight and win political battles, and this called for complex tactical operations, not least in that primary domain of political confrontation – public debate. On the basis of the evidence available in these historic audio-recordings, many of Bevan's debating successes hinged on establishing ludicrous or foolish or inconsistent personas for his Tory opponents, and in building identities and stances for himself in relation to them and working people which listeners could 'take away with them' and possibly adopt as their own. But he was also prepared to appropriate and to stylise some of the semiotic trappings of parliamentary authority, despite the fact that this semiotic would potentially conflict with the Tredegar mining semiotic. It would be entirely consistent with Bevan's politics to argue that the working classes should claim authority whenever they could, and not eschew the trappings of privilege.

6.5 DRAG AND CROSS-DRESSING PERFORMANCES

Stylistic crossing between social categories of various sorts has already emerged as an important theme in sociolinguistics. As we saw in section 5.8, the concept was carefully and insightfully articulated by Ben Rampton to explain ethnic styling. In a wider sense, there is always an element of crossing in the styling of speech, and certainly in the Bevan analysis just above. Allan Bell's audience design framework (section 3.2) can be interpreted as speakers shaping their sociolinguistic identities towards those of audiences under some circumstances. We have seen several different examples of speakers – paradoxical though it sounds – crossing into *their own* identities, ways of speaking that index their own sociolinguistic provenance, in a regional sense or another social group sense. Questions of personal and social authenticity lie behind these style operations, and I will try to draw them together in the final chapter. But there are more dramatic and dramatised instances of crossing to be considered first.

Transgender and transsexual identification are involved in a variety of performance roles and types, which Rusty Barrett (1999: 313–14) carefully explains. *Transsexuals* are people who feel that their gender identity doesn't correspond to the sex they were assigned at birth. They may try to close this gap through surgery or hormone therapy and thereby cross or 'pass' fully into the social role they feel is their own. There is no simple link between transsexual practice and sexuality, so transsexuals can be heterosexual, homosexual, bisexual or asexual. *Transvestites*, as Barrett says, identify with the gender that corresponds to their assigned sex. They derive satisfaction or benefit from cross-dressing – wearing clothes associated with the other sex, often selectively without trying to produce a whole image of the other sex. *Female impersonators* are professional cross-dressers who usually try to produce quite realistic images of famous women, usually glamorous and hyper-feminine ones. *Drag queens*, the focus of Barrett's own analysis, are almost always gay men. But drag queens perform for lesbian and gay audiences, often in gay bars and clubs, while female impersonators perform for mainly heterosexual audiences. *Glam queens* are a sub-category of drag queens who target similar visual (glamorous) personas to female impersonators.

There are different goals, stakes, benefits and risks associated with these different forms of transgender crossing. We can consider two strongly contrasting forms – Barrett's glam queens in the USA and the burlesque British theatre convention of the pantomime dame. Indexical styling at the level of accent/dialect is an important part of performance in each of the forms, in conjunction of course with other sorts of discursive construction and spectacular visual styling. They are very clearly *high* performance representations of gender and sexuality, highly focused, metacommunicative and metasocial.

Barrett studies African American drag (glam) queens who are professional entertainers. He focuses on their creation of a 'white woman' linguistic style, which can be understood as a response to complex ideological forces. Being a black gay man means having to resist several potential forms of oppression and prejudice. Barrett points out that AAVE is most commonly associated, stereotypically, with young, working-class heterosexual black men (as we saw in Cecilia Cutler's analysis of the Yorkville crew in section 5.6), and that there is a wider mythology of black males being sexually potent in the heterosexual domain. These assumptions promote racism among white gays and homophobia among African Americans. In consequence, 'African American gay men are often pressured to "decide" between identifying with African Americans or with white gay men' (Barrett 1999: 317).

Many African American men, gay or straight, do not use AAVE and there is a risk that non-AAVE-using African American men will be thought to have abandoned African American identity. At the same time, speaking 'standard' American English might be understood as an index of gayness.

Barrett says that the African American glam queens he studied project 'a polyphonous, multilayered identity by using linguistic variables with indexical associations to more than one social category' (1999: 318). They sometimes project their 'real' identities as African Americans, as gay men and as drag queens. But their main performance target is to project fictional identities as 'white women'. The drag persona of a white, heterosexual, upper-class woman inverts the 'real' social categorisation of these performers. Barrett says that the designation 'white woman' in this context refers primarily to class rather than to race, and expresses a US cultural ideal of femininity, 'being a lady'. This includes an ideal speech style, which Barrett models on Robin Lakoff's famous description of 'women's language' (Lakoff 1975). In ethnic and class dimensions, African American glam queens generally need to avoid AAVE and 'non-standard' speech (grammatically and phonetically). But they also adopt 'women's language' which, stereotypically, comprises several features. One feature is using specialist vocabulary linked to women's supposed interests (using precise colour terms, the vocabulary of sewing, etc.). Others are using so-called 'empty' adjectives like *divine* or *cute*, using tag questions in declarative utterances, using hedges and hyper-polite forms, also avoiding telling jokes, and 'speaking in italics', which refers to speaking on the assumption that no attention is being paid to one's speech (Barrett 1999: 322).

Barrett finds that glam queens performing 'white woman' keep to many of these stylistic characteristics. However they 'interrupt' this persona with markers that they are nevertheless 'really' African American gay men. In one example, a glam queen purports to apologise for her swearing, while swearing:

Extract 6.3
1 are you ready to see some muscles? [audience yells] (.) some dick?
2 excuse me I'm not supposed to say that (.) words like that in the microphone
3 like shit, fuck and all that (.) you know (.)
4 I am a Christian woman (.) I go to church
5 I'm <u>always</u> on my knees

(Re-transcribed from Barrett 1999: 324.)

The obscenities are stylised in the sense that they have an ambiguous status as the glam queen's own utterances. She of course mouths them, but quotatively, saying they are expressions she is *not supposed to* use (line 2). She styles the breaking down of the 'white woman' persona, partly through the strategic ambiguity of the phrase *always on my knees* in line 5. It refers both to her claim of being religious (presumably as an upper-class woman might be expected to be) and to performing oral sex on other men.

The same ambivalence can be achieved through dialect, as in Extract 6.4, where a glam queen is introducing the next performer.

> *Extract 6.4*
> 1 please welcome to the stage our next dancer
> 2 he is a butt-fucking tea honey [meaning 'wonderful'] (.) he is hot
> 3 masculine (.) muscled (.) and ready to put it to ya baby
> 4 anybody in here (.) hot (.) as (.) fish (.) grease?
> 5 that's pretty hot idn't it?
> 6 [switch to low pitch] hey what's up home boy?
> 7 [switches back to high pitch] I'm sorry that fucking Creole
> 8 always come around when I don't need it
>   (Re-transcribed form Barrett 1999: 324.)

Barrett points to the AAVE features of absence of *-s* inflection on *come* in line 8 and vocalised [l] on the word Creole in line 7 and the *home boy* address is to an African American man in the audience. The drag queen is voicing AAVE and obscene utterances within the act of apologising for using them. This self-referentiality and ambiguity are characteristic of the AAVE rhetorical mode called *signifying*, which is a classic form of stylisation. It is skilful, form-focused and knowingly ambiguous. It is a performance genre through which otherwise taboo forms of talk or relationally risky stances (like insults) can be produced without the consequences that normally follow. In the last of the terms I used to define stylisation in section 6.2, it is strategic inauthenticity.

The British theatrical genre of *pantomime* is not easy to explain to people unfamiliar with it, but it is utterly familiar to most Brits (see Coupland in pressa). 'Panto' is a generally low-budget, low-culture, burlesque form of music, comedy and drama staged at very many theatres through Britain over the months of November, December, January and February. Pantomimes are often said to be entertainment for children, although family groups make up most audiences. Each pantomime theme is a variation on one of a small number of traditional narratives, with roots in folk tales. Each theme tends to mingle ethnic and other social categories with abandon, but orientalism is a regular ingredient. *Aladdin*, like the animated Disney films of that title, builds its plot around an Arabian Nights magic lamp and a magic genie. But the performance also uses stage sets including 'old Peking', and the 'Wishy Washy' character's name refers to his menial job in a Chinese laundry. Pantomime plots always involve magic, intrigue, royalty, peasantry and a love-quest.

Typically, a noble prince, conventionally performed by a female, dressed in a tunic and high boots, falls in love with a beautiful girl from a poor family. The girl (played by an attractive young female) either has two large, ugly, vain sisters or a large, ugly, vain mother, referred to as a *Dame* and often named *The Widow Twankey* (these females are conventionally played by males). Characters, particularly the pantomime Dame or the ugly sisters, are starkly drawn and heavily stylised. Young love triumphs and royalist grandeur is subverted. The semiotic constitution of pantomime is bricolage (Hebdige 1979), intermixing light popular songs and comedy routines, exorbitant colours and costumes, and with vernacular, self-consciously 'common' values set against regal pomp and transparently evil figureheads. The interactional format involves a good deal of audience participation and ingroup humour. Hackneyed and formulaic plots are interspersed with disrespectful humour on topics of local or contemporary interest. Conventional teases appeal to children, who have to shout warnings to the heroine princess, for example when an evil emperor approaches, or to help the audience's friend (in this case Wishy Washy) to develop his quest (for example to find the magic lamp).

Extract 6.5 is from a version of *Aladdin* performed at a theatre in a small town in the South Wales Valleys. My description of coal-mining and class antagonism in the Valleys is again relevant, and social class is a highly relevant social meaning in the event. The extract captures the pantomime Dame/Widow Twankey's first entrance, close to the beginning of the show after the opening song performed by the full cast and live orchestra. The Dame's entrance is a tone-setting moment for the whole pantomime. She is the mother of Aladdin, the nominal hero, and she returns regularly through the pantomime, mainly to add the most burlesque dimension of humour on the periphery of the plot. Her styles of dress, hair (wig) and makeup are garish and extravagant. In Barrett's categories the Dame is a cross-dressing male, but with no attempt at realism or passing. The construction is deliberate caricature and a deliberately 'unsuccessful' female impersonation. The Dame is physically large and visually grotesque. Her character is pompous, vain and mildly salacious, but she is nevertheless funny and warm-hearted. Her transparent personal deficiencies are a familiar part of the character's performed identity, and they leave her open to be liked despite them.

Extract 6.5
1 [The Dame enters, waving, to music 'There is nothing like a dame']
2 Dame: **hello everyone**
3 Audience: hello
4 Dame: **hello boys and girls**
5 Audience: hello
6 Dame: **hello mums and dads**
7 Audience: hello
8 Dame: **grans and grandads** *brothers and sisters* **aunts and uncles**
9   **and all you lovely people back home** ooh hoo
10   *hey* (.) now I've met (.) all of *you*
11   *it's time for you to meet* [drum roll] all (.) of (.) [cymbal] me
12 Audience: [small laugh]
13 Dame: and there's a lot of me (.) to meet (chuckles)
14   *now my name is* (.) the **Widow T-wankey**
15   and d'you know what (.) *I've been a widow now* (.)
16   *for twenty-five years* [exaggerated sobs]
17 Audience: [mock sympathetically] o:h
18 Dame: yes (.) ever since my *poor husband died*
19   *oh what a man he was* (.) *he was gorgeous he was*
20   *do you know* (.) *he was the tallest man* (.) *in all of Peking* (.)
21   *and he always had* (.) *a runny nose* (chuckles)
22   *hey* (.) *do you know what we called him?*
23   '*Lanky Twankey with a Manky Hanky*'
24 Audience: [laugh]
25 Dame: *hey* (.) *and guess what* (.) *I've still got his manky hanky*
26   *to this very day* look look at that ugh
27 Audience: o:h [laughs]
28 Dame: *hey* [to orchestra members] *look after that for me will you?*
29   *you look like a bunch of snobs*
30 Audience: [laugh]
31 Dame: *anyway* (.) *I can't stand around here gossiping all day*
32   I have got a laundry to run
33   ooh (.) and I've got to find my two naughty boys (.)
34   Aladdin (.) and Wishy Washy (.)
35   *so* (.) *I'll see you lot later on is it?*
36 Audience: ye:s
37 Dame: [to camera] *I'll see you later on* (.) bye for now (.)
38   *tarra* (.) bye bye
39 [The Dame leaves waving, to music 'It's a rich man's world']

I do not give a detailed phonetic annotation of the Dame's variable accent on this occasion but I have marked her distinctively RP-like pronunciation sequences in boldface. Strongly Valleys vernacular speech is italicised. The most striking phonetic contrast is between the Dame's aspirationally posh, RP voice at the opening of the extract, and the broad vernacular Valleys Welsh English voice which she uses elsewhere in the extract, except at the end of line 14 when she says her name. The Dame's speech at lines 1–9 shows centralised onset of (ou) in all three tokens of *hello* and in *home*, contrasting with monophthongal [o:] which occurs later in the word <u>*nose*</u> (line 21). There is also fully audible [h] in all cases in these opening lines. Together, these features carry the first-level indexical meaning 'posh' as the extract opens, apparently outgrouping the Dame relative to the Valleys community in which the performance is geographically and ideologically situated. Aitch-less *hey* at line 10, and before that the schwa [ə] realisation of the first syllable of *brothers* (in place of RP [ʌ]), mark a strong shift from a conservative English RP voice into Valleys vernacular. The posh voice resonates most strongly at line 9 in the utterance *all you lovely people back home*, where the first two and last two words have significant RP and non-local tokens, [ju:] in *you*, [æ] in *back* and [əʊ] in *home*.

The abrupt stylistic shift at line 10 marks a cracked or unsustainable posh self-presentation. This chink in the Dame's accent armour of posh is confirmed to be as suspect as her dress-sense. The wider semiotic dimension here, as it was in the glam queens data, is once again fundamentally to do with authenticity and inauthenticity. After line 9, all tokens of (iw) have the Valleys local form, including *you* in line 11, said with contrastive stress. The Dame's self- introduction in line 14 pronounces the word *name* with the vernacular form [e:], although <u>*Widow*</u> <u>*T-wankey*</u>, when she mentions her name, has conservative RP central [ə] onset to (ou) and raised [æ] in *Twankey*. This achieves a neat and radical splitting of personas, between the introducing voice and the introduced voice, phonetically pointing up the Dame's inauthenticity even within the character being performed. The sequence setting up the *manky hanky* word-play (a *hanky* is a handkerchief or napkin and *manky* means 'dirty' and 'disgusting') is performed in a fully-formed local vernacular. All three vowels in the stressed syllables of *poor husband died* (line 18) are local Valleys variants. Similarly, aitchless *he* on the three occasions in line 19 and monophthongal *nose* in line 21 are prominent.

The Dame's mainly vernacular style is realised lexico-grammatically too. We have reduplicative *he was* at line 19 and the word *manky* as a childish and vernacular word. There is also the invariant tag *is it?* at line 35 (which, more usually in its negative form *isn't it?*, is a stereotype of Welsh English), and colloquial *tarra* for 'good bye' at line 38. Discursively too, the mock formality of the opening salutation and self-introduction is counter-pointed (and confirmed to have been mock) by later stances. The Dame's feigned grief at being widowed is subverted by the joke at the husband's expense and by references to the Dame's large bosom and hips (see lines 11 and 13). The disrespectful word play, *bunch of snobs* (*snobs* evoking 'snot' or nose effluent, visually rendered by a bright green stain on the handkerchief) addressed to the orchestra members, builds an allegiance against the conservative persona she feigns early on, and so on.

The similarity between the pantomime Dame and the African American drag queens is of course that both are instututionalised cross-dressers, men performing womanliness through dress and voice. There is a curiously shared similarity in social class demeanour too, because both transgender formats give priority to performing upper-class womanliness, although the drag queens need to approximate glamorous 'real ladies' far more than the pantomime Dame does. In the Dame's genre convention, the visual and vocal display of 'being a woman' is self-consciously ineffective and ludicrous. The male performer's sex is never 'successfully' restyled as female, in view of his projected femaleness being so shallow in the performance, and so deeply ritualised in pantomime. In both formats performers display the inauthenticity of their respective performances. But for drag queens, the identity discontinuity is far more radical than for the Dame, because their femaleness is more convincing until it is subverted. The Dame's main identity discontinuity is between a feigned poshness and a 'real' vernacular Welshness, where gender identity is ultimately fairly irrelevant. The Dame's posh demeanour is quite readily associable with 'Englishness' because the Welsh Valleys lack a clear sociolinguistic class structure and RP in the Valleys mainly indexes English ethnicity.

But each of these burlesque and extravagant stylisations does allow audiences to detach meanings that are significant to their own social and ideological circumstances. The pantomine (through many of its other characters and relationships as well as through the Dame's cracked persona) lives out a historical conflict between Welsh workers and English bosses, even though those real social structures have mainly disappeared from Welsh life, at least in the heavy industries that defined the Valleys. The relationship between the Dame and the audience, who are directly addressed in the text, also seems important in this regard. Extract 6.5 shows the Dame switching reference and address between the (fictional) *Aladdin* plot-world and the real Valleys audience-world and its *boys, girls, mums, dads* and so on. The Dame exists in both domains, but not as a 'straight' inhabitant of either.

Nevertheless, she does draw the audience into particular alignments with some of her espoused stances (e.g. against the suited orchestra members who she calls *a bunch of snobs*), with potential identity implications for audiences.

Both formats of gender performance we have considered in this section allow us to reach the same generalisation. Although high performance and heavily stylised representations complicate the links between sociolinguistic practice and social meaning, they can also expose those links quite strikingly and make them available for critical reassessment.

6.6 EXPOSED DIALECTS

The decontextualisation and transportability of performed speech is visible in many social domains. Accent/dialect varieties, and often just some of their fragments focused in specific performance routines, are recycled through different sorts of networks, both face-to-face and mass-mediated. This is one of the more obvious limitations of the concept of 'speech community', since varieties and features sometimes sweep across great distances with little regard for modernist socio-structural arrangements. Communities of practice, such as groups of adolescent school kids, do have particular parts to play in the dissemination of some such innovations and trends. But I am thinking of stylistic practices around accent/dialect which are most distinctive for how they do *not* respect boundaries between social groups. Many of them originate in the mass media, particularly television, in situation comedies, soap operas and product advertisements. They can rapidly reach awareness and some level of usage at a national level, and sometimes they can be close to global.

As a broad generalisation, it is true that popular culture on British TV has undergone a radical shift over the last thirty years to embrace regional vernacular speech. Regional vernaculars on networked television were at one time heard only in very limited contexts, such as in comedians' voices. It remains true that comic stand-up, on or off TV, is mainly delivered through broad regional voices associated with London, Liverpool, Birmingham, Belfast and other major cities. This emphasises the 'street' quality of their performances. But TV programming for children is another genre where 'the rise of the regional' (Mugglestone 2003: 273, see section 4.4) has been evident. That pattern regularly attracts criticism from conservatives, for example in the (London) *Times* feature headed *Mind ya grammar*,

Dick & Dom (19 October 2005, *News*, p. 3). The show in question is called *Dick & Dom in Da Bungalow*. When the *Times* carried this feature, *Dick & Dom in Da Bungalow* was the favourite TV programme of British 6–12-year-olds. Richard McCourt and Dominic Wood, both born in Sheffield in the north of England, were nominated as 'best presenters and entertainment show' at the British Academy Film and Television Awards (BAFTA). Game shows, quiz shows and 'reality television' competitions are also rich sites for vernaculars. The rapid growth in public participation television and radio – growth both in the range of formats and in the number of shows – has brought 'ordinary people' more and more into performance roles, where regionally marked speech seems to offer a shortcut to establishing 'personality'.

Vernaculars are therefore more available nowadays through the mass media. They are unlikely to function as models for wholesale patterns of language change because of their sheer range and diversity. But the significance of these developments lies in how the media contextualise vernacular speech in new ways, more than in a simple increase in exposure. In children's television, for example, Dick and Dom's voices do not index 'Sheffield-ness' as much as a mildly anti-establishment stance and an 'edginess' of language and world-view that is felt to appeal to kids and to older people in popular culture genres. This new media aesthetic does not assume any continuity between regional provenance and stylistic meaning. Dick and Dom's speech seems to be important for being non-normative in canonical broadcasting, rather than for being 'Sheffield English'. In the phrase *Da Bungalow* there is certainly no link to African American or Afro-Caribbean history, nor to Rap culture, except in the most tenuous of senses (very mild anti-establishment). Returning to Michael Halliday's broad distinction between 'dialect' and 'register' (section 1.3), we can say that the new aesthetic disconnects register from dialect in the conventional sense. It is the current, local, performative 'use' of speech that matters and dialect provenance is subordinated to that concern.

Product marketing through television advertisements has contributed to this process of indexical fracturing. The model and television presenter Melanie Sykes featured in a popular British TV advertisement for Boddington's beer, whose trademark regional association was with Manchester. The ad set up a highly glamorous and seductive visual set, with Sykes and a male partner dressed in high-fashion clothes and about to have cocktails. The only spoken line in the ad was Sykes's punchline, *do you wanna flake in that, love?*, referring to his glass of Boddington's beer, said in a broad Manchester accent ([e:] in *flake*, glottal stop [ʔ] in *that*, [ʊ] in *love*). A 'flake' is a chocolate stick conventionally available in a type of soft ice-cream cone. A strange association is made between the creamy head on a glass of beer and soft ice cream. The ad constructs a transparent dissonance between high- and low-culture designs: drinking beer versus drinking cocktails; Manchester voice versus an implied posh way of speaking. The thrust of the ad is difficult to pin down. Perhaps it promotes the implication that Manchester voice and Manchester beer are able to fit into both low-culture and high-culture domains. More likely it is designed to make the northern-sounding brand-name *Boddington's* memorable and to both endorse and undermine the northernness/ parochialism of the product's identity.

The quotability/transportability of the linguistic slogan *do you wanna flake in that, love?* is a key feature. The ad's success was marked by how the slogan (of course including its north-of-England pronunciation) was picked up and recycled in other media contexts and in everyday playful speech. There are countless similar examples. A Budweiser beer advertising campaign, broadcast in at least ten versions, was a global success in English-speaking cultures based around the greeting slogan *wassup* ('what's up?', pronounced something like [wæ ss'æ :::], with a nasalised long final syllable and said vigorously with facial contortions). The formula quickly outstripped its apparent origins as an AAVE expression and was simply enjoyed as an eccentric but possibly 'cool' vocal stylisation. The ads self-reflexively modelled people picking up on the expression, which they did outside as well as inside the studio. The ad's director, Charles Stone III, and its performers, Fred Thomas Junior, Scott Brooks and Paul Williams, are reported to have gone on to lucrative new contracts and starring roles. More than two million people a month were reported to be using the Budweiser internet site to download the ads.

Contemporary TV comedy shows also selectively sloganise vernacular speech and create their own quotables. A strong contemporary example, again from the UK, is the antagonistic teenage girl character created by Catherine Tate in her BBC show, and slogans incorporating the word *bovvered*. This is a dialect rendition of 'bothered', with consistent TH-fronting, [ð] to [v]. Peter Trudgill calls TH-fronting 'a remarkable phenomenon' which was formerly confined to the London area and to Bristol but has rapidly spread across England (Trudgill 1999: 137–8). Tate's character uses *bovvered* in multiple phrases like the following, often chained together in long sequences of dismissive reaction to authority figures: *I ain't bovvered* (.) *am I*

*bovvered? (.) am I bovvered though? (.) look at the face (.) am I bovvered? (.) face
(.) bovvered? (.) face (.) bovvered? (.) does this face look bovvered to you? ask me if
I'm bovvered (.) d'you fink I'm bovvered? (.) I ain't bovvered.* The routine
swept through the UK, being picked up quotatively by younger and
some older people. The 'phenomenon', as Trudgill calls it, is thoroughly marketised. Posters, telephone ring-tones and other sorts of
internet downloads are available, recycling 'bovvered' phrases and
sequences. *The Sun* newspaper reported that the singer Kylie
Minogue, diagnosed with cancer, herself recycled Catherine Tate's
TV catchphrase, saying *I have cancer – am I bovvered?* School kids com-
peted to produce the most innovative and/or surreal utterances and
routines extrapolating from the TV source and they were sometimes
willing to perform them for sociolinguists. Here are two connected
versions.

Extract 6.8
1 am I bovvered? (.) I used to have a big bag o bovvered
2 [touches and tips out an imaginary bag] no (.) no bovvered (.)
3 see (.) no bovvered

Extract 6.9
1 [stylised thinking face and posture] ooh wait (.) let me check my bovvered
2 pocket [pats a pocket which fictionally sometimes contains 'bovvered']
3 nah (.) no fuckin bovvered there neiver

The sequence in Extract 6.8 incorporates syntactic play where *bovvered*
becomes a noun and has a material thing-ness that allows it to be
placed in a bag and its presence/absence assessed. Extract 6.9 extends
this by adding a fictional 'bovvered pocket'. (I am grateful to Ellie
Martin and Kate Foley for these examples.)

The stylising of accent/dialect/language sequences, plucked from
their putative community sources and dropped into local performance contexts, does identity work targeted at speakers themselves,
showing them to be witty, aware, creative, etc. Critical sociolinguists
nevertheless sometimes argue that damage is done to people who are
normatively associated with the use of linguistic varieties that are
pastiched and recycled in this way. In other words, they reject my
suggestion, above, that high performance tends to break the historical
link to communities of users. One of the strongest arguments along
these lines in Jane Hill's account of 'junk Spanish' (Hill 1995). Junk
Spanish is the use of lexical items and fixed expressions of Spanish-
language origin in US English and elsewhere. Hill is referring to
expressions such as *no problemo, head honcho, el cheapo, no way José* and

probably most (in)famously, *hasta la vista baby* as a precursor to violence in a Hollywood movie. Hill argues that, through these and similar expressions, the dignity of Spanish as a linguistic code is undermined and Spanish culture pejorated. In this analysis junk Spanish conjures up stereotypes and racist representations of Mexicans in particular. To that extent, Hill says, they should be considered a manifestation of 'Anglo-racism', indirectly indexing 'whiteness' as an unmarked normative order (Hill 1995, 1998).

If Spanish speakers feel demeaned by junk Spanish then there is clearly a charge to be answered, and the political processes are difficult to read from outside a relevant cultural ecosystem. In my own case for example, I have limited experience of cultures where Spanish speakers are regularly disadvantaged. But it is at least relevant to note that stylistic appropriation is an extremely common process (as we have seen in Chapter 5 and other sections of this chapter). It is *not inherently* a subordination of one group by another, or an assertion of linguistic rights over another group's language. Some of the linguistic transformations that Hill draws attention to, such as inappropriate morphology (*no problemo*) and mispronunciation of Spanish (using American English pronunciation in the same example) do not themselves constitute subordination. Stylised performance can achieve not only *parody* but also *metaparody*, and it is useful to clarify these concepts.

We talk of parody when a cultural form, practice or text is being actively discredited and when performers position themselves outside or above the forms, practices or texts that they represent (Hutcheon 1985, 1994; Kelly 1994; Morson 1989). Morson says that parody: (a) evokes or indicates another text; (b) is antithetical to that other text; and (c) is intended to have higher semantic authority than the original text. But metaparody lacks that third feature. Metaparody 'mock[s] not only a "target" text but also [speakers'] own superior reworking of that prior text' (Kelly 1994: 56; Morson 1989: 67). The effect of metaparodic representation is often that audiences laugh *with* rather than *at* performers' representations. This is very similar to Bakhtin's distinction between uni-directional and vari-directional double-voicing (Bakhtin 1981, Rampton 1995: 222–3, 299–300, and see section 4.5).

There are metaparodic uses of junk Spanish, which perhaps should not therefore be said to be being 'junked'. An example from a film source is the Dude character in the Cohen Brothers' film, *The Big Lebowski*. Dude is a post-hippy Californian named Jeff Lebowski. He prefers 'Dude' as a form of personal reference and address, as he explains in the film. He tells another character he wants to be called

'Dude', or 'The Dude', or 'Duder', 'or El Dudarino if you're not into the whole brevity thing'. What seems to be being mocked here is not Spanish but the practice of using mock or junk Spanish. For many UK speakers too, it is impossible to use junk Spanish without a degree of *self*-targeted mocking that one is dipping into a stylised and in fact rather tired and cliché d repertoire. Other instances, of the mocking of Spanish or of other languages and speakers, are much more clear-cut in their pejorative and racist intent. Maggie Ronkin and Helen Karn (1999) analyse 'mock Ebonics' (mock AAVE) as it is caricatured on some Internet sites. The 'mocking' in this case is clearly motivated to demean African Americans and AAVE. People who post 'mock Ebonics' online parody AAVE, however impausibly, by implying that it can be easily derived from 'standard' English by applying a simple set of lexical and grammatical rules. But also, the linguistic structure of the examples they construct is overlaid on unquestionably racist content.

These examples re-emphasise the importance of engaging with local contextualisation in its particular aspects. As we have moved away from models of community-based speech variation into performative arenas of linguistic styling, it has become increasingly unsafe to read social meaning on the basis of distributional facts alone. An account of style that relies on speakers of type X using variety Y in context Z is analytically far too sparse and ignores those contexualisation processes that I summarised in section 5.3, and then appealed to in later analyses. That is, our reading of the socio-political values and loadings of particular stylistic practices – as between *wassup*, *bovvered*, *El Dudarino*, mock Ebonics, etc. – is crucially dependent on contextual framings and keying. Basic structural and categorial models cannot entertain these considerations.

7 Coda: Style and social reality

7.1 CHANGE WITHIN CHANGE

The narrative of this book has been a movement away from one way of looking at linguistic variation towards another – in fact from one very particular, consolidated, disciplined and productive perspective to a much more open, critical but speculative perspective. As I said near the beginning of the book, the first conception of style in a socio-linguistic context was a variationist one, defining style as a simple plane of linear variation within the speech of a single person. As the book has progressed, reflecting changes over time in the sociolinguistic analysis of style, it has become less and less satisfactory to work with *any* simple definition of style. In relation to general and literary stylistics, Jean Jacques Weber summarises these priorities as follows:

> meaning and stylistic effect are not fixed and stable, and cannot be dug out of the text as in an archaeological approach, but they have to be seen as a potential which is actualized in a (real) reader's mind, the product of a dialogic interaction between author, the author's context of production, the text, the reader and the readers' context of reception – where context includes all sorts of sociohistorical, cultural and intertextual factors (Weber 1996b: 3).

If we substitute a more complex notion of 'participants' for 'reader' in the above quote, including speakers, listeners and analysts as parties engaged with and impacted by stylistic meaning, then Weber's sentence stands as a useful summary of what a sociolinguistic stylistics, as I have argued for it in the book, can aspire to be and do.

Sociolinguistic style has outgrown its conceptual origins. If we continue to use the term, it has to encompass the whole field of making social meaning through deploying and recontextualising linguistic resources. And in that formulation, social meaning is itself a complex phenomenon, not merely referring to simple indexical relationships between language forms and membership of social groups. This makes style seem like the whole of discourse, apart from the fact that, in my own treatment here, I have generally remained within the conventional bounds of accent/dialect resources and meanings made around them. Even then, it has been important to stress the artificiality of dislocating anything we might think of as 'dialect' from discourse, because social meanings made through dialect are thoroughly embedded in more general discursive and semiotic processes.

This book's narrative relates intimately to other narratives. The general narrative of sociolinguistics as a discipline over the last fifty years, much more widely than in respect of style alone, shows the same movement away from reliance on a confident structural sociology to a more tentative social theory of practice. Approaching styling as social practice has allowed us to see a much wider range of social meanings, designs and consequences than a structural stylistics could. But these gains have been traded against the security – undoubtedly a false security – of simple explanatory models of style-shifting and of social organisation. The interpretive world of social practice is messy, complex and contingent. It doesn't allow us to be satisfied with a generalised account of 'what most people stylistically do', and that ceases to be a compelling issue. The main rationale for a practice view is, however, that it has a better chance of articulating the lived social world of meaning-making through language. When the focus is on variable forms of speech, a practice perspective can show how variation is made meaningful in, and embedded in, social interaction, rather than just being an attribute of speakers or a group tendency. It can help us address the old sociolinguistic question of why variation exists. The most inclusive answer is that it exists to make social meaning in discourse.

But sociolinguistics, and the study of linguistic variation within it, doesn't just 'happen' to be living out this particular change narrative. Intellectual fashions, like most other domains of fashion, can certainly be self-sustaining, but the move towards a constructionist and critical sociolinguistics is not just fashion. It has been a case of structuralist models only taking us so far in their ability to explain data at hand. A high level of abstraction in the definition of social groups and contexts and in the quantitative analysis of speech (see Chapters 2 and 3) has protected variationist sociolinguistics from confronting its explanatory limitations. In the study of what was called 'stylistic variation' across contexts, as we saw in earlier chapters, context simply could not be adequately handled via a determinist structural taxonomy. Styling achieves more than the demarcation of pre-defined situations or gross sorts of relational stance. John Gumperz makes this same point about taxonomies of speech events and genres:

Anthropologists and folklorists concentrating on performance
discovered that more often than not events were not clearly bounded.
Rather, the participants' definition of what the relevant context is
'emerged' in and through the performance itself ... The analytic issue
therefore shifts from language choice or style as traditionally
conceived within sociolinguistics, to the question of how and by what
signalling devices language functions to evoke context (Gumperz
1996: 365).

The narrative is therefore also a narrative of problems in the applica-
tion of tightly specified theoretical and methodological principles to
discourse data, and a progressive need to achieve better accountability
to those data. This in turn relates to what the aims of sociolinguistic
inquiry are taken to be. For understanding linguistic change, where a
language is viewed top-down as a system of variation, there are more
specific and narrow criteria for what is an adequate account of speech
variation data. Those criteria are far too narrow when the aim is to
understand social identity work through variation, for example.

But another narrative is the historical narrative of social life itself in
the social environments that sociolinguistics is trying to understand. I
have touched on this theme at a couple of points in the book (see
section 1.6, in particular), and it is the main issue in this short final
chapter. The movement away from a structural account of language in
society is a reflection of how society itself has begun to move beyond
what we have understood by social structure. This is the argument
that language – and language variation, as this book's concern – have
come to do rather different work in contemporary social life, by
comparison with their function in the seemingly more ordered
world that Labovian sociolinguistics encountered and modelled.
Intellectual paradigms, like people, are products of their times. Two
main issues are worth revisiting.

The first is the idea of *authenticity* and its relation to language and
sociolinguistic performance. At least implicitly, sociolinguistics has
made strong assumptions about authentic speech and about the
authentic status of (some) speakers. Sociolinguistics has often
assumed it is dealing with 'real language'. (There has even been a
sociolinguistics book series called the *Real Language Series*, where the
title stakes a claim for the importance of non-idealised speech and
language as data.) But 'real language' is an increasingly uncertain
notion. In late-modern social arrangements and in performance
frames for talk, do we have to give up on authenticity? How does
style play with, and play out, authenticity? The second issue is *mediation*. An idea of this sort is at the heart of stylistic performance and

reflexivity. It is the idea that there is, we might say, some reflexive chamber within which social meanings are made and inferred. Late-modernity is an era strongly associated with semiotic mediation, although it is usually the mass media that are in question. How does the mediation of language affect the quality of our social experience?

7.2 THE AUTHENTIC SPEAKER

> The first duty in life is to be as artificial as possible. What the second duty is no-one has as yet discovered. (Wilde 1894/1970: 433; Coupland 2003: 417)

Oscar Wilde's epigram grabs our attention, firstly, because it asserts something counter-intuitive. Most of us value truthfulness, consistency, coherence, integrity and so on, and we judge other people and ourselves partly against criteria like these. At the same time, the epigram hints at a widespread position in contemporary social science (post-dating Wilde by many decades) that is radically sceptical about the feasibility of authentic experience. Language and discourse are often given as a reason for this scepticism, in the broad sweep of argument about the social construction of reality (Berger and Luckmann 1971). The fact that language mediates our approach to the world is often taken to be the reason why there can be no directly authentic experience (Belsey 2005; Bendix 1997). The epigram also makes us think of Oscar Wilde's own rationale for favouring personal artificiality. As a gay man in the public eye in an intolerant world, he found that displaying his 'authentic self' did him no favours. We begin to sense the politics around authenticity. But what is authenticity and what might we mean by 'an authentic speaker'? There have been interesting debates about authenticity and sincerity, including Paddy Scannell's (1996) theorising of 'sincere' television representations, Joanna Thornborrow and Theo van Leeuwen's (2001) collection of papers on authenticity in the mass media and Lionel Trilling's (1972) literary theory of sincerity. Although there is little overall consensus in these sources, let me suggest that there are five main qualities of authenticity.

The first is *ontology*, meaning that things we consider authentic have a real existence, as opposed to a spurious or derived existence. The second is *historicity*. Because they are not 'made to order', authentic things generally have longevity; they have survived. Many things we consider authentic are durable and even timeless. Martin Montgomery

(2001: 398) explains that the earliest systematic uses of the word 'authenticity' were in relation to written documents and quests to establish what was and what was not an original written documentary source. A third quality of authentic things is their *systemic coherence*. Authentic things are 'properly' constituted in significant contexts. In the example of written documents, an authentic text is not just an old one. It is likely to be 'historic' as well as 'historical'. It fits into some significant institution or system. For example, if a text is an important religious or literary text, it has a particular place in the meaning-system of religion. Fourthly, there needs to be a degree of *consensus* in judging something to be authentic. So authenticity relates to the process of authorisation and to a particular source of authority. The significance of declaring something to be an authentic object, such as a painting, is to put its identity beyond challenge based on some expert assessment. Fifthly and most obviously, an authentic object has *value*. Because authentic things are ratified in a culture, they have definite cultural value. They are anchoring points – things one can hold on to.

Using this elaboration of the idea of authenticity, perhaps we can see more clearly how social styles, including linguistic styles, have been considered to be either more or less authentic, from different points of view. I have used the term 'vernacular speech' throughout the book to refer to something like 'the ordinary speech of ordinary people', without intending the concept to carry any specific ideological implications. But it's clear that variationist sociolinguistics has taken an ideological stance in favour of vernaculars, and that it has assumed that vernaculars are authentic speech products. Vernacular authenticity is based in beliefs about ontology – how language 'really is', on the ground; how we find it to be when we seek it out 'in the community', and when we observe it empirically without influencing it (recall the observer's paradox). Vernaculars also have historicity. They are the product of natural (inherent but also socially motivated) linguistic change in community speech-norms over time. The idea of systemic coherence is there too – the orderliness of the 'speech community' has been a recurrent theme in variationism. So is consensus – in-group norms for speech being recycled in dense networks, and community members conspiring to generate sociolinguistic structure. Vernacular speech clearly has value for sociolinguists. Not only is vernacular speech thought to be an anchor for solidarity and local affiliation, but we study vernaculars because we think they are worthy cultural objects.

In contrast, variationist sociolinguistics has (at least implicitly) discredited 'standard' or establishment ways of speaking, partly because it has constructed them to be *in*authentic. William Labov treats 'standard' speech as imposed variety and as a deviation from real, natural, orderly vernaculars. So, as Rusty Barrett pointed out (see Chapter 6), black speakers in the USA who do not use the 'full' AAVE sociolinguistic system have at times been considered 'lames' or marginal people, culturally speaking. There has been the assumption that style-shifting in general is a movement away from the true vernacular system, where the orderliness and coherence of the vernacular breaks down. It is very likely that the low level of attention paid to style in variationist sociolinguistics reflects the feeling that style is where sociolinguistic authenticity starts to crumble, which might make it a less worthy topic for investigation. I hope to have resisted this assumption in this book.

In passing we can note that the elite establishment has in fact defended 'standard' ways of speaking using pretty much the same criteria that sociolinguistics have appealed to in the defence of vernaculars. It has constructed 'standard' varieties to be more ontologically real, historic, coherent, consensual and valuable – in short, as more authentic. I am not suggesting that the establishment ideology is correct or even *equally* correct – it is hygienist, exclusionary and illiberal. I am just pointing out that phrases like 'real language' and 'the authentic speaker' resonate just as strongly for the establishment as they do for sociolinguists, and that each 'side' has invested heavily in the ideology of authenticity, feeling that they 'have authenticity on their side'. This is why sociolinguists' attempts to engage politically on behalf of 'non-standard' speech have not been as successful as they have deserved to be. The potential for point-of-view clashes and for discourse without shared assumptions is striking.

But the main point is that, when we start to unpack the ideological politics of linguistic authenticity, we can't avoid seeing authenticity, in this field at least, as a discursive construction (Bucholtz and Hall 2004). Authenticity's trick is to convince us that it is an absolute quality of things and people in our social world, and we do seem to have to believe this. But to attribute authenticity to ways of speaking is to fail to see the process of iconisation at work (section 1.4). 'Standard' speech (which I have been resolutely quote-marking throughout the book) and vernacular speech (which I haven't) can *each* be constructed to be authentic, and by implication, we can accept *neither* as truly authentic. The analysis of style, particularly when we interpret styling in terms of performance and stylisation, is where we see behind the mask of authentic speakerhood. Speakers invoke voices that *have had* historic, consensual meanings and values, but, in performance, they break the semiotic chains that are the basis of their supposed authenticity.

This gives us a useful way to interpret the high performance stylisations we saw in Chapter 6. The various speakers we analysed there were engaged in 'not being themselves' and using stylistic resources *both* to index social identities *and* at the same time to mark the fact that these were not identities that they authentically owned or inhabited. John and Roy, for example, were performing the genre of 'Welsh gossip through English' in the curious context of a discourse about historical facts. They were reflexively 'mentioning' this genre practice more than 'using' it. They were *deauthenticating* themselves as speakers and *deauthenticating* the practice they were alluding to and stylising. As I suggested in section 6.2, stylisation is precisely a means of complicating ownership of voice. We can make the same claim about the pantomime Dame and the African American glam queens. In the case of stylistic 'junking', the interpretive problem is to decide whether it is the normative users of a linguistic variety (e.g. Mexican Spanish speakers) that are being deauthenticated (through parody), or whether the speakers are, also or instead, deauthenticating themselves (through metaparody).

Some extreme forms of self-deauthentication through speech styling have been reported. John Maher describes the idea of *metroethnicity* in Japan (Maher 2005). He describes metroethnicity as a form of individualistic self-assertion that reinterprets ethnically or socially-linked ways of speaking. It does not buy into the ideology of 'language loyalty'. It is adoptive and fundamentally anti-essentialist. Speakers adopt or value ways of speaking for their ephemeral meaning of 'cool' and not at all as an endorsement of historical cultural associations. Metroethnicity, Maher says, is sceptical of 'heroic ethnicity'. It is a deliberately shallow form of ethnic identification and treats ethnic or social allegiance as a fashion accessory. So Irishness can be considered cool in Japan. The German language may be uncool, but German-accented English can be very cool, and so on. This is an extension of the media-based transformation and commodification of traditional meanings and values for varieties that we discussed in Chapter 6. Mikhail Bakhtin wrote about 'speech genres' being 'the drive-belts from the history of society to the history of language' (Bakhtin 1986: 65). But late-modern life seems able to break those 'drive-belts' on occasions and establish quite different values for varieties. This is where stylistic practice becomes most like bricolage (Hebdige 1979; Eckert 2005). We find appropriated semiotic resources being recombined into new meaningful relations.

Stylistic operations are not, however, restricted to this 'deconstructive' work. Authenticity is not fully 'in crisis' in late-modernity even though it is harder to find. Styling can also work to *(re)authenticate* identities. In Chapter 6 I argued that the distancing effect of stylisation opens up new opportunities for rethinking how a community of practice orients to its indexical linguistic forms and varieties. The result is not a simple 'new authenticity' but a new footing for reassessing value, historicity, coherence and so on – the various qualities of authentic experience. So we can think of 'authenticity in performance', or the construction of *second-level authenticities*. Performers often 'earn' degrees of authenticity precisely through their disavowal of first-order authenticities. Indeed it is an interesting speculation that, in late-modernity, authenticity needs to be earned discursively rather than automatically credited.

7.3   THE MEDIA(TISA)TION OF STYLE

Variationist sociolinguists have been consistently hostile to the idea that mass media are a regular or important factor in triggering linguistic change. In his substantial volume on social factors in linguistic change, William Labov says that 'all of the evidence generated in this volume and elsewhere points to the conclusion that language is not systematically affected by the mass media, and is influenced primarily in face-to-face interaction with peers' (Labov 2001a: 228). In the present book we haven't been concerned with linguistic change itself, only with the social contextualisation of variation in discourse and the making of local meanings from sociolinguistic resources. As I have already argued, for the present agenda, it would be rash to ignore how mass media package up sociolinguistic resources (cf. Lippi-Green 1997). Mass media do generate some new sociolinguistic resources and these are sometimes used and developed in everyday practice, however short-lived the phenomena might be. We considered a few examples in section 6.6.

The theoretical importance of media-influenced styling is, firstly, that mass media are increasingly active and important in delivering our accent/dialect/variation experience. We experience linguistic variation, extensively, as much from mass media sources as from face-to-face encounters. Mass media are replete with diverse accents and dialects, formatted into an increasingly wide range of popular genres. Face-to-face encounters, Labov argues, provide potentially *intensive* experience of local linguistic varieties (in the sense that foreign language teaching regimes can aspire to being intensive), allowing people to engage deeply with them. But mass media can *also* deliver intensive and intense experiences. Listening and viewing technologies encourage repeated exposure to linguistic/stylistic forms, such as audio- and video-recorded music, talk and mixed-modality performances, for example in advertisements, ring-tones and computer downloads. Repeated listening to particular music tracks through headphones is probably the paradigmatic case of intense engagement with styled performance.

Popular TV sitcoms can foreground distinctive set-piece expressions, positioning them at key narrative moments in dramatic sequences. This a similar process to the commercial sloganising we discussed in section 6.6. Think, for example, of the Rachel character in the global hit TV series *Friends*, and Rachel's use of *so* in expressions such as *I am so:: going to marry that guy*. The use of *so* as an intensifier in previously disallowed linguistic contexts (in the above instance, in the middle of a multi-part verbal expression) was rapidly borrowed into youth speak in the UK and doubtless elsewhere. But also, mass media can construct new social meanings for linguistic varieties by embedding them in new discourse contexts and genres. In Chapter 6 we considered the example of (notionally) 'stigmatised' north-of-England accent varieties becoming cool by being associated with innovative and slightly subversive children's TV programming in Britain. The mass media certainly play an important role in reshaping the sociolinguistic environment, which is of course a matter of normalised attitudes and ideological meanings for language as well as a matter of how language forms and varieties themselves are distributed.

But some speech styles and styling, *outside* mass media use and borrowings from mass media, increasingly have the feel of mediated discourse. In defining high performance, following Richard Bauman (section 6.1), I suggested that performing *for* as well as *to* audiences was a key criterion. Although my examples of high performance in Chapter 6 were mostly from focused and institutionalised speech events, I also argued that the high performance and (ordinary) performance are matters of degree rather than clearly distinct categories. 'Ordinary performance', if we take that to refer to set of styling conventions for face-to-face talk in everday settings, is still performance, and the various types of focusing that I listed are often detectable here too. Sociolinguistics has often treated its own empirical research settings as if they were platforms for speakers to produce 'everyday speech behaviour' rather than stages for performance. The classical sociolinguistic interview is a case in point, where devices used to trigger 'casual speech' (see Chapter 2) might be better described as stage-building for narrative performance. It is not surprising that some of the most influential early studies of style variation used data from social situations where people were, in one way or another, positioned as audiences receiving, in one sense or another, broadcast talk. (See Allan Bell's New Zealand radio newsreaders and the public domain elements of Sue's talk in the travel agency in my own research, Chapter 3.)

Correspondingly, sociolinguistics has often treated form-focused performance features of discourse as if they were 'ordinary' sociolinguistic variables. The best example is research on *be + like* as a quotative form, as in *she's sitting there and she's like 'oh my god!' (.) she's like 'that's your boyfriend?' (.) and I'm like 'yeah'* (re-transcribed from Tagliamonte and D'Arcy 2004: 493). The resource of *be + like* can be called 'quotative' because it is one way of introducing quoted or pseudo-quoted speech into a discourse. The feature has been diffusing vigorously through English varieties world-wide over the last twenty years. Sali Tagliamonte and Alex D'Arcy say the form is generally restricted to speakers between the ages of 15 and 35 and is favoured by girls and women. It is used most frequently in first-person contexts (*I was like 'give it back!'*) and, in recent years, it has mainly been used when 'quoting' non-lexicalised sounds (*every five seconds he's like [panting noise]*) and internal thoughts (*I was like 'this is bad news for me'*) (2004: 495, 509). (See also Tagliamonte and Hudson 1999; Dailey-O'Cain 2000.)

As Tagliamonte and D'Arcy say, these generalisations about social distribution help capture the pragmatic flavour of *be + like*. They show that younger speakers, particularly females, are coming to use *I'm like* apparently in preference to the 'standard' quotative *say* and to favour some particular 'contents of the quote' such as non-lexicalised sounds. But in another sense one could say that these speakers are ceasing to do 'reported speech' (which is the conventional analysis of *say + quote*). They are coming to do more performative utterance, including putting fabricated/reconstructed 'thoughts' and emotional expressive tokens in to their speaking. Survey-oriented sociolinguistic studies are picking up details of speakers' voicing practices, but rather obscuring the framing and keying designs that define these ways of speaking as identity performances. The superordinate phrase 'the quotative system' is necessary in order to locate the research within the variationist paradigm, where (see Chapter 2) we have to establish variants as being 'different ways of saying the same thing'.

Yet the discursive frames in which *be + like* become stylistically active are mediated ones. Performative voicing is done by distancing oneself as an animator of voices from the voices animated. Even in the first-person format, there is a separation of the animating self (the 'I' in the here and now of speaking) from the 'quoted' self (the 'I' at the moment and in the context of the earlier utterance). The animating self is therefore positioned as a potential audience to his/her own voiced utterance. Non-lexicalised emotional reactions to circumstances are not simply one set of 'contents of a quote'. They are elements of form-focused performance *for an audience*, where an emotion is styled and dramatised, and where an interpretive outcome is anticipated. Speech is disembedded from its immediate interactional context and held up for scrutiny – the micro-pause before a non-lexicalised sound is often a dramatic latency. These are, once again, the frames we have been associating with high performance and stylisation.

Ron Scollon considers mediation to be a quality of *all* spoken interaction. Similarly to Erving Goffman, he points to a speaker's awareness of the 'other' as an observer of the social action s/he is performing, and to how 'the identities imputed and claimed, negotiated and contested are constructed in part as a spectacle or pose for the observation of others' (Scollon 1998: 124). Of course there are particular social moments and genres where this sort of 'posing' is very clearly in evidence. Scollon analyses the distribution of handbills on the street or buying newspapers from news stands. These are public events where a social actor's demeanour and normative practice are on display and available for evaluation. We might think that mediation, in Scollon's sense, is therefore a special case and not a general quality of interaction. In the *be + like* instance, we might similarly argue that performance voicing is a routine that only certain social groups adopt on certain occasions.

On the other hand, there is a steady accumulation of domains and instances in contemporary life where the mediated quality of talk is discernible. Mobile phone and messaging technologies require people to represent themselves and their meanings with economy and aesthetic appeal. Spoken and textualised routines develop, in the context of reflexivity about communicative forms and designs and about identities. Communicative competence includes reflexive management of mediated self-identities and relationships in the use of new technologies. Ben Rampton has analysed how media-derived expressive forms, such as popular music and advertisement jingles, intrude into the ordinary sociolinguistic practices of school kids in the UK (Rampton 2006, Chapter 3). Deborah Cameron analyses how call centre workers – a group that epitomises workers in the new globalising economy of late-modernity – are subject to being scripted. They have preferred ways of speaking imposed on them (Cameron 2000, 2005). Cameron says this is often a symbolically feminised style, based on co-operation, nurturance, empathy and emotional expressiveness. These stylistic designs are again mediated, in the sense that they are pre-planned to have specific relational effects, but also of course in the more literal sense that they are formulaic stylistic projections designed to build relationships across large distances.

The compression of time and space that Anthony Giddens associates with late-modernity therefore impacts quite generally on communicative style. Mediated forms of language knowingly evoke much of the intimacy we have in the past associated with private rather than public domains of experience, and the division between these domains is being blurred. There are increasing demands for self-styling – the stylistic projection of an attractive individuated self, and particular stylistic projections (like the feminised intimate-in-public identity) have new economic value. The concept of mediation captures not only some aspects of the formal features of new ways of speaking but something of the generic design principles for contemporary social interaction. The future agenda for sociolinguistic stylistics should be to analyse the social conditions in which ways of speaking come to be naturalised or demanded of speakers. This gives us a final reason to argue – although I hope the argument has already been naturalised in this book – that 'style' is an indispensable and core part of the sociolinguistic programme.

References

Agar, M. (1991) The biculture in bilingual. *Language in Society* 20, 2: 167–82.

Alladina, Safder and Viv Edwards (eds.) (1990–1991) *Multilingualism in the British Isles*. London: Longman.

Anderson, Benedict (1983) *Imagined Communities: Reflections on the Origin and Spead of Nationalism*. London: Verso.

Androutsopoulos, Jannis (ed.) (2006) *Sociolinguistics and Computer-Mediated Communication*. (Thematic issue of *Journal of Sociolinguistics*, Volume 10, Issue 3.).

Antaki, C. and S. Widdicombe (eds.) (1998) *Identities in Talk*. London: Sage.

Auer, Peter and Frans Hinskens (2005) The role of interpersonal accommodation in a theory of language change. In Peter Auer, Frans Hinskens and Paul Kerswill (eds.) *Dialect Change: The Convergence and Divergence of Dialects in Contemporary Societies*. Cambridge: Cambridge University Press, pp. 335–57.

Austin. J. L. (1962) *How to Do Things with Words*. Cambridge: Harvard UP (Second edition 1975). Reprinted in Adam Jaworski and Nikolas Coupland (2006) *The Discourse Reader*. London: Routledge.

Bakhtin, Mikhail (1968) *Rabelais and his World*. Cambridge, Mass.: MIT Press.

(1981) *The Dialogic Imagination* (edited by M. Holquist and translated by C. Emerson & M. Holquist). Austin: University of Texas Press.

(1986) *Speech Genres and Other Late Essays* (Translated by Vern W. McGee and edited by Caryl Emerson and Michael Holquist). Austin: University of Texas Press.

Barrett, Rusty (1999) Indexing polyphonous identity in the speech of African American drag queens. In Mary Bucholtz, A. C. Liang and Laurel L. Sutton (eds.) *Reinventing Identities: The Gendered Self in Discourse*. New York and Oxford: Oxford University Press, pp. 313–31.

Barth, Frederik (1969) (ed.) *Ethnic Groups and Boundaries: The Social Organisation of Culture Difference*. Oslo: Universietsforlaget.

(1981) *Process and Form in Social Life: Collected Essays of Frederik Barth*, Vol.1. London: Routledge and Kegan Paul.

Baugh, John (1979) Linguistic style-shifting in Black English. PhD dissertation, University of Pennsylvania.

(1983) *Black Street Speech: Its History, Structure and Survival*. Austin: University of Texas Press.

Bauman, Richard (1977) *Verbal Art as Performance*. Prospect Heights, Ill.: Waveland Press.

(1992) Performance. In Richard Bauman (ed.) *Folklore, Cultural Performances, and Popular Entertainments*. New York and Oxford: Oxford University Press, pp. 41–9.

(1996) Transformations of the word in the production of Mexican festival drama. In Michael Silverstein and Greg Urban (eds.) *Natural Histories of Discourse*. Chicago and London: University of Chicago Press, pp. 301–27.

Bauman, Richard and Charles Briggs (1990) Poetics and performance as critical perspectives on language and social life. *Annual Review of Anthropology* 19: 59–88.

Bauman, Richard and Joel Sherzer (eds.) (1989) *Explorations in the Ethnography of Speaking*. Cambridge: Cambridge University Press.

Bayley, Robert (2004) The quantitative paradigm. In J. K. Chambers, Peter Trudgill and Natalie Schilling-Estes (eds.) *The Handbook of Language Variation and Change*. Oxford: Blackwell Publishing, pp. 117–41.

Beck, Ulrich (1992) *Risk Society: Towards a New Modernity*. London: Sage.

Beck, Ulrich, Anthony Giddens and Scott Lash (1996) *Reflexive Modernization: Politics, Tradition and Aesthetics in the Modern Social Order*. Cambridge: Polity Press.

Bell, Allan (1984) Language style as audience design. *Language in Society* 13: 145–204.

(1992) Hit and miss: Referee design in the dialects of New Zealand television advertising. *Language and Communication* 12: 327–40.

(1999) Styling the other to define the self: A study in New Zealand identity making. *Journal of Sociolinguistics* 3, 4: 523–41.

(2001) Back in style: Reworking audience design. In Penelope Eckert and John R. Rickford (eds.) *Style and Sociolinguistic Variation*. Cambridge and New York: Cambridge University Press, pp. 139–69.

Belsey, Catherne (2005) *Culture and the Real*. London: Routledge.

Bendix, Regina (1997) *In Search of Authenticity: The Formation of Folklore Studies*. Madison: University of Wisconsin Press.

Berger, P. and T. Luckmann (1971) *The Social Construction of Reality*. Harmondsworth: Penguin.

Bernstein, Basil (1971–1990) *Class, Codes and Control*, 4 Volumes. London: Routledge and Kegan Paul.

(1996) *Pedagogy, Symbolic Control and Identity: Theory, Research, Critique*. London: Taylor and Francis.

Bhabha, Homi (1994) *The Location of Culture*. London: Routledge.

Bishop, Hywel, Nikolas Coupland and Peter Garrett (2005) Conceptual accent evaluation: Thirty years of accent prejudice in the UK. *Acta Linguistica Havniensia* 37: 131–54.

Blom, Jan-Petter and John Gumperz (1972) Social meaning in linguistic structures: Code-switching in Norway. In John Gumperz and Dell Hymes (eds) *Directions in Sociolinguistics: The Ethnography of Communication.* Oxford: Basil Blackwell, pp. 407–434.

Blommaert, Jan (1999) *Language Ideological Debates.* Berlin: de Gruyter.

(2005) *Discourse.* Cambridge: Cambridge University Press.

Bourdieu, Pierre (1977) *Outline of a Theory of Practice.* Cambridge: Cambridge University Press.

(1984) *Distinction: A Social Critique of the Judgement of Taste* (Translated by R. Nice). London: Routledge.

(1991) *Language and Symbolic Power.* Cambridge: Polity Press.

Bourhis, Richard Y. and Howard Giles (1977) The language of intergroup distinctiveness. In Howard Giles (ed.) *Language, Ethnicity and Intergroup Relations.* London: Academic Press, pp. 119–35.

Britain, David (1992) Linguistic change in intonation: The use of High Rising Terminals in New Zealand English. *Language Variation and Change* 4, 1: 77–104.

Brown, Penelope and Stephen Levinson (1987) *Politeness: Some Universals of Language Use.* Cambridge: Cambridge University Press.

Brown, Roger and M. Ford (1961) Address in American English. *Journal of Abnormal and Social Psychology* 62: 375–85. Also appears in J. Laver and S. Hutcheson (eds.) (1972) *Communication in Face to face Interaction.* Harmondsworth: Penguin Books.

Brown, Roger and A. Gilman (1960) The pronouns of power and solidarity. In T. A. Sebeok (ed.) *Style in Language.* Cambridge, Mass.: MIT Press, pp. 253–77.

Bucholtz, Mary (1999a) 'Why be normal?' Language and identity practices in a community of nerd girls. *Language in Society* 28: 203–223.

(1999b) 'You da man': Narrating the racial other in the production of white masculinity. *Journal of Sociolinguistics* 3, 4: 443–60.

(2003) Sociolinguistic nostalgia and the authentication of experience. *Journal of Sociolinguistics* 7, 398–416.

Bucholtz, Mary and Kira Hall (2004) Theorizing identity in language and sexuality research. *Language in Society* 33: 469–515.

Bühler, Karl (1934) *Sprachtheorie.* Jena: Fischer.

Butler, Judith (1997) *Excitable Speech: A Politics of the Performative.* New York and London: Routledge.

Cameron, Deborah (1990) De-mythologising sociolinguistics: Why language does not reflect society. In John Joseph and Talbot Taylor (eds.) *Ideologies of Language.* London: Routledge, pp. 79–93.

(1995) *Verbal Hygiene.* London: Routledge.

(2000) Styling the worker: Gender and the commodification of language in the globalized service economy. *Journal of Sociolinguistics* 4, 3: 323–47.

(2005) Language, gender and sexuality: Current issues and new directions. *Applied Linguistics* 26, 4: 482–502.

Cameron, Deborah and Don Kulick (2003) *Language and Sexuality*. Cambridge: Cambridge University Press.

Chambers, J. K. (1995) *Sociolinguistic Theory: Linguistic Variation and its Social Significance* (Second edition 2003). Oxford: Blackwell.

(2004) Studying language variation: An informal epistemology. In J. K. Chambers, Peter Trudgill and Natalie Schilling-Estes (eds.) *The Handbook of Language Variation and Change*. Oxford: Blackwell Publishing, pp. 3–14.

Chambers, J. K. and Peter Trudgill (1999) *Dialectology*. Cambridge: Cambridge University Press.

Chambers, J. K., Peter Trudgill and Natalie Schilling-Estes (eds.) (2004) *The Handbook of Language Variation and Change*. Oxford: Blackwell Publishing.

Cheshire, Jenny (1998) Linguistic variation and social function. In Jennifer Coates (ed.) *Language and Gender: A Reader*. Blackwell: Oxford, pp. 29–41.

(2000) The telling or the tale? Narratives and gender in adolescent friendship networks. *Journal of Sociolinguistics* 4, 2: 234–62.

(2004) Sex and gender in variationist research. In J. K. Chambers, Peter Trudgill and Natalie Schilling-Estes (eds.) *The Handbook of Language Variation and Change*. Oxford: Blackwell Publishing, pp. 423–43.

Clark, Herbert H. (1993) *Arenas of Language Use*. Chicago: University of Chicago Press.

Coates, Jennifer (2003) *Men Talk: Stories in the Making of Masculinities*. Oxford: Blackwell.

(2004) *Women, Men and Language* (Third edition). London: Pearson Longman.

Coupland, Justine (ed.) (2000) *Small Talk*. London: Longman.

Coupland, Justine, Nikolas Coupland and Jeffrey D. Robinson (1992) 'How are you?': Negotiating phatic communion. *Language in Society* 21: 207–230.

Coupland, Nikolas (1980) Style-shifting in a Cardiff work setting. *Language in Society* 9: 1–12.

(1984) Accommodation at work: Some phonological data and their implications. *International Journal of the Sociology of Language* 46: 49–70.

(1985) 'Hark, hark the lark': Social motivations for phonological style-shifting. *Language and Communication* 5: 153–72.

(1988) *Dialect in Use: Sociolinguistic Variation in Cardiff English*. Cardiff: University of Wales Press.

(1995). Pronunciation and the rich points of culture. In J. Windsor Lewis (ed.) *Studies in English and General Phonetics: In Honour of Professor J. D. O'Connor*. London: Routledge, pp. 310–19.

(2000a) 'Other' representation. In Jef Verschueren, Jan-Ola Ostman, Jan Blommaert and Chris Bulcaen *Handbook of Pragmatics: Instalment 2000.* Amsterdam & Philadelphia: John Benjamins Publishing Co.

(2000b) Sociolinguistic prevarication over standard English. Review article of Tony Bex and Richard J. Watts (eds.) (1999) *Standard English: The Widening Debate. Journal of Sociolinguistics* 4, 4: 630–42.

(2001a) Introduction: Sociolinguistic theory and social theory. In N. Coupland, S. Sarangi and C. N. Candlin (eds.) *Sociolinguistics and Social Theory.* London: Longman/Pearson Education, pp. 1–26.

(2001b). Language, situation and the relational self: Theorising dialect style in sociolinguistics. In Penelope Eckert and John R. Rickford, (eds.) *Style and Sociolinguistic Variation.* Cambridge and New York: Cambridge University Press, pp. 185–210.

(2001c) Dialect stylisation in radio talk. *Language in Society* 30: 345–75.

(2001d) Age in social and sociolinguistic theory. In Nikolas Coupland, Srikant Sarangi and Christopher N. Candlin (eds.) *Sociolinguistics and Social Theory.* London: Longman, pp. 185–211.

(2003) Sociolinguistic authenticities. *Journal of Sociolinguistics* 7: 417–31.

(in pressa) The discursive framing of phonological acts of identity: Welshness through English. In Catherine Evans Davies, Janina Brutt-Griffler and Lucy Pickering (eds.) *English and Ethnicity.* London: Palgrave.

(in pressb) Aneurin Bevan, class wars and the styling of political antagonism. In P. Auer (ed.) *Social Identity and Communicative Styles: An Alternative Approach to Variability in Language.* Berlin: Moutande Gruyter.

(in pressc) 'Hark hark the Lark': Multiple voicing in DJ talk. In D. Graddol, D. Leith, J. Swann, M. Rhys & J. Gillen (eds.) *Changing English.* London: Routledge in association with the Open University.

Coupland, Nikolas and Hywel Bishop (2007) Ideologised values for British accents. *Journal of Sociolinguistics* 10, 5:.

Coupland, Nikolas, Hywel Bishop, Betsy Evans and Peter Garrett (2006) Imagining Wales and the Welsh language: Ethnolinguistic subjectivities and demographic flow. *Journal of Language and Social Psychology* 25, 4: 351–76.

Coupland, Nikolas, Hywel Bishop and Peter Garrett (2003) Home truths: Globalisation and the iconisation of Welsh in a Welsh-American newspaper. *Journal of Multilingual and Multicultural Development* 24, 3: 153–77.

Coupland, Nikolas, Justine Coupland and Howard Giles (1991) *Language, Society and the Elderly: Discourse, Identity and Ageing.* Oxford: Blackwell.

Coupland, Nikolas, Justine Coupland, Howard Giles and Karen Henwood (1988) Accommodating the elderly: Invoking and extending a theory. *Language in Society* 17, 2: 1–42.

Coupland, Nikolas, Peter Garrett and Angie Williams (2005) Narrative demands, cultural performance and evaluation: Teenage boys' stories for their age-peers. In Joanna Thornborrow and Jen Coates (eds.) *Sociolinguistics of Narrative*. Amsterdam/Philadelphia: John Benjamins, pp. 67–88.

Coupland, Nikolas and Howard Giles (eds.) (1988) *Communicative Accommodation: Recent Developments*. (Double special issue of *Language and Communication*, Vol. 8, 3/4.)

Coupland, Nikolas and Adam Jaworski (2004) Sociolinguistic perspectives on metalanguage: Reflexivity, evaluation and ideology. In Adam Jaworski, Nikolas Coupland and Dariusz Galasiński (eds.) *Metalanguage: Social and Ideological Perspectives*. Berlin and New York: Mouton de Gruyter, pp. 15–52.

Coupland, Nikolas, Srikant Sarangi and Christopher N. Candlin (eds.) (2001) *Sociolinguistics and Social Theory*. London: Longman.

Cukor-Avila, Patricia and Guy Bailey (2001) The effects of the race of the interviewer on sociolinguistic fieldwork. *Journal of Sociolinguistics* 5: 254–70.

Cutler, Cecilia A. (1999) Yorkville crossing: White teens, hip hop, and African American English. *Journal of Sociolinguistics* 3, 4: 428–42.

Dailey-O'Cain, Jennifer (2000) The sociolinguistic distribution of and attitudes toward focuser *like* and quotative *like*. *Journal of Sociolinguistics* 4: 60–80.

Dickey, E. (1997) Forms of address and terms of reference. *Journal of Linguistics* 33: 225–74.

Douglas-Cowie, Ellen (1978) Linguistic code-switching in a Northern Irish village: Social interaction and social ambition. In Peter Trudgill (ed.) *Sociolinguistic Patterns in British English*. London: Edward Arnold, pp. 37–51.

Downes, William (1998) *Language and Society* (Second edition). Cambridge: Cambridge University Press.

Duranti, Alessandro (1997) *Linguistic Anthropology*. Cambridge: Cambridge University Press.

Eastman, Carol M. and Roberta F. Stein (1993). Language display: Authenticating claims to social identity. *Journal of Multilingual and Multicultural Development* 14, 3: 187–202.

Eckert, Penelope (2000). *Linguistic Variation as Social Practice*. Maldon, Mass. and Oxford: Blackwell Publishers.

  (2001) Style and social meaning. In P. Eckert and J. Rickford (eds.) *Style and Sociolinguistic Variation*. Cambridge: Cambridge University Press, pp. 119–26.

(2002) Demystifying sexuality and desire. In Kathryn Campbell-Kibler, Robert J. Podesva, Sarah Roberts and Andrew Wong (eds.) *Language and Sexuality: Contesting Meaning in Theory and Practice*. Stanford: CSLI Publications, pp. 99–110.

(2003) Elephants in the room. *Journal of Sociolinguistics* 7, 3: 392–7.

(2004) Variation and a sense of place. In Carmen Fought (ed.) *Sociolinguistic Variation: Critical Perspectives*. New York: Oxford University Press, pp. 107–118.

(2005) Stylistic practice and the adolescent social order. In Angie Williams and Crispin Thurlow (eds.) *Talking Adolescence: Perspectives on Communication in the Teenage Years*. New York: Peter Lang, pp. 93–110.

Eckert, Penelope and Sally McConell-Ginet (1992) Think practically and look locally: Language and gender as community-based practice. *Annual Review of Anthropology* 21: 461–90.

Eckert, Penelope and John Rickford (eds.) (2001) *Style and Sociolinguistic Variation*. Cambridge: Cambridge University Press.

Eggins, Suzanne and J. R. Martin (1997) Genre and registers of discourse. In Teun A. van Dijk (ed.) *Discourse Studies: A Multidisciplinary Introduction*, Vol. 1, *Discourse as Structure and Process*. Thousand Oaks, Calif.: Sage, pp. 230–56.

Ervin-Tripp, Susan (1973) *Language Acquisition and Communicative Choice*. Stanford: Stanford University Press.

Fairclough, Norman (1992a) Introduction. In N. Fairclough (ed.) *Critical Language Awareness*. London: Longman, pp. 1–29.

(1992b) The appropriacy of appropriateness. In N. Fairclough (ed.) *Critical Language Awareness*. London: Longman, pp. 33–56.

(1995a) *Media Discourse*. London: Edward Arnold.

(1995b) *Critical Discourse Analysis*. London: Longman.

Feagin, Crawford (2004) Entering the community: Fieldwork. In J. K. Chambers, Peter Trudgill and Natalie Schilling-Estes (eds.) *The Handbook of Language Variation and Change*. Oxford: Blackwell Publishing, pp. 20–39.

Ferguson, Charles A (1996) *Socio-linguistic Perspectives: Papers on Language in Society, 1959–1994*. New York and Oxford: Oxford University Press.

Figueroa, Esther (1994) *Sociolinguistic Metatheory*. Oxford: Pergamon Press.

Firth, John R. (1957) *Papers in Linguistics 1934–1951*. London: Oxford.

Foucault, Michel (1984) The order of discourse. In M. Shapiro (ed.) *Language and Politics*. New York: New York University Press, pp. 108–138.

Foulkes, Paul and Gerard Docherty (1999) Urban Voices – overview. In Paul Foulkes and Gerard Docherty (eds.) *Urban Voices: Accent Studies in the British Isles*. London: Arnold, pp. 1–24.

Gal, Susan and Judith Irvine (1995) The boundaries of languages and disciplines: How ideologies construct difference. *Social Research* 62: 967–1001.

Garrett, Peter (forthcoming) *Language Attitudes*. Cambridge: Cambridge University Press.

Garrett, Peter, Nikolas Coupland and Angie Williams (1999) Evaluating dialect in discourse: Teachers' and teenagers' responses to young English speakers in Wales. *Language in Society* 28: 321–54.

(2003) *Investigating Language Attitudes: Social Meanings of Dialect, Ethnicity and Performance*. Cardiff: University of Wales Press.

(2004) Adolescents' lexical repertoires of peer evaluation: 'Boring prats' and 'English snobs'. In Adam Jaworski, Nikolas Coupland and Darius Galasinski (eds.) *Metalanguage: Social and Ideological Perspectives*. The Hague: Mouton, pp. 193–225.

Genessee, F. and R. Y. Bourhis (1988) Evaluative reactions to language choice strategies: The role of sociostructural factors. *Language and Communication* 8: 229–50.

Giddens, Anthony (1984) *The Constitution of Society*. Cambridge: Polity.

(1991) *Modernity and Self-identity: Self and Society in the Late Modern Age*. Cambridge: Polity Press (in association with Basil Blackwell).

(1996) Living in a post-traditional society. In Ulrich Beck, Anthony Giddens and Scott Lash, *Reflexive Modernization: Politics, Tradition and Aesthetics in the Modern Social Order*. Cambridge: Polity Press, pp. 56–109.

(2002) *Runaway World: How Globalisation is Shaping our Lives*. London: Profile Books.

Giles, Howard (1973) Accent mobility: A model and some data. *Anthropological Linguistics* 15: 87–105.

(2001) Couplandia and beyond. In Eckert and Rickford. *Style and Sociolinguistic Variation*. Cambridge: Cambridge University Press, pp. 211–19.

Giles, Howard, Justine Coupland and Nikolas Coupland (eds.) (1991) *Contexts of Accommodation: Developments in Applied Sociolinguistics*. Cambridge: Cambridge University Press.

Giles, Howard and Nikolas Coupland (1991) *Language: Contexts and Consequences*. Milton Keynes: Open University Press.

Giles, Howard and Patricia Johnson (1981) The role of language in ethnic group relations. In John C. Turner and Howard Giles (eds.) *Intergroup Behaviour*. Oxford: Blackwell, pp. 199–243.

Giles, Howard and Peter Powesland (1975) *Speech Style and Social Evaluation*. London: Academic Press.

Goffman, Erving (1959) *The Presentation of Self in Everyday Life*. New York: Doubleday.

(1971) *Relations in Public*. London: Allen Lane.

(1974) *Frame Analysis*. Harmondsworth: Penguin.

(1981). *Forms of Talk*. Oxford: Blackwell.

Gregory, Michael and Suzanne Carroll (1978) *Language and Situation: Language Varieties and their Social Contexts*. London: Routledge and Kegan Paul.

Gumperz, John J. (1982) *Discourse Strategies*. Cambridge: Cambridge University Press.

(1996) Introduction to Part I. In John J. Gumperz and Stephen C. Levinson (eds.) *Rethinking Linguistic Relativity*. Cambridge: Cambridge University Press, pp. 359–73.

Gumperz, John J. and Dell Hymes (eds.) (1972) *Directions in Sociolinguistics: The Ethnography of Communication*. New York: Holt, Rinehart and Winston.

Hall, Stuart (1996) Introduction: Who needs 'identity'? In Stuart Hall and Paul du Gay (eds.) *Questions of Cultural Identity*. London: Sage, pp. 1–17.

Halliday, M. A. K. (1978) *Language as Social Semiotic: The Social Interpretation of Language and Meaning*. London: Edward Arnold.

(1996) Linguistic function and literary style: An inquiry into the language of William Golding's *The Inheritors*. In Jean Jacques Weber (ed.) *The Stylistics Reader: From Roman Jabobson to the Present*. London: Arnold, pp. 56–91.

Hammersley, Martyn and Paul Atkinson (1995) *Ethnography: Principles in Practice* (Second edition). London: Routledge.

Hanks, William F. (1996) Exorcism and the description of participant roles. In Michael Silverstein and Greg Urban (eds.) *Natural Histories of Discourse*. Chicago and London: University of Chicago Press, pp. 160–200.

Hannerz, Ulf (1996) *Transnational Connections*. London: Routledge.

Hasan, Ruqaia (1996) *Ways of Saying: Ways of Meaning*. London: Cassell.

Hebdige, Dick (1979). *Subculture: The Meaning of Style*. London: Methuen.

Hewitt, Roger (1986) *White Talk Black Talk; Inter-racial Friendship and Communication Amongst Adolescents*. Cambridge: Cambridge University Press.

Hewstone, Miles and H. Howard Giles (1986) Social groups and social stereotypes in intergroup communication: A review and model of intergroup communication breakdown. In William B. Gudykunst (ed.) *Intergroup Communication*. Baltimore: Edward Arnold, pp. 10–26.

Hill, Jane H. (1995) Junk Spanish, covert racism, and the (leaky) boundary between public and private spheres. *Pragmatics* 5: 197–212.

(1998) Language, race and white public space. *American Anthropologist* 100, 3: 680–89.

Hill, Jane H. and Kenneth Hill (1986). *Speaking Mexicano*. Tucson: University of Arizona Press.

Hill, Jane H. and Judith T. Irvine (eds.) (1993) *Responsibility and Evidence in Oral Discourse*. Cambridge: Cambridge University Press.

Hinskens, Frans, Peter Auer and Paul Kerswill (2005) Introduction: The study of dialect convergence and divergence – conceptual and methodological considerations. In Peter Auer, Frans Hinskens and Paul Kerswill (eds.) *Dialect Change: Convergence and Divergence in European Languages*. Cambridge: Cambridge University Press, pp. 1–48.

Holmes, Janet (1994) New Zealand flappers: An analysis of T Voicing in New Zealand English. *English World-Wide* 15, 2: 195–224.

(1997) Setting new standards: Sound changes and gender in New Zealand English. *English World-Wide* 18, 1: 107–142.

Holmes, Janet and Miriam Meyerhoff (1999) The community of practice: Theories and methodologies in language and gender research. *Language in Society* 28: 173–83.

Hutcheon, Linda (1985) *A Theory of Parody*. New York: Methuen.

(1994) *Irony's Edge: The Theory and Politics of Irony*. London: Routledge.

Hymes, Dell (1962) The ethnography of speaking. In T. Gladwin and W. C. Sturtevant (eds.) *Anthropology and Human Behaviour*. Washington: Anthropological Society of Washington, pp. 15–53.

(1964) Toward ethnographies of communication. In John J. Gumperz and Dell Hymes (eds.) *The Ethnography of Communication*. Washington DC: *American Anthropologist* (Special Issue), pp. 1–34.

(1972). Models of the interaction of language and social life. In John J. Gumperz and Dell Hymes (eds.) *Directions in Sociolinguistics*. New York: Holt, Rinehart and Winston, pp. 35–71.

(1974) *Foundations in Sociolinguistics: An Ethnographic Approach*. Philadelphia: University of Pennsylvania Press.

(1975) Breakthrough into performance. In Dan Ben-Amos and Kenneth S. Goldstein (eds.) *Folklore: Performance and Communication*. The Hague: Mouton.

(1996) *Ethnography, Linguistics, Narrative Inequality: Toward an Understanding of Voice*. London: Taylor and Francis.

Irvine, Judith T. (1996). Shadow conversations: The indeterminacy of participant roles. In Michael Silverstein and Greg Urban (eds.) *Natural Histories of Discourse*. Chicago and London: University of Chicago Press, pp. 131–59.

(2001) 'Style' as distinctiveness: The culture and ideology of linguistic differentiation. In Penelope Eckert and John R. Rickford (eds.) *Style and Sociolinguistic Variation*. Cambridge and New York: Cambridge University Press, pp. 21–43.

Jakobson, Roman (1960) Concluding statement: Linguistics and poetics. In T. A. Sebeok (ed.) *Style in Language*. Cambridge, Mass.: MIT Press, pp. 350–77.

Jaworski, Adam and Justine Coupland (2005) "You go out, you have a laugh and you can pull, yeah, but ..." Othering in gossip. *Language in Society* 34, 5: 667–94.

Jaworski, Adam and Nikolas Coupland (eds.) (2007) *The Discourse Reader* (Second edition). London: Routledge.

Jaworski, Adam, Nikolas Coupland and Dariusz Galasiński (eds.) (2004) *Metalanguage: Social and Ideological Perspectives*. The Hague: Mouton.

Jaworski, Adam and Annette Pritchard (eds.) (2005) *Discourse, Communication and Tourism*. Clevedon: Channel View Publications.

Jenkins, R. (1997) *Rethinking Ethnicity: Arguments and Explorations*. London: Sage.

Johnson, Fern L. (2000) *Speaking Culturally: Language Diversity in the United States*. Thousand Oaks: Sage.

Johnstone, Barbara (1995) Sociolinguistic resources, individual identities and the public speech styles of Texas women. *Journal of Linguistic Anthropology* 5: 1–20.

(1996) *The Linguistic Individual: Self-expression in Language and Linguistics*. Oxford and New York: Oxford University Press.

(1999) Uses of Southern speech by contemporary Texas women. *Journal of Sociolinguistics* 3: 505–522.

(2004) Place, globalization and linguistic variation. In Carmen Fought (ed.) *Sociolinguistic Variation: Critical reflections*. New York: Oxford University Press, pp. 65–83.

Johnstone, Barbara and Judith Mattson Bean (1997) Self-expression and linguistic variation. *Language in Society* 26: 221–46.

Jones, Daniel (1917) *English Pronouncing Dictionary* (First edition). London: Dent.

Joos, Martin (1962) *The Five Clocks*. New York: Harcourt, Brace.

Kelly, Katherine E. (1994) Staging repetition: Parody in postmodern British and American theatre. In Barbara Johnstone (ed.) *Repetition in Discourse: Interdisciplinary Perspectives*, Vol. 1. Norwood, NJ.: Ablex, pp. 55–67.

Kiesling, Scott Fabius (1998) Men's identities and sociolinguistic variation: The case of fraternity men. *Journal of Sociolinguistics* 2: 69–99.

Kristiansen, Tore (2004) Social meaning and norm-ideals for speech in a Danish community. In Adam Jaworski, Nikolas Coupland and Darius Galasinski (eds.) *Metalanguage: Social and Ideological Perspectives*. Berlin and New York: Mouton de Gruyter, pp. 167–92.

Kristiansen, Tore, Peter Garrett and Nikolas Coupland (eds.) (2006) *Subjective Processes in Language Variation and Change. Acta Linguistica Havniensia*, Volume 37.

Kress, Gunther and Theo Van Leeuwen (2001) *Multimodal Discourse: The Modes and Media of Contemporary Communication*. London: Arnold.

Kulick, Don (2003) Review of Jennifer Coates (2003) *Men Talk: Stories in the Making of Masculinities. Journal of Sociolinguistics* 7: 628–30.

Labov, William (1966) *The Social Stratification of English in New York City*. Washington DC: Center for Applied Linguistics.

(1972a) *Language in the Inner City: Studies in the Black English Vernacular*. Oxford: Basil Blackwell.

(1972b) *Sociolinguistic Patterns*. Philadelphia: University of Pennsylvania Press.

(1972c) Some principles of linguistic methodology. *Language in Society* 1: 97–120.

(1982) Objectivity and commitment in linguistic science. *Language in Society* 11: 165–211.

(1990) The intersection of sex and social class in the course of linguistic change. *Language Variation and Change* 2: 205–254.

(1994) *Principles of Linguistic Change: Internal Factors*. Malden, Mass. and Oxford: Blackwell Publishers.

(2001a) *Principles of Linguistic Change: Social Factors*. Malden, Mass. and Oxford: Blackwell Publishers.

(2001b) The anatomy of style-shifting. In Penelope Eckert and John R. Rickford (eds.) *Style and Sociolinguistic Variation*. Cambridge: Cambridge University Press, pp. 85–108.

(2006) *The Social Stratification of English in New York City* (Second edition). Cambridge: Cambridge University Press.

Lakoff, Robin (1975) *Language and Woman's Place*. New York: Harper and Row.

Lavandera, Beatriz R. (1978) Where does the sociolinguistic variable stop? *Language in Society* 7: 171–83.

Lave, Jean and Étienne Wenger (1991) *Situated Learning: Legitimate Peripheral Participation*. Cambridge: Cambridge University Press.

Leckie-Tarry, Helen (1995) *Language and Context: A Functional Linguistic Theory of Register*. London: Pinter.

Lee, David (1992) *Competing Discourses: Perspective and Ideology in Language*. London: Longman.

Le Page, Robert B. and Andrée Tabouret-Keller (1985) *Acts of Identity: Creole-based Approaches to Language and Ethnicity*. Cambridge: Cambridge University Press.

Lippi-Green, Rosina (1997) *English with an Accent: Language, Ideology and Discrimination in the United States*. London and New York: Routledge.

Livia, Anna and Kira Hall (1997) *Queerly Phrased: Language, Gender and Sexuality*. New York: Oxford University Press.

Macaulay, Ronald (1997) *Standards and Variation in Urban Speech*. Amsterdam: John Benjamins.

(2001) The question of genre. In Penelope Eckert and John R. Rickford, (eds.) *Style and Sociolinguistic Variation*. Cambridge and New York: Cambridge University Press, pp. 78–82.

(2005) *Talk That Counts: Age, Gender, and Social Class Differences in Discourse*. New York: Oxford University Press.

Machin, David and Theo van Leeuwen (2005) Language style and lifestyle: The case of a global magazine. *Media, Culture and Society* 27, 4: 577–600.

Maher, John C. (2005) Metroethnicity, language and the principle of Cool. *International Journal of the Sociology of Language* 175/6: 83–102.

Malinowski, Bronislaw (1923). The problem of meaning in primitive languages. Supplement to C. Ogden and I. Richards *The Meaning of Meaning*. London: Routledge and Kegan Paul, pp. 146–52.

Manning, Paul (2004) The streets of Bethesda: The slate quarrier and the Welsh language in the Welsh Liberal imagination. *Language in Society* 33: 517–48.

Mead, George Herbert (1932) *Philosophy of the Present*. LaSalle, Ill.: Open Court.

(1934) *Mind, Self and Society*. Chicago: Chicago University Press.

Mees, Inger and Beverley Collins (1999) Cardiff: A real-time study of glottalization. In Paul Foulkes and Gerard Docherty (eds.) *Urban Voices: Accent Studies in the British Isles*. London: Arnold, pp. 185–202.

Mendoza-Denton, Norma (2004) Language and identity. In J. K. Chambers, Peter Trudgill and Natalie Schilling-Esrtes (eds.) *Handbook of Language Variation and Change*. Malden and Oxford: Blackwell Publishing, pp. 474–99.

Milroy, James 2001. Language ideologies and the consequences of standardization. *Journal of Sociolinguistics* 5, 4: 530–55.

Milroy, James and Lesley Milroy (1985) *Authority in Language: Investigating Language Prescription and Standardisation*. London: Routledge.

(1997) Varieties and variation. In Florian Coulmas (ed.) *The Handbook of Sociolinguistics*. Oxford: Blackwell, pp. 47–64.

Milroy, Lesley (1987) *Observing and Analysing Natural Language*. Oxford: Blackwell Publishers.

(2004) Language ideologies and linguistic change. In Carmen Fought (ed.) *Sociolinguistic Variation: Critical Reflections*. New York: Oxford University Press, pp. 161–77.

Montgomery, Martin (2001) Defining 'authentic talk'. *Discourse Studies* 3, 4: 397–404.

Moore, Emma (2003) Learning Style and Identity: A Sociolinguistic Analysis of a Bolton High School. Doctoral dissertation, University of Manchester, UK.

Morgan, Kenneth O. (1989) *The Red Dragon and the Red Flag: The Cases of James Griffiths and Aneurin Bevan*. Aberystwyth: The National Library of Wales.

Morson, Gary (1989) Theory of parody. In G. S. Morson and C. Emerson (eds.) *Rethinking Bakhtin*. Evanston, Ill.: Northwestern University Press, pp. 63–86.

Mugglestone, Lynda (2003) *Talking Proper: The Rise of Accent as Social Symbol*. Oxford: Oxford University Press.

Newbrook, Mark (1999) West Wirral: Norms, self reports and usage. In Paul Foulkes and Gerard Docherty (eds.) *Urban Voices: Accent Studies in the British Isles*. London: Arnold, pp. 90–106.

Niedzielski, Nancy and Dennis Preston (2003) *Folk Linguistics*. Berlin and New York: Mouton de Gruyter.

Ochs, Elinor (1992) Indexing gender. In A. Duranti and C. Goodwin (eds.) *Rethinking Context: Language as an Interactive Phenomenon*. Cambridge: Cambridge University Press, pp. 335–58.

Ochs, Elinor and Bambi Schieffelin (eds.) (1986) *Language Socialization across Cultures*. Cambridge: Cambridge University Press.

Peirce, Charles Sanders (1931–58) *Collected Writings* (8 Vols.) (edited by Charles Hartshorne, Paul Weiss and Arthur W. Burks). Cambridge, Mass.: Harvard University Press.

Potter, Jonathan and Margaret Wetherell (1987) *Discourse and Social Psychology: Beyond Attitudes and Behaviour.* London: Sage.

Pratt, Mary Louise (1987) Linguistic utopias. In Nigel Fabb, D. Attridge, A. Durant and C. MacCabe (eds.) *The Linguistics of Writing: Arguments between Language and Literature.* Machester: Manchester University Press and New York: Methuen, pp. 48–66.

Preston, Dennis (1996) "Whaddayaknow": The modes of folk linguistic awareness. *Language Awareness* 5, 1: 40–74.

Rampton, Ben (1991). Interracial Panjabi in a British adolescent peer group. *Language in Society* 20, 3: 391–422.

(1995) *Crossing.* London: Longman.

(1999) (ed.) *Styling the Other.* Special issue of *Journal of Sociolinguistics* 3, 4.

(2000) Speech community. In J Verschueren, J.-O. Ostman, J. Blommaert and C. Bulcaen (eds.) *Handbook of Pragmatics.* Amsterdam: John Benjamins, pp. 1–34. (Also at http://www.kcl.ac.uk/depsta/education/ ULL/wpull.html)

(2006) *Language in Late Modernity: Interaction in an Urban School.* Cambridge: Cambridge University Press.

Reid, Euan (1978) Social and stylistic variation in the speech of children: Some evidence from Edinburgh. In Peter Trudgill (ed.) *Sociolinguistic Patterns in British English.* London: Edward Arnold, pp. 158–171.

Richardson, Kay (2006) The dark arts of good people: How popular cuture negotiates 'spin' in NBC's The West Wing. *Journal of Sociolinguistics* 10, 1: 52–69.

Rickford, John R. and Faye McNair-Knox (1994) Addressee- and topic-influenced style-shift: A quantitative sociolinguistic study. In Douglas Biber and Edward Finegan (eds.) *Sociolinguistic Perspectives on Register.* New York and Oxford: Oxford University Press, pp. 235–76.

Riggins, S. H. (1997) (ed.) *The Language and Politics of Exclusion: Others in Discourse.* Thousand Oaks: Sage.

Romaine, Suzanne (1984a) *The Language of Children and Adolescents: The Acquisition of Communicative Competence.* Oxford: Basil Blackwell.

(1984b) The status of sociological models and categories in explaining linguistic variation. *Linguistische Berichte* 90: 25–38.

Ronkin, Maggie and Helen E. Karn (1999) Mock Ebonics: Linguistic racism in parodies of Ebonics on the Internet. *Journal of Sociolinguistics* 3, 3: 360–80.

Said, Edward (1978) *Orientalism.* London: Routledge and Kegan Paul.

Sankoff, Gillian (2004) Adolescents, young adults, and the critical period: Two case studies from 'seven up'. In Carmen Fought (ed.) *Sociolinguistic Variation: Critical Perspectives.* New York: Oxford University Press, pp. 121–39.

Scannell, Paddy (1996) *Radio, Television and Modern Life: A Phenomenological Approach*. Oxford: Blackwell.

Schilling-Estes, Natalie (1998) Investigating 'self-conscious' speech: The performance register in Ocracoke English. *Language in Society* 27: 53–83.

(2004a) Investigating stylistic variation. In J. K. Chambers, Peter Trudgill and Natalie Schilling-Estes (eds.) *The Handbook of Language Variation and Change*. Malden, Mass. and Oxford: Blackwell Publishing, pp. 375–401.

Schilling-Estes, Natalie (2004b) Constructing ethnicity in interaction. *Journal of Sociolinguistics* 8, 2: 163–95.

Scollon, Ron (1998) *Mediated Discourse as Social Interaction*. London and New York: Longman.

Sebba, Mark (1993) *London Jamaican: Language Systems in Interaction*. London: Longman.

Sebeok, Thomas (1960) *Style in Language*. Cambridge, Mass.: MIT Press.

Shepard, Carolyn A., Howard Giles and Beth A. Le Poire (2001) Communication accommodation theory. In W. Peter Robinson and Howard Giles (eds.) *The New Handbook of Language and Social Psychology*. Chichester: John Wiley, pp. 33–56.

Silverstein, Michael (1976) Shifters, linguistic categories and cultural description. In K. H. Basso and H. A. Selby (eds.) *Meaning in Anthropology*. Albuquerque: University of New Mexico Press, pp. 11–55.

(1979) Language structure and linguistic ideology. In Paul R. Clyne, William F. Hanks and Carol L. Hofbauer (eds.) *The Elements: A Para Session on Linguistic Units and Levels*. Chicago: Chicago Linguistics Society, pp. 193–247.

(1993) Metapragmatic discourse and metapragmatic function. In John A. Lucy (ed.) *Reflexive Language*. Cambridge: Cambridge University Press, pp. 33–58.

Smith, David (1999) *Wales: A Question for History*. Bridgend: Seren.

Snow, Catherine E. and Charles A. Ferguson (1977) *Talking to Children: Language Input and Acquisition*. Cambridge: Cambridge University Press.

Sutcliffe, David (1982) *British Black English*. Oxford: Basil Blackwell.

Swales, John (1990) *Genre Analysis: English in Academic and Research Settings*. Cambridge: Cambridge University Press.

Tagliamonte, Sali and Alex D'Arcy (2004) *He's like, she's like:* The quotative system in Canadian youth. *Journal of Sociolinguistics* 8, 4: 493–514.

Tagliamonte, Sali and Rachel Hudson (1999) *Be like* et al. beyond America: the quotative system in British and Canadian youth. *Journal of Sociolinguistics* 3: 147–72.

Thakerar, Jitendra, Howard Giles and Jenny Cheshire (1982) Psychological and linguistic parameters of speech accommodation theory. In Howard Giles and Robert N. St. Clair (eds.) *Advances in the Social Psychology of Language*. Cambridge: Cambridge University Press, pp. 205–255.

Thornborrow, Joanna and Theo van Leeuwen (eds.) (2001) *Authenticity in Media Discourse.* Thematic Issue of *Discourse Studies*, 3, 4.

Trilling, Lionel (1972) *Sincerity and Authenticity.* Cambridge, Mass.: Harvard University Press.

Trudgill, Peter (1974) *The Social Differentiation of English in Norwich.* Cambridge: Cambridge University Press.

   (1981) Linguistic accommodation: Sociolinguistic observations on a socio-psychological theory. In C. Masek, R. Hendrick and M. Miller (eds.) *Papers from the Parasession on Language and Behavior, Chicago Linguistics Society.* Chicago, Ill.: University of Chicago Press, pp. 218–37.

   (1986) *Dialects in Contact.* Oxford: Blackwell.

   (1999) Norwich: Endogenous and exogenous linguistic change. In Paul Foulkes and Gerard Docherty (eds.) *Urban Voices: Accent Studies in the British Isles.* London: Arnold, pp. 124–40.

   (2001) The sociolinguistics of modern RP. In Peter Trudgill *Sociolinguistic Variation and Change.* Edinburgh: Edinburgh University Press, pp. 171–80.

   (2004) Social differentiation. In J. K. Chambers, Peter Trudgill and Natalie Schilling-Estes (eds.) *The Handbook of Language Variation and Change.* Malden, Mass.: Blackwell Publishing, pp. 373–4.

Ullman, Stephen (1966) *Language and Style.* Oxford: Blackwell.

Urban, Greg (1993) The represented functions of speech in Shokleng myths. In John A. Lucy (ed.) *Reflexive Language: Reported Speech and Metapragmatics.* Cambridge: Cambridge University Press, pp. 241–59.

   (1996) Entextualization, replication and power. In Michael Silverstein and Greg Urban (eds.) *Natural Histories of Discourse.* Chicago: University of Chicago Press, pp. 21–44.

van Leeuwen, Theo (2001) What is authenticity? *Discourse Studies* 3, 4: 392–6.

Verschueren, Jef (2004) Notes on the role of metapragmatic awareness in language use. In Adam Jaworski, Nikolas Coupland and Dariusz Galasinski (eds.) *Metalanguage: Social and Ideological Perspectives.* Berline and New York: Mouton de Gruyter, pp. 53–73.

Volosinov, N. V. (1983) *Marxism and the Philosophy of Language* (Translated by L. Matejka and I. R. Titunik). Cambridge, Mass.: MIT Press.

Wales, Katie (1989) *A Dictionary of Stylistics.* London: Longman.

Wardhaugh, Ronald (2002) *An Introduction to Sociolinguistics.* Oxford: Blackwell Publishers.

Watts, Richard J. (2003) *Politeness.* Cambridge: Cambridge University Press.

Weber, Jean Jacques (1996a) *The Stylistics Reader: From Roman Jakobson to the Present.* London: Arnold.

   (1996b) (ed.) Towards contextualized stylistics: An overview. In Jean Jacques Weber (ed.) *The Stylistics Reader: From Roman Jakobson to the Present.* London: Arnold, pp. 1–8.

Weinreich, Uriel, William Labov and Marvin Herzog (1968) Emprical foundations for a theory of language change. In Winfred P. Lehmann and Yakov Malkiel (eds.) *Directions for Historical Linguistics: A Symposium*. Austin, Tex.: University of Texas Press, pp. 95–188.

Wenger, Etienne (1998) *Communities of Practice*. Cambridge: Cambridge University Press.

Wilde, Oscar. 1894/1970. Phrases and philosophies for the use of the young. *Chameleon* 1: 1–3 (December). Reprinted in Oscar Wilde (1970) *The Artist as Critic: Critical Writings of Oscar Wilde* (edited by Richard Ellman). London: W. H. Allen, pp. 433–38.

Williams, Ann and Paul Kerswill (1999) Dialect levelling: Change and continuity in Milton Keynes, Reading and Hull. In Paul Foulkes and Gerard Docherty (eds.) *Urban Voices: Accent Studies in the British Isles*. London: Arnold, pp. 141–62.

Williams, Gwyn A. (1985) *When was Wales?* London: Black Raven Books.

Williams, Raymond (1977) *Marxism and Literature*. Oxford: Oxford University Press.

Wolfram, Walt (1969) *A Sociolinguistic Description of Detroit Negro Speech*. Washington DC: Center for Applied Linguistics.

(1993) Ethical considerations in language awareness programs. *Issues in Applied Linguistics* 4: 225–55.

(1998) Scrutinizing linguistic gratuity: A view from the field. *Journal of Sociolinguistics* 2: 271–9.

Wolfram, Walt, and R. W. Fasold (1974). *The Study of Social Dialects in American English*. Englewood Cliffs: Prentice Hall.

Woolard, Kathryn A. (1995) Changing forms of code switching in Catalan comedy. *Catalan Review* IX (2): 223–52.

(1999) Simultaneity and bivalency as strategies in bilingualism. *Journal of Linguistic Anthropology* 8 (1): 3–29.

Zahn, C. and Hopper, R. (1985) Measuring language attitudes: the speech evaluation instrument. *Journal of Language and Social Psychology* 4: 113–23.

Index

CPSIA information can be obtained at www.ICGtesting.com
Printed in the USA
BVOW050721090911

270880BV00001B/88/P